#**494**

OPERA FACULTATIS PHILOSOPHICAE
UNIVERSITATIS MASARYKIANAE

SPISY FILOZOFICKÉ FAKULTY
MASARYKOVY UNIVERZITY

MUNI
ARTS

Myths and Traditions of Central European University Culture

Lukáš Fasora – Jiří Hanuš

MASARYK
UNIVERSITY
PRESS

KAROLINUM PRESS

BRNO AND PRAGUE 2019

KATALOGIZACE V KNIZE – NÁRODNÍ KNIHOVNA ČR

Fasora, Lukáš, 1972-
Myths and traditions of Central European university culture / Lukáš Fasora, Jiří Hanuš ; translation Graeme Dibble. – First published. – Brno : Masaryk University Press ; Prague : Karolinum Press, 2019. – 245 stran. – (Opera Facultatis philosophicae Universitatis Masarykianae = Spisy Filozofické fakulty Masarykovy univerzity, ISSN 1211-3034 ; 494)
Německé resumé
Přeloženo z češtiny. – Obsahuje bibliografii, bibliografické odkazy a rejstřík

ISBN 978-80-210-9412-3 (Masarykova univerzita ; brožováno). – ISBN 978-80-246-4380-9 (Karolinum ; brožováno)

* 378.4 * 378 * 37.014.5 * 316.75-028.78 * 37.0(091) * (437.3) * (4-191.2) * (048.8)
– universities – Czechia
– universities – Europe, Central
– universities and colleges – Czechia
– universities and colleges – Europe, Central
– educational policy – Europe, Central
– cultural traditions – Europe, Central
– history of education – Europe, Central
– monographs

378 - Higher education [22]

Reviewers: Jiří Štaif (Charles University)

Petr Svobodný (Institute of the History and Archive of Charles University)

ISBN 978-80-210-9412-3 (Masarykova univerzita. Brno) (paperback)
ISBN 978-80-246-4380-9 (Karolinum. Praha) (paperback)
ISBN 978-80-210-9413-0 (Masarykova univerzita. Brno) (online : pdf)
ISBN 978-80-246-4497-4 (Karolinum. Praha) (online : pdf)

ISSN 1211-3034
https://doi.org/10.5817/CZ.MUNI.M210-9413-2019

Contents

MYTHS AND TRADITIONS OF CENTRAL EUROPEAN UNIVERSITY CULTURE (AN INTRODUCTION FOR INTERNATIONAL READERS)

In this brief introduction we would like to outline the main ideas which led us to writing this publication and the main thematic elements which we discussed with our academic colleagues from various Czech and international higher-education establishments.

The first thing to mention is that one of the recurring concepts was the fact that universities are a special kind of *institution*. Some of them date back to the Middle Ages – therefore, important questions regarding their historical continuity have to be considered. At present they are linked to three organizational groups – the church, the state and the city. At the same time, they are related to power and education, which power and social status often co-create and define. They create a unique system, containing a social role and a system of transferred symbols and traditions. Universities have probably gained in importance in the modern age and represent a path which more and more people embark on. And as historians we were naturally interested in the issue of how universities as a specific institution "bring up" their supporters, how they look after their legacy, and how specialist interests and social trends intersect within them. As part of the history of the institution we were also interested in how universities differ amongst each other, how reciprocal relationships develop and how the university operates within its own specific region.

It took some time before we agreed on the main interpretational key to use to describe historical events and trends as well as current issues. When laying the groundwork we decided on the terms "myths" and "traditions" in order to avoid older concepts concerning Central European universities, which were mainly associated with celebrating the university's existence, with a specific ideology or with an obviously nationalist story. Therefore, we chose a more general interpretational scheme which, we believe, allowed us to examine more thoroughly specific university structures which have been handed down and are occasionally reflected upon. Our interest in myths can be explained using the example of the so-called *founding myth*. Universities, like states, churches, or nations in the modern era, have their own founding myths which do not necessarily have to be religious in character, but are often rooted in a kind of basic anthropological need to strengthen the institution, unify it and maintain its legacy. For our university in Brno, this founding myth was the fifty-year struggle over its establishment, involving the "clash between Czechs and Germans", intervention by important figures including the politician and later president of Czechoslovakia, Tomáš G. Masaryk, and lastly, the republican and secular models which connected the university to the establishment of the new democratic state (Masaryk University was founded some three months after an independent Czechoslovakia was declared!). It is very interesting for us how universities, and not only our own, use these founding myths, how they emphasize specific parts of them and how they create sub-institutions to cultivate the "university's memory". Another example might be the myth in the form of a large *metanarrative* such as the Marxist-Leninist story of the class struggle, of the "Battle of Armageddon of the world proletarian revolution followed by a golden era of jubilation in a classless society" (Stanislav Komárek), a story which influenced thousands of academics in the 20th century. In relation to this we felt there was enormous significance in the symbolic behaviour of universities and their celebrations, as through them we can see how a university has existed, how it presents itself to the public and how it demonstrates its usefulness to society.

From the outset we realized that we would require more than a national framework, despite the fact that the Czech Republic offers a variety of universities for comparative purposes: medieval, modern and those established as recently as after 1989; Metropolitan universities and regional ones, universities with a more general focus and those with particular specializations, etc. However, we had greater ambitions – for several reasons we wanted to take a look at universities within Central Europe. After the collapse of the Soviet empire it would seem that the *Central European region* is reawakening from a slumber of several decades and is starting to regain its cultural as well as political identity. Central Europe once more makes political "sense", which does not mean that there are not significant differences between the countries of Central Europe. It is noteworthy that several of the universities were established within the Austrian empire which shaped Central European state unity over a long period, and thus offers a similar, comparable environment. This is why we have occasionally focused on Slovakia, Poland, Germany and Austria. Naturally, there were also instances when we had to take into account the global context, as Central European universities are now part of an international network consisting of universities from Western Europe, America and even Asia. Another key word in our book is *network* because we are aware of the fact that the interdependence of science and education has always been a part of university life – as long as obstacles, such as ideological ones, were not in its path. The term *network* also relates to a specific type of academic and formative communication which is promoted at universities.

The identity of the Central European university has also been shaped by the dark period *under the great ideologies* of the 20th century. This is also something they share – most importantly through the loss of university freedom during the war and sometimes also the complete paralysis of university activity as a result of the Nazi's anti-nationalist measures, and also in the form of a "spiritual plague" during the communist era which curtailed the free exchange of information and scientific knowledge, while its class politics affected many people who were involved in academia, making their academic and personal lives a misery. In this sense, it is precisely in Central Europe where we can reflect on the perennial attempts to discover the meaning of university traditions and the very foundations of university culture.

However, our book also hopes to open discussions on current as well as historical topics. Of these, four probably have priority today: firstly, the contradiction between unavoidable internationalization (the use of English, exchange visits of teachers and students, guest lecturers, etc) and maintaining a distinct national character, which seems to be at least as important; secondly, the contradiction between unavoidable reforms which are required through changes in our understanding of education, economic pressure and the needs of society, and the necessity to preserve traditions which allow the university to settle in a specific region and area; thirdly, the contradiction between the traditional emphasis on specific disciplines and their methodologies, and the much-vaunted interdisciplinarity which is required in relation to project and grant policies which universities are heavily involved in; and fourthly, the contradiction between the requirements of scientific research and teaching – i.e. the relationship between them. These four themes certainly do not encompass all of the issues and contradictions in today's higher-education institutions, but they do represent a kind of basis which is also connected to the complex issue of financing higher education. A basis from which it is possible to move on to discussions which this modest publication also hopes to initiate.

Naturally, the book Myths and Traditions of Central European University Culture was also written for ourselves. We are not only observers of university culture from the outside – we are steeped within it, and it is from the inside that we try to orientate ourselves in the place we work and live. This is probably reflected in some of the book's priorities as well as its weaknesses.

Lukáš Fasora, Jiří Hanuš, May 2019

MYTH: AN ATTEMPT AT UNDERSTANDING UNIVERSITY HISTORY

Given that most of the chapters in this book refer to the concept of myth, which is used by the authors as one of the keys to understanding the cultural history of universities, and indeed the history of institutions in general (state institutions, church institutions, etc.), it is worth explaining from the outset what is understood by myth here and in what sense this term is being used.

Religious studies scholars usually associate myth and its origins with cult and cult drama. "*If the task of modern drama is to 'hold up a mirror to nature', as Hamlet says to the actors, then the task of cult drama is to make the story present so that it becomes the here and now for those involved. Artistic drama presents what happened in the past or what according to the writer's imagination will happen in the future; cult drama not only presents the story but replays it.*"[1]

Of course, this basic assessment cannot be fully applied in our case. The conception of myth as a "cult drama scenario" and the joining (making present) of myth through cult drama cannot be transferred anachronistically to the modern age, which we must deal with as a priority. After all, in the religious studies conception, myth is bound up with events involving gods, demi-gods and other superhuman beings, which man participates in by means of the cult.[2] Moreover, all of this is set in a time when the cultic can be regarded as the factual. This archaic conception was captured, for example, by Alois Jirásek in his Old Czech Legends: "*...the Lúčans' witches* [probably priestesses/oracles – author's note] *and the Czechs' witches decided the next day's battle in advance – it was to be lost by the Lúčans.*"[3] The view of modern man is different, at least in the sense that he believes his methods

---

1   Heller, Jan – Mrázek, Milan: *Nástin religionistiky.* Prague 2004, p. 207.
2   Ibid.
3   Ibid, p. 205.

of controlling nature to be more sophisticated and is unlikely to search for direct agents behind natural events (and yet is all the more capable of searching for "conspiracies" behind political events!) In this conception myths also have their own logic, which it is difficult for contemporary people to understand and accept. Ancient myths are not "legends" with a historical core, as one might suppose. Myths contain much that is illogical, improbable or impossible. It is not possible to insert a modernly conceived system into a myth. What belongs in a myth, as J. Heller and M. Mrázek accurately say, is the expression "so that", rather than a mere explanation of the world: "*...so that there will be a harvest and people won't go hungry, so that death will no longer reign in the village – so that the threat of disaster will be removed.*" Cult is performed precisely with a view to this "so that".[4]

On the other hand, it is clearly not possible to set up an absolute contradiction between the understanding of myths among our forebears and our modern view. Certainly, much has changed (the understanding of nature, the individual conception of man, the increasing adoption of an urban lifestyle as opposed to the traditional rural one, the withdrawal of religion from the public sphere etc.); on the other hand, complete discontinuity with the past is unimaginable. On the contrary, many – often unexpected – connections can be found. With some authors, these connections have a "comparative" form in the sense of total interconnectedness, analogousness and indeed equality of values.[5]

Before mentioning them, we would like to address one very widespread conception according to which "myth" is contrasted with "reality" and the historian's task is merely to "demolish" myths in history. There are countless examples of this conception. For example, in magazines for young people we can encounter articles in which so-called myths about the Wild West are created or destroyed. In this case the historian is the one called upon to explain that in images from the period there are few occurrences of a gunslinger with a pair of colts slung low on his hips and a repeater, and that it is not true that the criminal white men massacred the noble Indians.[6] Of course, the task of historians is *also* to explain that the colt of the time was extremely heavy, so it was quite enough to carry one, and in an armpit holster, and that the majority of Indians lost their lives as a result of epidemics and intertribal fighting that was genocidal in nature. (Incidentally,

---

4   Ibid, p. 207.

5   This is particularly evident in the Jungian school, cf. e.g. Campbell, Joseph: *Mýty. Legendy dávných věků v našem denním životě*. Prague 1998. According to Jung, the role of myth is to link us with the realm of the unconscious. Through its images it awakens forces in us which have always been inherent to the human soul and which harbour the knowledge of the species, wisdom, which has helped man to make his way through the centuries. Cf. Campbell, *Mýty*, p. 23.

6   Cf. e.g. Visingr, Lukáš: Sedm statečných mýtů o Divokém západě: Jak to (možná) bylo doopravdy. In: *Bobří stopa* 3/2017 (autumn), pp. 3–5.

historians would probably lose out on work if they refused to get involved in this "search for how it really was"!)

Nevertheless, it seems to us that myths cannot be understood merely as "the opposite of reality", with our only task being to "overturn" myths. Instead, we will concern ourselves with a) possible sources of inspiration for understanding myth across epochs on the basis of new findings about the function of myth and findings from other disciplines and b) the use of these findings to formulate these findings for our purposes – i.e. processing some aspects of cultural university history.

First the question of inspiration. The first thing to mention is deliberations on the basic content of the human psyche. In this connection there is sometimes reference to basic thought patterns which are not only lexical but also pictorial (eidetic) in nature. In this regard one of the basic terms is "archetype", which refers to a Jungian concept. What is important for our purposes is that, according to C. G. Jung and other authors, "particular archetypal images surface from the unconscious into the conscious of individuals and *entire collectives,* often in the form of myths or myth-like phenomena of the modern age – or, to be more exact, particular mythologems, which is a term for their smallest constituent part not further divisible in a meaningful way."[7] Stanislav Komárek accurately points out that *"...according to Jung, the goal of human life is the so-called integration of archetypes, i.e. consciously grasping them and incorporating them into one's own psyche, which thus becomes more linked-up and coherent and (...) contributes to the understanding of one's own identity (salvation is essentially conscious self-identity), one's place in society and the world, and the increased creativity and meaningfulness of the individual destiny."[8]* This fact is, of course, significant mainly for describing the development of an individual (for example, the inadequacy of the fundamental personal "metamorphosis" in modern humans), but also for collective perception – whether it relates to the perception of the living world or the cultural world. In this connection it is worth quoting another one of Komárek's observations: *"Innate patterns of feeling and behaviour affect virtually every sphere of a person's activities, and it is remarkable to see, for example, man's inherent sense of ceremony and strict observance of rituals as it is reflected in particular areas of human activity (strict rules for religious ceremonies, magical procedures, scientific experiments and the bureaucratic or military 'liturgy' must always be stringently and strictly observed; otherwise the system 'does not work' or 'has no effect'). It can be said that the vast majority of what people have created in their cultural/civilizational efforts is a kind of rationalization and ma-*

---

7   Here we proceed from the Jungian interpretation of Stanislav Komárek, whose numerous essays are often an exploration of "hidden" connections and parallels.

8   Komárek, Stanislav: *Příroda a kultura. Svět jevů a svět interpretací.* Prague 2000, p. 12.

terialization of vaguely archetypal ideas on these subjects and it is not as 'fundamentally alien' to people as is sometimes claimed." [9]

On the basis of these quotations, it is possible to question the total discontinuity between pre-modern and modern history and, on the contrary, point out anthropological connections "inherent to man" in connection with the history of institutions like schools and universities. Within this area of history, this inherent conception can primarily be linked with the world of "symbols", so typical of the education system. This is clearly not just about an understanding of the symbol as a "sign" (anchor equals hope), but also about something that operates nonverbally (or in an intersection of verbal and nonverbal expression) in an exceptionally powerful way – i.e. not just in the sphere of rationality but also emotionality. In this connection it is enough to recall a whole range of phenomena which occur in the university setting (the symbols of individual faculties and the symbols of the university placed above them, the rituals of graduation ceremonies and student initiation rites, the respecting of hierarchies and discussions about their importance, the social role and status (and mask) of the teacher, the casting of aspersions on colleagues and co-workers, the problem of the team competitor/rival and so on and so forth) and it is more than likely that inspiration in the spirit of Jungian "archetypes" is worth considering. [10]

The second source of inspiration comes from philosophy. It is based on the distinction between *poiesis, praxis* and *theória* known from as far back as the Platonic period. While poiesis is creating and producing and praxis is the sphere of negotiation (politics), theória is "viewing the truth for its own sake", i.e. science. The university in its ideal, platonic form is therefore a community of people who dedicate themselves for a limited time (students) or their whole lives (teachers/scientists) to discovering, mediating and acquiring many fragments of a universe of methodically discovered truths. Moreover, this idea comes to the fore in two old names for the university: *universitas magistrorum et scholarium* and *universitas litterarum.* [11] However, in this connection there is still something of fundamental importance to be added. In the European historical context, this basic idea of the university (as a community of people who search for and are "committed" to the whole of the truth) has led to universities being regarded as a "third power" in society (along with the state and church), a power that has its own virtues:

---

9   Ibid, p. 13.

10   Jungianism is also characterized by excellent comparative observations – across cultures and civilizations. This aspect requires a degree of caution. It is not possible to examine these interesting aspects here, so we would refer the reader to publications by Stanislav Komárek, quoted above, who deals with these issues within a wide range of cultural and natural phenomena.

11   Cf. Lobkowicz, Nikolaus: Die Idee der Universität. *Vereinszeitung des A. G. V. München,* LIX (1980), pp. 2–5.

thoughtfulness, readiness to listen to arguments in a dialogue and an appreciation of distinguishing the paths leading to the truth.

We can also call this idea of the university "platonic" in the sense that although it functions as a kind of model, it is one that is probably never achieved in practice. Mikuláš Lobkowicz put it this way: *"In reality universities had to wage a constant struggle with the state and the church, often in relation to privileges and power; it was not uncommon for universities to let themselves be abused by other powers. In addition, because they had a tradition, they were always sceptical of innovations, and indeed sometimes – as was the case at the end of the 17th century and in the 18th century – so sclerotic that creative scientists, with the help of the relevant rulers, formed their own societies, in which true scientific progress then took place. On the other hand, it was not uncommon for universities to yield to trends of the time, so they often became a haven for ideological charlatans instead of a space for thinking. Finally, universities have long been an object of ridicule because of the indiscipline of their students and the nuttiness of their professors..."*[12] In other words, the difference between the "idea" and "realization" has always been and still is considerable, even though it is possible to speak of those in the history of universities who came very close to this ideal (generally in connection with Oxford and Cambridge, because they stood aside from revolutions and defined the social elites themselves).

However, this is not just about the discrepancy between the ideal and the reality, because this idea (which, for that matter, we can rightly consider a myth par excellence) is not simply the past. It underlies many modern thoughts about reforming universities (take, for example, the classic case formulated by John H. Newman in his famous work *The Idea of a University*, partly applied in practice at the Catholic university in Dublin[13]) and is also present in the reasoning of present-day higher-education staff and (possibly) civil servants. The idea still remains in the minds of many of those involved with the standard used for measuring the often "grim reality", the standard which raises hopes of getting closer to the ideal. This is obviously complicated by the fact that the modern age has expanded the possibilities on offer – apart from the original ideal, there are many other ideals

---

12 Lobkowicz: Mikuláš: *Duše Evropy*. Prague 2001, p. 55.

13 "It is remarkable that Newman's *Idea of a University* emerged from a project that – measured by the original intentions – actually failed. The basic aim was achieved: after several years of preparatory work, which included a lecture campaign comprising what is now the first part of the *Idea of a University*, Newman founded the Catholic University of Ireland in Dublin in 1854. He also became its first rector; however, after four years he resigned from this post and returned to England. Throughout its existence, the Catholic University of Ireland contended with a number of problems, from financing difficulties through low student numbers to the fact that it did not have the right to award officially recognized university degrees (with the exception of medical ones). The main cause of these obstacles was probably the fact that following centuries of British oppression (political, economic, linguistic and religious) Ireland lacked a sufficiently strong Catholic middle class which could give rise to a university undergraduate body." Cf. Soukup, Daniel: Jednota filozofie a různost věd. Introduction to J. H. Newman's book *Idea univerzity*. Olomouc 2014, p. 6.

that attempt to formulate the aims of this institution in the modern age. In any case, these ideas, however "platonic", are still with us in the form of some modern-day myths, and the university setting guarantees that they are continually updated. The idea of the university is a myth which forms a permanent "backbone" for these institutions. Even though from time to time someone will forget how important the backbone is as a support for the body, the university tradition and a certain continuity within it enables new deliberations on the fulfilment of the ideal.

The third stimulus is offered by the literary/academic deliberations of Claudio Magris, expressed in his now "classic" book *The Habsburg Myth*. In the foreword Magris not only explains the meaning of the term myth, but also its application to the area of literature he is researching: "*The term myth – which in itself means that reality is modified and distorted in such a way as to extract the anticipated basic truth from it, that hypothetical metahistorical core capable of synthesizing the basic meaning of reality – takes on a special added significance in this case. The Habsburg myth is not an ordinary process of the usual poetic transfiguration of reality, but rather the total substitution of one reality (a socio-historical one) for another (a fictitious and illusory one): it is therefore the sublimation of a specific living society into the picturesque, safe and ordered world of a fairy tale.*"[14] What is important here is that according to Magris this "fairy tale" world was able to characterize some aspects of Habsburg society and culture, and "not without finesse and the requisite depth". So this is not just about worshipping the old world and viewing the good old days through rose-tinted glasses. Quite the reverse. The mythicizing of the Habsburg world evokes the past, but at the same time it distorts it, mocks it and at the same time makes use of it – it becomes a tool for prudent political strategy, an attempt to find a principle of cohesion for the increasingly anachronistic and intolerable form of the state. Here the expression "fairy tale" is apposite, even though the works of the writers analysed are very far removed from classic fairy tales. Nevertheless, they attempt to express their commitment to the values of the past, draw attention to specific ideals and deflect attention from the oppressive reality. Magris added something else of fundamental importance on this subject: "The Austrian myth acquired a distinct ability to penetrate into society, which used it to imbibe human consciousness and human sensitivity, and it eventually succeeded in almost completely transforming the contradictory Austrian reality into a peaceful and safe world."[15] The truth of this statement is, of course, debatable, but the basic idea is not – even the modern (literary) myth has a certain power to alter social reality. In this book, works of literature will not be analysed to this extent but rather mentioned in passing. However, we must bear in mind the lesson Magris teaches us: There is truth in fairy tales and they are capable of altering human consciousness.

---

14   Magris, Claudio: *Habsburský mýtus v moderní rakouské literatuře*. Brno 2001, p. 17.
15   Ibid, p. 18

The fourth source of inspiration is represented by anthropological and social-science deliberations about the functions of modern-day myths and methodological complexes. It is no coincidence that these conceptions are predominantly found among authors dealing with modern nationalism and the creation of modern national identities and their vitality. According to these authors, "myth" is a basic tool of what is termed cultural reproduction, a tool for creating human communities. They refer to myths, rituals and symbols as "languages" that communities use to create, self-identify, demarcate and maintain their existence.[16] In this sense, myth makes it possible to understand many phenomena of the 18th–20th centuries, especially modernization, social communication, cultural transfers and especially the emergence of modern nationalism. Myths also determine the strategy of communities; they are used in publicity and social control and abused by ideological propaganda. This social-science conception, which has gradually been adopted by historians too, certainly has its limits and dangers. Its advantages include aspects that have been noted in recent decades by historians of the modern age during research into the great ideologies and ideological regimes of the 19th and 20th century. These ideologies not only discovered, interpreted and exploited "ancient myths", but also created new ones. Thus, communist or fascist regimes, for example, can be described as "myth-making". And not only that. Modern ideologies and their power applications are like islands floating in the universal myths of the modern age, sometimes without even being aware of it. One of the most frequently mentioned is the "myth of progress", which forms a background to modern ideologies and the modern world with its understanding of tradition, culture, authority, science and technology, and especially of man and his possibilities.

It is abundantly clear that in this social conception myths (whether they are narrowly focused or more generally widespread) can also be applied to the area of university history. Here it is important to recall the relationship institutions had with the great ideologies of the time (just consider the Czech example of building *national* universities(!) and the role of these institutions in the formation of a Czech national identity). The myth of progress is directly embodied in society by the creation and further development of educational institutions. It is surely not insignificant that the 19th-century "myth of progress" has been thoroughly analysed by historians (to give just two examples, the British historian Christopher Dawson[17] and the Czech, later exiled, historian Bohdan Chudoba[18]). According to Dawson, this myth consists of the theory of evolution (Spencer, Darwin) applied

---

16   Cf. Hoskins, Geoffrey – Schopflin, George (eds.): *Myths and Nationhood*. New York 1997. This publication contains excellent and at the same time digestible contributions working with the social conception of myth in research into recent decades.

17   Dawson, Christopher: *Pokrok a náboženství*. Prague 1947.

18   Chudoba, Bohdan: *O dějinách a pokroku*. Brno 1939.

to social progress, 18th-century deism and its influence on the preferences of practical philanthropy, Enlightenment philosophy emphasizing an optimistic view of human nature (Rousseau), and above all the influence of German idealism (Lessing, Hegel). Dawson states that the idea of progress reached its apotheosis in the first half of the 19th century and dominated the major trends in European thinking: rationalist liberalism, revolutionary socialism and transcendental idealism.

A similar emphasis on the intellectual history of progress and its antepositions can also be observed in the present day, in the monumental work by the historian Bedřich Loewenstein *Faith in Progress*.[19] Here the Czech historian not only dissected "faith in progress" as a monolithic phenomenon but pointed to its changing and yet pluralistic face in the modern age. Among other things, he dealt with the "myth of revolution" as the preferred myth of the 20th century and analysed German and Russian thinkers who not only reflected on this myth, but to some extent also created it. In the 1990s, just as in the late 1960s, both Europe and the USA were grappling with the nature of postwar development, and systemic contradictions could not help but affect the area of science and its cultivation at universities. With regard to the history of the USA, Loewenstein gives the example of James William Fulbright (1905–1995), the committed senator and advisor to J. F. Kennedy famous for creating the student exchange programme, who became involved in shaping American politics and promoted "mentoring" and "partnership" in international politics as well as in schools.[20]

For that matter, some German authors, for example, associate the idea of progress with the "Humboldtian myth" and the difficult-to-translate expression "*Bildung*", i.e. education, which also implies modern rationality and the (Enlightenment) notion of possible – and sometimes sustained – progress in the education of man in all its constituent parts: rational, emotional and volitional.[21] Incidentally, the Humboldtian myth will be referred to many times in the book, in various connections.

Finally, the fifth source of inspiration was found with the contemporary Czech historian Jiří Štaif. He discusses his understanding of "myth" and "social rituals" in the work Writing Biographies and Authorial Self-Reflection, which is an exposition of his conception of a biographical book about František Palacký. Here Štaif analyses the term "symbolic communication" and explains his own approach within this context: "*I paid some attention to biographical issues specifically with regard to Palacký. What I was primarily interested in was how to explain the historical fact that his image "settled" in the modern memory of Czech national society as one of its constants.*

---

19   Loewenstein, Bedřich: *Víra v pokrok. Dějiny jedné evropské ideje*. Prague 2009.

20   Ibid, p. 482.

21   Mittelstraß, Jürgen: *Die unzeitgemässe Universität*. Frankfurt am Main 1994, pp. 95–104.

What seemed key to me was the myth that saw him as the symbolic Father of the Czech nation. I originally thought that this conception of the cultural integration of national society was only typical of "late" national movements. However, in time, through the influence of Mircea Eliade, I came to realize that this kind of myth can function even in the modern age, because it makes it possible to develop the integrating role of the patriarchal father responsible for his "children". It offers them the opportunity to seek and find in him "their own" certainty amid the uncertainties of the modern age, even after he is no longer physically alive, for as long as they believe he is their authoritative compass. As a symbolic father, Palacký is thus to assume moral responsibility not only for the birth of his children, but also for their lives, as well as the lives of their descendants. As his "offspring" they have the assurance that he is always "watching over them".[22] Of course, when it comes to the history of institutions such as colleges, universities or academies, the biographical method can only be partially employed. Nevertheless, the way our colleague from Prague approached his material seems to us extremely productive and also applicable to the history of such traditional institutions as universities.

These five examples should suffice to outline the basic assumptions of our work and explain our understanding of the crucial word "myth" as it will be used in this work. As part of the summary of the conception presented, the following should be added:

1. The conception of "myth" used in the above connotations can be a useful tool for the history of university culture even in the modern era. This is primarily because it makes it possible to reveal intentions of those involved which would otherwise be incomprehensible and to grasp long-term trends underlying university traditions and operations. It can shed light on the world of symbols and at the same time it is possible to interpret its new meanings within the framework of changing social conditions.

2. This conception obviously needs to be applied to the relevant areas of university life in its institutional and personnel sphere. For the historian there is also the necessity of not pre-empting the "language of the sources", which always has priority, but the theoretical concept allows the segments of university culture that we consider the most significant to be discussed in isolation in individual chapters.

3. Clearly, the cultural history of university institutions cannot be exhausted using a single method, even if we consider it a pivotal one. For that reason, other approaches to social, political and cultural history will also appear in this book – it can thus be said to represent a combination of methods, taking into account the importance of biographical aspects in a work of this

---

22 Štaif, Jiří: Psaní biografie a autorská sebereflexe. *Dějiny – teorie – kritika* 1/2015, p. 120. Here the author explains his motivation for writing the book *František Palacký. Život, dílo, mýtus*. Prague 2009.

type: we believe that what is critical in university life is not just "structures", but above all the people who create and influence those structures.

4. We are aware that university culture cannot be accurately described without taking into account the political context in a comparative European (Central European) perspective. However, our comparison can only be of limited scale and applicability – it is more about taking soundings of selected institutions and countries in an attempt to capture major similarities and differences.

5. The world of universities is not a world where teaching and research, schools and state, teachers and students coexist in harmony, but a world full of rivalry, conflicts and problems, at every conceivable level. These problems cannot be swept under the carpet; on the contrary, it is necessary and it is incumbent on the historian to uncover and duly interpret them. This is especially sensitive in connection with recent decades, a period when the witnesses of past events are still alive. A particularly sensitive approach is required by the interpretation of events linked with moments of political and ideological upheaval (in the Czech setting e.g. 1968, 1989).

6. Universities are generally a place of social mobility and the formation of national elites, a place where the struggle for university and more generally applicable freedoms takes place, a place where new ideas (which are applicable to society and sometimes "subversive") are formulated, but sometimes also a place of "intellectual bubbles" which the outside world occasionally fails to penetrate. Elitist tendencies manifest themselves across the university spectrum, and for the historian it is extremely interesting to observe how they take on diverse forms in diverse historical situations.

7. The authors' decision to write a history of university culture goes hand in hand with a conviction that "culture" is something of fundamental importance in the life of modern states and institutions. It is an element which is often rooted very deeply in national societies, mentalities and reputations, and its permanence and specificity is more important than its variability and universality. In other words: we are of the opinion that an "institutionalized" culture is not easily interchangeable and contains a certain national and intellectual "flavour", some aspects of which may be non-transferable. Culture, made up of unique historical phenomena, can to a certain extent be regarded as "myth", which we live off and use as a source of inspiration for creative life.

We are aware, however, that our approach and the research presented here is only a kind of introduction to the issue. It does not represent a synthetic view of the whole area of university culture – such an ambition would simply have been unreasonable. Nevertheless, we believe that the following chapters offer food for thought and for subsequent discussion, especially in the university setting, which may help to invigorate the regular course of university life.

THE MYTH OF UNIVERSITY FREEDOM

This chapter will aim to highlight the issues surrounding the origin of universities. University culture refers back to a very old medieval concept, which is a fact that has to be taken very seriously as the institution of the university as we know it today with its faculties, courses, lectures and titles, comes to us from the medieval world. We can safely say that cathedral schools and certain informal groups acquired their form during the 12th century. But how would we characterize a university? Some authors see their characteristic features in the canon of required texts from which teachers lectured and added their own views, forming academic programmes which conferred titles, in some cases independently of other institutions and offices. In the thirteenth century, we see for the first time a certain freedom of "universality" – the rightful holder of a title could teach anywhere in the world (ius ubique docendi). It was a type of legal "university stamp". As in other spheres of medieval society, the fundamental matter was the granting of privileges (mainly by religious dignitaries at universities). The Czech scholar Pavel Spunar sees the main characteristics of medieval universities as being their administrative and spiritual autonomy, which was strictly guarded from the outset (the outward expression of authority was an academic community directed by a rector, who was elected from among them and who exercised jurisdiction over the members of the university), in a community which was created by the participation of people from all social groups (social background did not play a decisive role for the students or teachers!), and by a new border between clerics and laymen (the term *clerikus* was not unambiguously understood and there appeared attempts to transfer it from the religious to the secular sphere). According to Spunar, an "intellectual class" began to form in Italy in the 13th century, where student lawyers were no longer considered as laymen, but as clerics, even though they had not been religiously ordained.[23]

Freedom in the modern sense of the word did not exist in the Middle Ages. Privileges were understood as "the presentation of freedom" in a world divided by the estates. There was no concept at the time of a universality of rights.[24] The freedom of universities was at first linked to the freedom of the clerics, which was also granted by secular rulers. It is clear from the start that they fought for these privileges, and that the character of the university as an intellectual corporation matured with these struggles. Documents exist which tells us about the right to suspend lectures, about professors' salaries, even about the right to strike (*Parens scientiarum* Gregory IX).[25]

On the other hand, the early universities differed from later ones in many respects: for example, universities did not have libraries, sometimes not even their own buildings, the most common and most popular subject was law, which was seen as preparation for other vocations. The main subjects taught were the 'seven free arts', as well as civil and canonical law, cosmology, medicine and theology. From the outset, universities received a tremendous boost for their development from the intellectual renaissance which was occurring in the emerging Western world. The core of teaching and education lay in the 'disputation', which was designed to stimulate the ability to argue logically (the scholastic argumentation is best described in Summa Theologica by St Thomas Aquinas, the learned Dominican).[26] A future master had to demonstrate his knowledge of a specific canon of books, after which he could apply for a licence to teach, and this process was accompanied by an act of loyalty. Sometimes the licentiate would also receive a master's title. Again, the concept of "freedom" here is part of a precisely defined framework. In terms of the medieval concept of independence, we have to add that the university began at that time to represent a certain "power" in society, and its self-confidence grew in this regard. It is possible to recall a chapter from Czech history which relates to the time of Charles IV and the Hussite period, and is illustrative of the role which the university (Central European by this stage) played in scholarly disputes and how it assumed powers. In religious disputes, universities had the tendency to place themselves as the arbiter of the true interpretation of Biblical texts, Christian traditions, as well as history. One example of this was the history of the medieval and early modern age councils.[27]

The Modern Age continued to be linked to these university origins. This is best shown in the relationship towards the main figures in medieval scholastics,

---

23   Spunar, Pavel et al.: *Kultura středověku*. Prague 1995, p. 87.

24   Cf. Hanuš, Jiří (ed.): *Lidská práva. Národ na obecnou platnost a kulturní diferenciace*. Brno 2001.

25   Woods, Thomas E.: *Jak katolická církev budovala západní civilizaci*. Prague 2008, p. 45.

26   Cf. Floss, Pavel: *Architekti křesťanského středověkého myšlení 1*. Prague 2004. A scholastic interpretation from its origins to the later period.

27   Cf. Schatz, Klaus: *Všeobecné koncily. Ohniska církevních dějin*. Brno 2014.

the study of intellectual life in the Late Middle Ages, and a rational understanding of issues in general. Naturally, there was a significant distance in this period from the medieval basis of science, and not only in the sense of time, but also an intellectual distance. Jacques Le Goff saw one of these transitional phases as the end of the 14th and the start of the 15th century, when universities "opened up to humanism", in particular in Italy (Bologna, Padua). This signalled a development in Greek studies and interest in ancient writings in general, the rejection of scholastics as a "rigid system", an emphasis on the duo of philology and rhetoric (as opposed to the duo of dialectics – scholastics), interest in the "beautiful language" – but also a certain aristocratic behaviour as the humanist "writes for the enlightened" (the home of humanism was more the ruler's court than a student hostelry!). "*From the start its world was designed as a protective hand for the powerful, for the maintenance of offices and material wealth.*"[28] It is also important that humanism pushed intellectuals from the towns to the countryside, specifically to rural residences, as was described by Erasmus in *The Profane Feast.*[29] Humanism also brought a rift between science and teaching, which was connected to the expansion of book publishing and libraries. During this period, independence was an even greater chimera than it had been previously – scholars gladly worked in the service of rulers and courts: here too we cannot apply a contemporary postmodern perspective.

We have presented these two historical situations (outlined in almost unacceptable brevity) for an important reason. When describing the main interpretive stereotypes as part of the history of universities, we might come across dual-type problems. The independence of the medieval and humanist type of scholarship and its institutions cannot hide a certain continuity through all of the changes which universities went through, even from the 18th to the 21st centuries. On the contrary, this modern period often returned to its medieval and humanist origins and mythologised them, even if this was not done within the holistic European cultural mainstream, but instead some parts of it. Therefore, for example, the Catholic universities which were founded in the 19th and 20th centuries sometimes openly declared their respect for these medieval traditions, even if the forms of teaching and their relationship towards other institutions, in particular towards the state, were more fitting for that period. On the other hand, we can see the exact opposite in the Modern Age – the attempt to escape from this tradition, the attempt to radically break from earlier periods. It is unsurprising that such attempts are also often types of "mythologies" (for example, communist attempts led to a kind of mythology about the contemporary rejection of old university forms, as we will see later). The independence of universities in the

---

28   Goff Le, Jacques: *Intelektuálové ve středověku.* Prague 2009, p. 130.

29   Cf. Svatoš, Michal – Svatoš, Martin: *Živá tvář Erasma Rotterdamského.* Prague 1985.

past was also mythicised or even directly parodied, and during the Modern Age, the Middle Ages were generally (and entirely non-historically) considered to be an era lacking in freedom, of intellectual repression, whilst knowledge was better during the humanist period, in particular because the first reflections on science appear, which Enlightenment and post-Enlightenment thinkers thought signified the origins of real education. The Modern Age, therefore, mythologised both its present and the past, as it had to come to terms with the fact that universities were very old institutions, institutions whose origins harked back to the "darkness" of religious medieval Europe. On a more general level, we can talk about the idea of "progress", which to a certain degree logically saw the Middle Ages and its organisations as "outdated", or in the worst case, "reactionary". This second view, which creates the impression that later must mean "more progressive" and, therefore, "better", would appear to be the most controversial modernist idea.[30] It was research into the Middle Ages from the second half of the 20th century which showed the richness, variety and also logic of the school and university councils of the time.

Society and knowledge

The British historian Peter Burke has helped us to uncover on a general level the myths relating to education and "knowledge", and their relationship towards the autonomy of universities in the period after the European Enlightenment. He examines the relationship between society and knowledge and its fundamental aspects in his important book *A Social History of Knowledge*, particularly in the second volume.[31]

At first he determines the position of "knowledge and society" on the basis of how knowledge is used. It is a type of framework which also describes the position of universities and other educational institutions in the Modern Age, particularly in Europe and America. The most important idea which evidently determines the overall character of the epoch is the *idea of practical knowledge*, i.e. turning away from "pure" science, from "knowledge for knowledge's sake". What we have said in the previous paragraphs applies here – we have to avoid mistaken ideas about previous historical periods. To a certain degree, knowledge and education had always been practical, despite the fact that the requirements and applications of this "practicality" differed. However, it can be said that in the 18th century there was a significant expansion in practical knowledge and applied knowledge in rela-

---

30   In a Czech context, one of the first historians to criticize the "idea of progress" was Bohdan Chudoba in: Chudoba, Bohdan: *O dějinách a pokroku*. Brno 1939.

31   Burke, Peter: *Společnost a vědění II. Od encyklopedie k Wikipedii*. Prague 2013.

tion to the practical orientation of the natural sciences and to economic growth (it is possible to name emerging institutions in Germany, Great Britain and the USA). In the USA in the second half of the 19th century the slogan "revealing the truth for the benefit of the people" began to spread, which was a call to scientists and inventors, but also to millionaires and philanthropists (Andrew Carnegie and others). The idea of utility became established thanks to the growth in trade and industry, and it appeared at the turn of the 20th century that universities were losing out to competition from other more practically orientated institutions. Commerce brought with it further difficulties and problems, for example, the question of the ownership of knowledge and the issue of acquiring information, which became increasingly important.

This understanding of utility, however, did not survive for long. Further expansion in practical research in the modern era was the result of military conflicts. These introduced the scientization of warfare, modernization, the development of military intelligence services and technology in general. From there it is only a small step to those who lead the war – rulers and governments. Even here there was movement away from the collection of practical information, as ordered by Enlightened rulers, to the acquisition of information using technological means, as we see today, for example, with the intelligence services. Undoubtedly, the needs of empires also played a role in this development, in particular those at the turn of the 20th century which on the one hand educated and trained colonial officials, and on the other, collected material from their colonial possessions. This was the case for both the older colonial powers (Great Britain, France), as well as those which joined them in the 19th century (Germany).

This transformation in the social paradigms had to influence university knowledge and the specific form of the university, including its understanding of "autonomy" and "independence". Universities also provided an education for bureaucrats, altering their programmes to become more practical and useful, and offering professional training in new areas such as engineering, accounting, journalism and physical education. One special area was the more practically oriented business studies (e.g. the Wharton School in Pennsylvania and the Graduate School of Business in Chicago), which also partly served as "model institutions" for Western Europe.

The collaboration between universities and the state apparatus spread widely. Governments and government agencies began to draw more upon academic research, particularly from the social sciences: "*This collaboration between the state apparatus and the university developed markedly at the Russian Research Center at Harvard. The university itself did not come up with the idea for the center, rather it was the director of the US Army Information and Education Section, who turned to the Carnegie Corporation with the project. The FBI "interfered in the center's affairs", subjecting researchers to preliminary screenings and assuming it would have any appropriate findings at its disposal prior to publication. Under pressure from the FBI, the center's director, the historian Stuart Hughes, was dismissed for displaying leftist sympathies."*[32]

This resulted in significant changes in the standing of universities and educational centres in the modern era – approximately from the 18th century. Universities had to adapt to

1) the growing power of the state, its needs and demands;
2) the industrial revolution, industrialization and modernization, which brought with them the need for greater practicality and utility
3) the competing requirements between society and the state, and even military conflicts;
4) competition with other schools, institutions and organizations.

This was the framework in which the freedom of the university developed – or was restricted.

A dependency network

It is on a macro-level that we can see the necessity and, at the same time, the relative speed with which universities began to change. We might also be aware of a "dependency network" which the universities were part of.[33] They became part of an enormous educational system, which on the one hand meant a demand for education due to the modernization of society, while on the other, it represented a large number of competitors. However, it became increasingly dependent on the state and its needs, usually accompanied by the declining role of religion and church in society. A plural society no longer required an "arbiter of the truth" as in the Middle Ages, but it still valued the diplomas which were awarded to graduates.

Specific historical situations, meanwhile, demonstrate that the idea that on one side is the "church" or the "state" or a "rich firm", attempting to restrict the "freedom" of the university, which is on the other side, striving to maintain its independence, is false, or at least inaccurate. Naturally, such situations may occur, but the more complicated cases are more frequent.

One example is the situation in France after 1870, which was culturally influential for the subsequent period (equally influential was the period of the Napoleonic Wars and the Prussian model that followed). The French republicans came to believe that "he who controls the schools, controls the world". In particular they

---

32   Ibid, p. 183.

33   Contemporary historiography uses the idea of "information networks" not only for the recent past, but also as the key to understanding the entire modern era, basically since the era of the Reformation. Cf. Ferguson, Niall: *The Square and the Tower: Networks, Hierarchies and the Struggle for Global Power*. London 2017.

had in mind the primary schools with their moral and civic education, which was to replace the old-fashioned religious education that was anathema to republican ideals. Historians do not hesitate to add that in the case of spreading republican values, this was a kind of ideological substitute: *"During the Third Republic, French village teachers became missionaries for republican layman values and competed with the village priests over who would win the hearts and minds of the local population."*[34] At the same time, it led to a sharp rise in literacy not only in France, but also in western and central Europe, and to a certain extent in Russia as well. It is worth remembering that France witnessed the introduction of new school laws by Jules Ferry, which brought in compulsory free education (1881 and 1882). The expansion of literacy not only affected the development of the markets and all areas of society, but also interest in acquiring higher school qualifications, including university ones. High schools, which were originally designed for the elites, gradually opened up to everyone (Gymnasien, lycées, ginnasi). Social mobility developed – in the 1860s the Parisian lycées had been dominated almost exclusively by the elites, while half of the graduates from provincial secondary schools came from the families of farmers, shopkeepers, clerks, workers and soldiers. At this time, some countries (Italy) were already traditional the classic secondary schools and universities for educating an excessively intellectual proletariat, a "class of parasites", people who were incapable of finding work. For comparative purposes, at the start of the century this represented an annual growth of 1,700 – 1,800 people.[35] The education of women also underwent serious discussion and changes too began to occur, albeit slowly. In the school year of 1911/1912, women constituted only 4.8% of all registered students at German universities, in 1914 women made up one-tenth of students at Parisian universities, and the gates to the famous École Normale Supérieure were opened to them in 1910. Women in Austria-Hungary had been allowed to register at the Faculty of Arts since 1897 and at the Faculty of Medicine since 1900.

But regarding the most fundamental matters: in several European countries, schools and education in general were considered to be a national undertaking, with universities often responsibly and "joyfully" taking part in this task. The slogans of the period emanating from France proved to be infectious. Liberalism, social cohesion through education, dreams about a rapid end to illiteracy, competition between countries through the widely expanding school networks and emerging universities – these were the ideals which spread across Europe before and after the First World War. It is clear that in such a context, universities could only preserve their "independence" to a certain degree: this was due to an awareness of the "national undertaking" and the ideology from a growing secularism.

---

34   Rapport, Michael: *Evropa devatenáctého století.* Prague 2011, p. 263.
35   Ibid, pp. 267–268.

The French university scene was fittingly characterized by Christophe Charle, an expert on university and intellectual history. He showed that despite all of the ideological attempts at cultural diffusion, French higher education was still very fragile at the turn of the 20th century, due to its diversification, its mimicking of the German model, and the new understanding of science and the position of the teachers: "*If in France a university in the German or English sense of the word was impossible, this was mainly because of the permanent crisis surrounding the social definition of teachers. Apart from some short and exceptional moments, they never managed to have some kind of collective consciousness, the most basic social project or the ideal of a united professional group. The Napoleonic reorganization aligned them with all the other clerks. The model of the supreme authority was represented by the highest officials of state office ("grand corps") and was based on the culmination of functions and mobility within the state apparatus, and not on intellectual excellence as judged by your peers, as was the case in German-speaking countries and then the rest of Europe. This ideal of the professor-scientist was a late import from the German model, and the group of university teachers continued to be periodically doubted.*"[36] From this it emerges that university teachers were divided according to mutually incompatible models of behaviour and opposing social and intellectual strategies, and were, therefore, unable to build any common professional basis which would be capable of a dialogue with the outside world (with political authorities, local and social demands, economic powers, students, etc.). Ultimately, the conflicts within universities were mostly a reflection of external tensions. Therefore, this was a particularly complex system where the specific French conditions of post-revolution developments, international competition and a change in social mentalities, played their role. Charle argues that after the period of stagnation and the radical changes at the turn of the 19th century, social changes led to the French university system losing all of its autonomy, which it then began trying to "discover" with difficulty in the last thirty years of the 19th century. In other countries there were conflicts between the old autonomous area of the universities and social, political and intellectual forces which tried to limit this autonomy in the name of "external imperatives", whether these were economic developments, social requirements, international intellectual competition or a new political situation.

From the above we can see the fragility and fragmentation of the modern university environment, and the almost permanent struggle for independence and autonomy, a struggle which had varying degrees of success. It is clear that this struggle was carried out within the specific conditions of the different multinational empires (Great Britain, Austria-Hungary, Russia), and the different national states, which gave a modern tone to education (France, Germany).

---

36   Charle, Christophe: *Le République des universitaires*. Paris 1994, introduction.

The great ideologies of the 19th and 20th centuries

However, there can be no doubt that the greatest attack on the freedom and con-tinuity of university development, and on the foundations of university education, was led by the great ideologies of the 20th century and the state parties and politi-cal organizations which adhered to these ideologies and attempted to spread them within their own societies as well as outside. These were mainly the ideologies of National Socialism and communism as developed in Germany and the Soviet Un-ion, or in those countries which were dependent on these powers during certain historical periods.[37] The National Socialist and communist systems affected both the university systems in the given countries as well as education in general, as they sought the unconditional subjugation and control of all its citizens, in par-ticular the youth. It is possible to view these political ideologies as "political reli-gions" as they wanted to convince people of the undisputed truth of their "sacred texts", their faith in a charismatic leader and in human redemption through obe-dience, self-sacrifice, unconditional commitment and unwavering effort. Accord-ing to an American professor from the University of California, James A. Gregor, the two totalitarian ideologies had a long pre-history which contained scientific or pseudo-scientific systems, and which, therefore, were of interest to academics and intellectuals from these countries. In the case of National Socialism this was a tradition of racism (Gobineau, Chamberlain), German culture (Wagner), and its own ideology (Rosenberg). In the case of communism, this was post-Hegelian German materialist philosophy (Marx, Engels) and a whole spectrum of European thinkers, as well as Russian socialists and anarchists. For both National Socialism and communism, this range of ideas, projects, utopian visions and plans to solve the problems of modernity led to an intellectual assemblage which was often at-tractive to intellectuals both within and outside of universities.

As regards the research into universities which were affected by the great ide-ologies of the 20th century, it is possible to mention the work of Michael Grüttner and his team which resulted from a conference held to mark the anniversary of the University of Jena in 2008. This looked at both the history of German universi-ties and the history of science in the broadest sense of the word. The fundamental methodological issues which were described by Ralph Jessen and Jürgen John in

---

37 There is no room here to develop the complex and much-discussed issue of "totalitarianism" or "totalitarianisms" of the 20th century. From the enormous library devoted to this issue we might mention the Czech researcher Bedřich Loewenstein, who examined this problem in relation to the works of Hans-Joachim Maaz, Norbert Elias, Maw Weber and other writers. Cf. Loewenstein, Bedřich: Totalitarismus a moderna, in: *My a ti druzí. Dějiny, psychologie, antropologie.* Brno 1998, pp. 306–313. Some original Czech thinkers who looked at the phenomenon of totalitarianism included the German Studies scholar and philosopher Rio Preisner (1925–2007) and his trilogy *Kritika totalitarismu.*

the journal Jahrbuch für Universitätsgeschichte in 2005[38], can be summarized as follows. The authors focused on some very interesting areas: how scientists' self-understanding changes, how scientific institutions operate within different political systems and how academics have reacted to the ideological changes in modern history, how science has developed within and outside of universities in both democratic and totalitarian systems, how the continuity of science has worked and why discontinuity in development occurred, and how all of this operated in German universities in an entirely unique way. These contributions are invaluable to those who are interested in the institutional and personal failings during the 1930s and 1940s and in the decline of science. On the other hand, it is surprising in its evaluation of postwar developments as it also critically evaluates the period of de-Nazification implemented to only a small degree by German democrats. This is not surprising not only in relation to the attacks in the 1950s by East Germany on West German lawyers, but also regarding the open discussion on de-Nazification at the end of the 1960s and the subsequent well-known dispute between historians (when the careers of the generation linked to Nazism came to an end, large research projects began to examine professions and organizations, such as the DFG (Deutsche Forschungsgemeinschaft) and MPG (Max Planck Gesellschaft). Meanwhile, research into the history of science in East Germany is still in its infancy. This is why revealing the subservience and instrumentalization of science remains an important undertaking, which the authors of this book are aware of and encourage.

University institutions "between autonomy and adaptation" was examined from an international perspective by the authors of a volume compiled by John Connelly and Michael Grüttner published in 2003. Alongside Soviet and German universities with their Central European satellites, they also include examples from Italy (universities under Mussolini's dictatorship), Spain (universities during the dictatorship of Franco) and even China (the Sovietization of Chinese universities 1949–1952). The history of Czech universities was presented in Jan Havránek's clear and cogent paper,[39] which places communist higher education and the history of science within the context of developments during the First Republic. There is a comparison of the situations in Bohemia, Moravia and Slovakia, and he characterizes the transformation from a democratic to communist education system from 1945 to 1948, mentioning the important elements of the communist

---

38 Jessen, Raplh and John, Jürgen: Wissenschaft und Universitäten im geteilten Deutschland der 1960er Jahre, in: Jahrbuch für Universitätsgeschichte, Band 8, Franz Steiner Verlag 2005.

39 Havránek, Jan: Die tschechischen Universitäten unter der kommunistischen Diktatur. In: Connelly, John – Grüttner, Michael: *Zwischen Autonomie und Anpassung: Universitäten in den Diktaturen des 20. Jahrhunderts.* Paderborn 2003. The comparisons in this volume are only partial because some authors (Connelly, Stiffler) only look at a certain time period during the communist dictatorship, pp. 157–171.

dictatorship which developed in universities: action committees in universities, the exclusion of "non-progressive" teachers, changes to curriculum procedures, the Sovietization of the syllabus, the ideological "transformation" of teachers, classes in Marxism-Leninism, etc. He also persuasively describes the waves of Stalinization and de-Stalinization of the university system and the situation after the Prague Spring of 1968 – the period of Normalization. He sees in certain modern traditions, such as the tragic story of the students Jan Opletal (1915–1939) and Jan Palach (1948–1969), a crucial element in awakening the independence of university students. Other contributions look at specific features of different countries (the resistance of teachers to the regime in the 1950s in Hungary and Poland, the standing of the church and its educational institutions in Poland, the "national" aspects in Hungarian intellectual thought, the differences between authoritarian Spain, Italy and Nazi Germany, etc.), as well as certain similarities, in particular within the postwar communist bloc. Typical here was the "cultural revolution" which was partly related to the pre-war left-wing avant-garde. Jan Křen gave a quite precise characterization of the Stalinist-style "cultural revolution", where he convincingly described the situation in the 1950s in artistic, cultural and scientific spheres within the framework of Central European history: *"Artistic and intellectual work was strictly limited and all of those who were thought unsuitable in the cultural community were mercilessly expelled; the spectrum of these restrictions was wide and ranged from ending careers and banning publications to police intervention. Among the victims of communist repression, the creative intelligentsia from the arts and humanities were represented in exceptionally large numbers. One of the paradoxes of the age was the way in which artists and movements from entirely opposing directions met in the artistic and social expulsion – the leaders of the pre-war left-wing avant-garde, artists from the democratic centre, and representatives from conservative agrarian ruralism and Catholic Modernists. Those who were unwilling to cooperate faced tragic fates, suicides, death sentences, long years in prison or emigration; the Nazi era aside, no other period brought such losses to the cultural community in these countries."*[40] All that can be added is that this was also certainly the case for intellectuals from universities. Havránek and Hroch's main thesis was later expanded upon by the historian Josef Petráň (1930–2017) in his extensive work on the history of Charles University's Faculty of Arts,[41] where he also provided a Central European background, both in relation to the Faculty of Arts and Charles University, as well as the origins and development of the Czech Academy of Sciences, which according to its founders was to "create a lever for universities" and "at the same time, establish a way to systematically abolish older scientific institutions which did not submit to the central control

---

40 Křen, Jan: *Dvě století střední Evropy*. Prague 2005, p. 629.

41 Petráň, Josef: *Filozofové dělají revoluci. Filozofická fakulta Univerzity Karlovy během komunistického experimentu (1948–1968–1989)*. In cooperation with Lydia Petráňová. Prague 2015.

and supervision of the communist regime."[42] Petráň's work can also be considered as an example for other institutional histories – it contains both a history of structural changes as well as the personal stories of teachers, scientists and students. It also convincingly demonstrated that despite all of the efforts of the Stalinist functionaries and all of the restructuring and difficulties faced by the teaching body, Charles University's Faculty of Arts and other institutes had an intellectual basis which the communist regime failed to completely destroy. Naturally, it was impossible to talk about "independence" and "autonomy" during the period 1948–1989, apart from certain moments of liberalization, which were followed by consolidation in terms of ideology and personnel. Even here there only existed "dreams of independence".

The failure of intellectuals

Petráň's work, in particular certain passages (including those dedicated to the Czech linguists Jan Mukařovský and František Trávníček), lead us to an issue which usually falls under the remit of the history of ideas – the so-called failure of or betrayal by intellectuals when faced by strong ideological pressure (existential or often life threatening). This is a complex matter which also relates to university culture for at least three reasons:

Firstly, it is not entirely clear what is meant by the word "intellectual". It is a term which holds different meanings in different historical periods and in different countries (France, Russia, England). In Central Europe, the French interpretation has a relatively strong tradition (intellectuals as the "conscience of the nation"), which is not only due to the goals of the national movements within the multi-ethnic Austrian state, but also the cultural transfer of the French meaning with its roots in the famous case connected to the Manifesto of the Intellectuals, published in relation to the Dreyfuss affair in Paris in 1898.[43] In more recent times, resistance to the communist regime has also played its role – for example, the Czech Charter 77 had a very strong "moral dimension", referring to the "voice of conscience".

Secondly, the theme of betrayal by intellectuals is only partially applicable to university culture because intellectuals are not just scientists or people who went through university. On the contrary, sometimes they are people who stand apart from universities, which they view as socially sterile and obstacles to true social

---

42   Ibid, p. 223.

43   The standing of intellectuals has been examined over the long term by Czech thinkers such as Mikuláš Lobkowicz, an emigre working in Germany (Munich, Eichstätt). Cf. Lobkowicz, Mikuláš: *Duše Evropy*. Prague 2001. In particular the chapter „Intelektuál: prorok, nebo metafyzický revolucionář?", pp. 60–69.

engagement. Intellectuals like to comment on the present (it is almost one of the "defining marks" of intellectuals), unlike "strict" academics who only observe their science and the allegedly objective reality hidden underneath the "daily froth".

When we look at the European university and interpretations of it, we cannot overlook the relative importance which universities and colleges attach to moral or immoral behaviour, especially in relation to revolutions and the authoritarian and totalitarian regimes of the 20th century. Universities in Central Europe were not able to completely rid themselves of the influence of intellectuals and their ideals – the universities in Prague and Brno are good examples.

The theme of betrayal by intellectuals is endless. There are more and more discussions in universities and elsewhere about the number and role of intellectuals who stood on the side of fascism, Nazism and communism. Interpretations are often based on emotional standpoints, and often popularize different individuals and their motivations without much critical evaluation. This is the case for universities across Europe where there are high-quality works on the "failings" of this type and of individuals from the West such as Carl Schmitt, Martin Heidegger, Knut Hamsun, Giovanni Gentili, Jean Paul Sartre and Herbert Markuse. Central and Eastern Europe, though, have followed with more superficial or moralistic interpretations.[44] It was certainly the case that intellectuals from universities and colleges, as well as people for whom the word intellectual was used more as a pejorative term, had a problem in the 20th century defending their independence against ideologies and attacks by ideological regimes, leading to considerable ethical problems.

The complexity of the whole matter is also due to the fact that although certain prominent authors succumbed to the allure of great utopian projects and ideologies, their works were also some of the best to be published in their field. In German culture this could be applied to the political philosopher Carl Schmitt (1888–1985), who alongside his Nazi ravings wrote important books on legal and political thought. From a Czech perspective, one example was the theologist from Charles University, Josef L. Hromádka (1889–1969), who in addition to his important work in the fields of dogmatic and ecumenical theology and inspirational pastoral work, also worked on behalf of the communist regime after 1948, and even created a complicated theological construct to substantiate and justify these activities.[45]

The difficulty in interpretation is down to the fact that intellectuals and academics bombarded the public with publications which were often interesting and influential, where they explained their positions and defended any of their fail-

---

44 This does not mean that important, high-quality works do not exist. Some have been translated into Czech, such as Kervégan, Jean–François: *Co s Karlem Schmittem?* Prague 2015.

45 Morée, Peter – Piškula, Jiří: *„Nejpokrokovější církevní pracovník". Protestantské církve a Josef Lukl Hromádka v letech 1945 – 1969.* Benešov 2015.

ings, which naturally their opponents did not forget to use in their critical publications. Central Europe is also a relatively rich area for similar discussions, albeit that these are more expressions of journalistic and media gratitude than critical, academic analyses. This is probably because in the Czech historical community the genre of intellectual history and the history of ideas has not been particularly well developed, while there also remains a certain academic reticence towards sensitive ethical themes.

A good example of a national discussion was one which was carried out over several decades and partly involved the world of academia – the debate surrounding the memoirs of the literary historian Václav Černý (1905–1987), which were first published in exile and then again after 1989.[46] Černý approached the "failure of intellectuals" in a very sharp and caustic manner, without attempting to hide his subjective viewpoint. Regarding Charles University, he not only cogently described its fall after 1948 and the tragedy of the university act of October 1950 (which he compared to the White Mountain catastrophe), but he also evaluated structural and personnel issues: *"The act suspended free intellectual thought at the university and in this sense put an end to its reason for existing; university humanism replaced by the trough of prescribed ideology and party propaganda. Intellectually independent people now had no business being there – neither professors nor students. There were several waves of expulsions of nonconformist teachers, regardless of the outcome for the school, science and the students. Then a vetting pogrom of students was organised based on their social background and beliefs, ignoring their talents, the future of national culture, or any justice or human sensitivity for young people. Informing, denunciation and spying on teachers and students was carried out at an official level."*[47] Černý was also criticized by the democratic intelligentsia (he was "damned" by orthodox communists and strongly criticized by reformists) for his sweeping generalizations as well as passing his private experiences for general trends. However, this writer demonstrated the irreplaceable role of the intellectual-academic in the public environment at a time when it was necessary to publish personal accounts. His work and the writings of others show that during the totalitarianism of the 20th century, it was a matter of preserving the absolute basics in education and morality on which creative human freedom rests.

Fortunately, the theme of "the failure of intellectuals" also contains the aspects of their "non-failure", i.e. the ability to resist all forms of totalitarianism and ideology. If we were to produce one example from many, practically a role model, then we could name the Czech theoretician, art historian and archaeologist

---

46 Černý, Václav: *Paměti I–III*. Brno 1992–1994.

47 Černý, Václav, c. d., III. vol, p. 271.

Růžena Vacková (1901–1982).[48] Naturally, she paid a high price for her protest: in February 1948 she was the only teacher from Charles University to take part in a student march to address President Edvard Beneš at the Castle, and at the same time spoke up for those teachers deemed unsuitable by the new regime. Her strong moral position did not go unpunished: she was sacked from her post in 1952 and sentenced to 22 years in prison as part of the "Mádr et al" show trial. From 1952–1967 (sic!) she spent time in prison in Znojmo, Nový Jičín, Pardubice, Ruzyně and Pankrác, Opava, Ilava and Ostrava nad Ohři. She became a credit to Czech higher education as even in the difficult conditions in jail she was able to communicate her thoughts and she often lectured for her fellow inmates.[49] Vacková thus became an example of freedom within complete "non-independence", which is something quite exceptional.

University freedom as an arduous undertaking

It might appear that the collapse of the USSR in 1989 and the liberation of Central Europe from dictatorship – which in the 1970s and 1980s meant censorship and the rejection of a plurality of ideas and personal legal recourse within universities and academia – also meant an end to those ideologies which had stifled science and academics throughout the entire 20th century. It might have looked this way at the start of the 1990s across a whole swathe of countries which had once more acquired their independence. State independence should also have meant independence for all of its institutions. However, initial enthusiasm soon cooled as it became apparent that it was impossible to introduce democratic structures overnight, and that the destruction had not only hit institutions, but also people's thinking and mentality. In any case, much was accomplished. Large and small universities in Central Europe gradually regained their lost self-assurance and re-established their former eminence as well as their international contacts, which had previously been directed entirely towards countries from the "Eastern Bloc". Added to this trend was also a kind of optimism, as in the 1990s there was the general conviction that it was possible in the new era to establish a multitude of new institutions, as there seemed to be a hunger for education which could not be satiated in just the large intellectual centres, but also in the regions.

Soon, however, problems began to appear. At first some intellectuals began to point to the fact that the end of communist utopia and concepts of "a class-free happy tomorrow" did not spell the end of all utopias, that we were still exposed

---

48   Cf. Gjuričová, Adéla: 20. stoletím s čistým štítem i utkvělými představami: Růžena Vacková. In: Marek, Pavel – Hanuš, Jiří (eds.): *Osobnost v církvi a politice*. Brno 2006, pp. 546–556.

49   Vacková, Růžena: *Vězeňské přednášky*. Prague 1999.

to several destructive influences (which was also the case for universities!), which forced us to adapt our ideas about independence and forced us – as the older ideologies did – into a type of behaviour which took away our freedom. Here we can look at three warnings from various facets of university life in Central Europe. According to the Krakow philosopher Ryszard Legutko (1949), one major contemporary problem that causes us great confusion is mass culture, which penetrates into and upsets the entire education system. In his view, therefore, we have been naïve to expect that a democratization of culture would lead to progress in the grand march of intellectual and aesthetic development, introducing life and dynamism to the existing hierarchy. Mass culture becomes a danger which democratic institutes are incapable of confronting and instead succumb to it: *"Education increasingly turns towards mass ideas and, therefore, the intellectual horizon typical for the majority. One interesting example is to observe the changes in school textbooks and manuals where references to mass culture, the mass aesthetic and an imagination formed by television or mass entertainment predominate. There is a widespread belief that education which ignores these relationships is ineffective. Children are perceived as a democratic electorate who have to be approached using various forms of persuasion and whom it is necessary to cajole, enliven, encourage, but how they will finally make decisions will depend entirely on them."*[50] Legutko's warning is not only applicable to primary and secondary schools, but also to universities, as it is there where they have to contend with the results of such educated youth. It is clear that "mass culture" is a phenomenon which goes hand in hand with democratic societies and its ideas of equality, and thus it is very difficult to avoid its influence.

The famous Austrian thinker Konrad Liessmann (1953) has a similarly critical, albeit less pessimistic outlook, and his works on university education and the character of our age have been widely translated and discussed in Central European intellectual circles. In his most famous book, Liessmann criticized the semi-education or even non-education spreading across universities and colleges, which are characterized by their emphasis on the different world rankings (PISA), attempts at reforms which bring a worse situation than before (the Bologna Process), and instead he called for the old (basically Humboldtian) model where universities did not chase after performance points. His observations concerning university autonomy deserve attention: *"This so-called university autonomy, which has taken root in many areas over recent years, gives the impression that it responds exactly to the demands for freedom in study and research. Universities have a guaranteed budget to cover at least the basic equipment and essential needs for teaching, and can to a large extent make decisions concerning employees and the listed fields of study. It is naturally curious that at those universities where the transfer to autonomy had been completed that the space for free decision-making had not expanded, but had in fact been restricted on*

---

50   Legutko, Ryszard: *Ošklivost demokracie a jiné eseje*. Brno 2009, pp. 24–25.

all levels. University autonomy in institutional and economic terms does not mean a free university. Autonomy can often be a euphemism for insufficient administration, which the state leaves to the universities themselves in order to save money. And through budgets, academic surveys and European directives, universities remain just as dependent on politicians as before. The joint financing by external sources, the existence of accreditation and evaluation agencies, and the interference by university boards to a greater extent in university affairs leave obvious marks."[51]

It is not necessary to agree with all of the Austrian philosopher's conclusions. On the other hand, it is interesting that similar criticisms have also appeared independently in different places. For example, the aspect of universities being subject to "practical interests" and the implementation of market principles within universities has been criticized by a group of British humanist and science scholars, and they also pointed to the paradox mentioned by Liessmann – what was initially had been emphasized as the quality of a university eventually became a burden which bureaucratized universities, and when combined with government intervention tended to damage the overall system.[52] The fact that critics have been heard from different areas saying similar things would suggest it is not just the work of some bitter cultural pessimists who do not want important reforms (even though such people can be found in universities!).

In recent years, however, criticisms concerning the bureaucratization of universities and the restriction of freedom have been connected to the European Union, its projects and overall strategy for higher education development. Many people have warned that the aim of a united policy pushed forward by the current liberal ideology (multiculturalism, gender and environmental themes, political correctness, the rejection of traditional values, the illusion of technology's ability to solve all problems), and the complex project mechanisms, confuse and place a burden on the existing national higher education systems. The application of the Union's "calendar plans" destroy academic creativity (as did the communists' Five-Year Plans). Gottfried Schatz (1936), a professor of biochemistry from Basel has warned, for example, that: *"Knowledge is precious, but we should not overestimate it. Our schools, our universities and our politicians responsible for research focus too much on knowledge and thus often suppress independent and critical thinking, i.e. science. The public and also, unfortunately, many research experts believe that research is a strictly logical process, which requires the researcher to patiently place stone upon stone until the meticulously planned building is finished. Innovative research, however, works exactly the other way round: it is intuitive, rarely predictable, full of surprises and sometimes even chaotic, all of which also applies to innovative art. Both innovative art*

---

51 Liessmann, Konrad Paul: *Teorie nevzdělanosti. Omyly společnosti vědění.* Prague 2010, p. 84.

52 Cf. Ohrožení britských univerzit (Rada na obranu britských univerzit a Manifest reformy), Kontexty V., 1 (2013), pp. 45–49.

and science cannot be compared to strolls along clean streets, but rather to expeditions into unknown territories, where artists and scientists often get lost."[53] There are also some Czech university professors who are not afraid to criticize the Union's existing education policy as "social engineering" of a sort. For example, the biologist and philosopher Stanislav Komárek has repeatedly brought attention to the growth in the number of diplomas, the expansion of the term "university" ("The University of Local Studies and Tourist Management in Smallville"), the disintegration of the term "cultural heritage" and the erosion of the meaning of education.[54] He states: "*When I see the gigantic and uncommonly generous programmes of the European Union under the pressure of integrating European education and research in often bizarre bureaucratic projects, where they have calculated precisely the number of institutions from different regions of the continent which have to work together, along with the percentage of women and young people involved, then I can't help but feel anxious.*"[55] Although many university researchers do not express themselves so succinctly, they are also often thinking the same thing.

Conclusion

The myth of freedom and autonomy, and the exaggerated expectations concerning both values, can be seen in issues which face us today. These should be described and analysed by academics and intellectuals who are part of the university environment and know its weaknesses. In addition, it is necessary to give a precise definition of the borders of the "independence" of science as well as university institutions. The 20th century showed how important this independence is, while the present teaches us how delicate a fabric independence creates, how complex the issue of free research is within institutions and how problematic and counterproductive attempts at reforms (even necessary ones) can be. University freedom is a fragile flower which not only needs care, but the right type of care. Otherwise it will die.

---

53   Schatz, Gottfried: *Skutečné vzdělání namísto pouhého zprostředkování znalostí.* Kontexty VII., 3/2015, p. 33.

54   Cf. Komárek, Stanislav: *Evropa na rozcestí.* Prague 2015, pp. 259–261.

55   Ibid, p. 260.

THE HUMBOLDTIAN MYTH

"The Humboldtian myth is like a shield which academics always raise whenever university reforms appear on the horizon."[56] *"Humboldt is carried into every debate about higher education like a monstrance."*[57] *"Humboldt is the name of the besieged ivory towers' line of defence."*[58] *"The Bologna Process is in fact the struggle between the bourgeois Humboldtians and the plebeian Bolognians."*[59] These are just a few of the opinions about the work and myth of a man who, despite having not invented the concept of early modern Central European university education based on the unity of research and teaching, was largely responsible for its implementation. The story of Wilhelm Humboldt, who created from chaos a university of world renown and provided direction for the development of (Central European) university culture, is a theme which occupies anyone in academia who is interested in the idea of the *universitas* within a wider historical and cultural context. In 2013 Petr Pabian and Karel Šima's mainly sociological view of Humboldt described his utopian vision of the university as an ideology, arguing that the great majority of the (academic)

---

56 Lundgren, Peter: Mytos Humboldt in der Gegenwart. Lehre – Forschung – Selbstverwaltung, In: Ash, Mitchell (Hg.): *Mythos Humboldt. Vergangenheit und Zukunft der deutschen Universitäten*. Wien – Köln – Weimar 1999, pp. 145–169, p. 166.

57 Markschies, Christoph: Was von Humboldt noch zu lernen ist? 11 Thesen. In: Kovce, Philip – Priddat, Birgit (Hg.): *Die Aufgabe der Bildung. Aussichten der Universität*. Marburg 2015, pp. 239–246, here p.240.

58 Weisbrodt. Bernd: Der wandelbare Geist. Akademisches Ideal und wissenschaftliche Transformation in der Nachkriegszeit, In: (Hg.): *Akademische Vergangenheitspolitik. Beiträge zur Wissenschaftskultur der Nachkriegszeit*. Göttingen 2002, pp. 11–38, here p. 26.

59 Krull, Wilhelm: Hat das Humboldtsche Bildungsideal noch eine Zukunft? In: Rudersdorf, Manfred – Höpken, Wolfgang – Schlegel, Martin (Hg.) *Wissen und Geist. Universitätskulturen*. Leipzig 2009, pp. 207–219, here p. 207.

public are still under its sway, even consciously and gladly so because of fears about the consequences of university reforms over the past decades.[60] Our objective is to look at "Humboldt" as a myth, and in this respect our position is historical on the one hand, though somewhat more indulgent on the other, as we are not as direct in calling for some kind of "liberation".[61] However, like our colleagues, we also ask: What is the purpose of this narrative, who does it benefit?

The Humboldtian myth has shown incredible resilience across epochs and regimes, demonstrating how strongly resistant the medieval academic community is to change. Konrad Jarausch says that this myth provides the basis for academic exceptionalism and academics' demands to be treated differently to other professions. This claim ostensibly ignores the fact that over the last fifty years the number of universities in Central Europe has quadrupled and the number of students matriculating has increased fifteen-fold. The narrators of the Humboldtian myth have even managed to turn their position "outside of time and social reality" to their advantage, stubbornly clinging to their privileges as the foundation of their identity as members of the academic community. According to Jarausch, this attachment to the Humboldtian vision in today's academic community is merely an empty slogan which has nothing in common with the reality of mass universities, and the Humboldtian cultural circle only impedes any reforms to universities. This is viewed from a global perspective, particularly by American and Asian authors, as the most traditional and least open to reform.[62] There is even a euphemism which compares the Humboldtian mythical narrative to an illness.[63]

Stories about the Prussian philologist and organizer of higher education are also well known in non-German countries which historically have shared the model of the Humboldtian university, inspired in part by the Prussian reforms – i.e. in Germany's eastern neighbours, in Italy and in the Balkans.[64] In today's universities in the Czech Republic and Austria we no longer encounter myths about the national reformer Leo Thun, or Hungary's Jozef Eötvös, only the myth about

---

60 Šima, Karel – Pabian, Petr: *Ztracený Humboldtův ráj. Ideologie jednoty výzkumu a výuky ve vysokém školství.* Prague 2013, esp. pp. 11–13, 25

61 Ibid, pp. 138–143.

62 E.g. Fallon, Daniel: *The German University. A heroic ideal in conflict with the modern world.* Boluder/ Colorado 1980; Neave, Guy – Blückert, Kjell – Nybom, Thorsten (ed.).: *The European research university. An historical parenthesis?* New York 2006.

63 Jarausch, Konrad: Das Humboldt–Syndrom. Die westdeutschen Universitäten 1945–1989 – ein akademischer Sonderweg?, In: Ash, Mitchell G. (Hg.): *Mythos Humboldt. Vergangenheit und Zukunft der deutschen Universitäten.* Wien – Köln – Weimar 1999, pp. 58–79, here p. 75.

64 Livescu, Jean: Die Entstehung der rumänischen Universitäten im Zusammenhang der europäischen Kulturbeziehungen (1850–1870). In: Plaschka, Richard Georg – Mack, Karlheinz (Hg.): *Wegenetz europäischen Geistes. Wissenschaftzentren und geistige Wechselbeziehungen zwischen Mittel- und Südosteuropa vom Ende des 19. Jahrhunderts bis zum Ersten Weltkrieg.* Wien 1983, p. 21–35; Barbagli, Marzio: *Educating for unemployment: politics, labor markets, and the school systém – Italy 1859–1973.* New York 1982.

Humboldt.[65] Over the years his story, which is basically about political compromise, has had other narratives added to it, and we are at present dealing with a myth which has the largest mobilizing influence within the academic community. "Humboldt" stirs up emotions – as an argument it appears in the debates about the present state and future of the university, and it has been held up as a slogan by representatives standing on one side or the other of the debate on reforming higher education.

Meanwhile, the historical core of the Humboldtian myth retreats into the background. Apart from a handful of historians, it is rare for anyone to see the important context of the reforms. Wilhelm von Humboldt was one of the participants in the crucial debates concerning the future of higher education in Prussia and Germany around 1800 – a time when the whole university education system was in crisis – something which offers parallels to the state of universities today. Sylvia Paletschek even talks about the "extinction" of German universities during this period[66]: around the year 1800, half of the universities had closed – a total of 22 German-speaking universities (including universities in Cologne, Strasbourg, Bonn, Erfurt and Münster). Their fate was decided by the constitutional changes which had been introduced in Germany as a result of the French invasions. It is important to recall that of the approximately 300 German states from the era of the Napoleonic Wars, only around thirty survived. The universities lost their sovereign, their patron and their political protection. But the crisis was mainly due to internal reasons – society viewed university education as unnecessary and outdated. Many of the formerly large and famous universities only had a handful of students registered: for example, Duisburg only had 38 students, Erfurt 43.[67] It is also often forgotten that this university apocalypse was not only confined to German lands: of the 143 universities in Europe in 1789, only 60 remained twenty years later. During the revolution and the time of Napoleon, all 22 universities were closed in France as they were viewed by the revolutionary regime as a body which limited and threatened freedom of expression. Professional academies appeared in their place which quickly grew in prestige, with some of them also being more research oriented. Universities were perceived as being incompatible with the challenges of the modern age, which required a rational and scientific approach towards the world. The word "university" was seen as being so hopelessly

---

65 Engelbrecht, Helmut: *Geschichte des österreichischen Bildungswesens*, Bd. 4, Von 1848 bi zum Ende der Monarchie. Wien 1986, pp. 221–251; Szögi, László: Die Universitäten in Ungarn. Gründungswelle vom späten Mittelalter bis ins 20. Jahrhundert. In: Wörster, Peter (Hg.): *Universitäten im östlichen Europa. Zwischen Kirche, Staat und Nation– Sozialgeschichtliche und politische Entwicklungen*. München 2008, pp. 235–268, esp. pp. 255–259.

66 Paletschek, Sylvia: *Die permanente Erfindung der Tradition. Die Universität Tübingen im Kaiserreich und in der Weimarer Republik*. Stuttgart 2001, p. 27.

67 Mittelstraß, *Die unzeitgemäße Universität*, p. 20, 71.

old fashioned and historically discredited that only a few Prussian educational specialists used it in debates when describing the future institutions of higher education.[68]

The Humboldtian concept of the university was born from the interaction between ideological allies and opponents, the result of which (and also its symbol) – the University of Berlin (1810) – was a compromise. This grew from the shared conviction of the members of Prussia's educated elite that the "old university" had had its day and that fundamental changes were necessary. There was a powerful group of politicians and officials at the head of the Prussian state who saw a way out of the crisis in university education through the transference of some of the university's activities, specifically its lower arts faculties, to the gymnasium. The upper faculties were to be replaced by professional academies. The spokesperson for this group, the legal expert Julius von Massow, was a Prussian minister whose department was responsible for the reform of higher education. On the other hand, the theologian and philosopher Friedrich Schleiermacher, who held high positions within the Prussian Lutheran Church and scholarly societies, was regarded as the spokesperson of the conservative wing of reformers, who advocated revitalizing the university through a reform of its educational goals and curricula. The philosophers Immanuel Kant and Johann Gottlieb Fichte also had considerable influence on the public debate on higher education. In addition to organizational issues, they both added the theme of higher education fulfilling the ideal of searching for truth and attaining social progress through education within an enlightened society. Thanks largely to Fichte, the legal-political issue of the future of the university became an ethical topic with a considerable mobilizing influence on public opinion; as part of his vision of the university, Fichte incorporated his dream of a better humanity which would be attained through the courses at generally focused arts faculties.[69]

If we look at this entire project from a distance, it is quite remarkable that such an ethically grounded argument, far removed from the reality of a complicated era full of dramatic political and social changes, eventually found an audience amongst the Prussian court and the public. Some authors have looked for a connection between the profound crisis of the Prussian state and its crushing defeat at Jena in 1806, when the shock of defeat prompted attempts to re-establish the state from its very foundations.[70] Fichte's ethically based involvement in the debates was even mocked by his contemporaries – for example, one of his colleagues said that *"the university is in fact Fichte institutionalized"*, by which he meant the

---

68 *Geschichte der Universität in Europa.* Band IV. Hg. Von Walter Rüegg. München 2008, p. 27; *Hodnocení kvality vysokých škol jako světový problém.* Prague 1997, p. 105.

69 Mittelstraß, *Die unzeitgemäße Universität*, pp. 20–24; Rolfe, Gary: *The University in Dissent. Scholarship in the corporate university.* London – New York 2013, p.13 ff.

70 *Geschichte der Universität in Europa.* Band IV. Hg. von Walter Rüegg. München 2008, p. 47.

undisguised idealism and even utopianism of the whole project.[71] The public was evidently receptive to ancient platonic ideas about schools which would educate philosopher-kings, a place where education would not be determined by "*bureaucrats and pedants, but by philosophers and scientists.*"[72]

The next development in the Humboldtian educational project has been well researched, but there are still different opinions concerning its interpretation. Sceptics highlight it as an idealistic project which was far removed from reality; they talk about the "short-lived dream" of an ideal university which became a reality and worked well for only a relatively short period of time – a few decades is but an episode in the long history of higher education. The pessimists point to the fact that the Humboldtian concept was always only partially viable, underlining the compromised nature of the project from the outset. They overlook its ethical mission and focus on utilitarian criteria, particularly criteria which are quantifiable. Neither is there any shortage of general criticism of the Humboldtian project as something which has brought more negatives than positives, and it is also possible to find those who mock the two-hundred-year academic debate on the Humboldtian university as just further proof of the hopeless state of the university which is impossible to reform and is incompatible with the world that surrounds it. Optimistic voices are to be heard less often. The defence of Humboldt is carried out with some embarrassment, evidently from concerns about being stigmatized as being a nostalgic, distant professor, who is ready to remain in his ivory tower at any cost. However, when they do appear, they offer a revitalized, updated, enlightened vision of a better society through education. Fichte would be pleased to see his ethical argument resurface here about the beneficial influence of a properly functioning university on humanity. Naturally, the difference is that neither the parliaments or the public of the "liberal democracies" listen to that argument in the way that scholars and royal officials did in early modern Prussia.

Which elements of the Humboldtian reforms proved to be of long-term significance for the development of the university in Central Europe? Although there is no complete agreement amongst scholars, it is possible to speak of two central arguments which still resonate strongly within academia:

a) *University autonomy and academic freedom.* The university is a community of scholars which should be governed only by a committee chosen from inside the academic community. This arrangement effectively immunizes academics against unwanted political and economic pressure, and within this framework of guaranteed freedom it is possible for them to develop their teaching and research in the appropriate direction – including directions which peers may view as unnecessary, erroneous or too expensive. The

---

71 Mittelstraß, *Die unzeitgemäße Universität*, p. 22.

72 Ibid, p. 24.

university is an ethical community of people seeking the truth, their performance cannot be measured using a utilitarian standpoint, as the view of the present is not sufficiently relevant. Through its activities the university, more than any other institution, combines the past, present and future of mankind.

b) *Combining research and teaching.* High-quality university education is unimaginable without the wealth of experience that educators have from their research work. The basic rules of research work and their transdisciplinary scope encompassing the "totality of knowledge and truth" is one of the main benefits of a university education in comparison with other higher levels of education.

Marita Baumgartner provided a unique insight into the social history of professors during the golden era of Humboldt. It is an illuminating overview of the difference between ideals and reality. In 1914 the following disciplines (according to hierarchy) made up the core of the humanities professorships: philosophy, classical philology, German studies, Romance languages and literature, and English studies. The majority of universities also had Oriental studies, Sanskrit, comparative linguistics, history, archaeology and art history. Hierarchically the natural sciences consisted of mathematics, physics, chemistry, mineralogy, botany, zoology and geography. Baumgartner described the dense network of family ties between academics throughout the whole of the 19th century: 2 out of 3 humanities professors had a relative who was an academic, every eleventh professor was the son of a professor, every tenth professor had a wife who was the daughter of a professor, every seventh had a son in academia. Baumgartner makes direct mention of professorial dynasties which ruled over the universities. She also states, however, that these ties were much more numerous and stronger in the 16th and 17th centuries. The situation was similar in the natural sciences, where the tendency to create dynasties was only marginally weaker. In the provincial universities, a professorship was attained at the age of 37–38 while the overall German average was 39. The metropolitan university in Berlin was considered to be the pinnacle of one's career and, as a result, professors were accepted at an older age. In the natural science disciplines the average age of a professor was slightly lower, and the practical training at the metropolitan universities in Berlin and Munich was the same. Compared with today, professors held on to their chairs much more tenaciously – in the humanities only one in seven professors had experience of teaching abroad, while it was one in every thirteen in the natural sciences. Arts researchers would usually travel to German-speaking countries, whilst the natural scientists utilized the wider university circles and were considered more integrated into the international networks.[73] The ideological core

---

73 Baumgartner, Marita: *Professoren und Universitäten im 19. Jahrhundert.* Göttingen 1997, esp. pp. 55–86, 93–130, 181–182, 240–243.

of the Humboldtian university became clearer the moment the whole concept became threatened. Robert Anderson states that the golden era of the Prussian university model was clearly linked to the period of pre-industrialized Germany with its relatively small middle class prior to the country's unification. The rapid modernization of society after 1870 was no longer compatible with the Humboldtian concept.[74] Around 1900 it was obvious that the system was going through a crisis and that fundamental reforms were necessary. Jürgen Mittelstraß mentions three spectres which have hovered over "Humboldtians" since then: a reduction in the cultural level of students going to university; the mass nature of university study; and the movement of research away from the university, requiring its supporters to constantly defend its rationale and two central arguments.[75] The concept undoubtedly had more problematic areas, but from the perspective of the history of Central Europe in the 20th century, these three issues became highly significant and were the greatest threats to the viability of the Humboldtian university.

By 1900, university lecture halls were already overcrowded and the whole infrastructure was under such intense pressure that the issue of publicly financing universities became an acute problem. At the same time, there was political pressure to make education more accessible, though within the financial means of public budgets. Sylvia Paletschek pointed out that the 1870s–1880s saw a type of competition between political representatives of the German states and the free cities over which universities would be better equipped.[76] This ethos disappeared in Germany around the year 1900.[77] On the periphery of the Humboldtian circle – for example, in Czech, Polish, Greek[78] or Norwegian areas[79] – its effects lasted somewhat longer, particularly in connection with the birth of nation states where universities were their calling cards, but even here this ethos began to disappear during the interwar period when faced with the extremely high costs of higher education for a wider section of the population.[80] The expanding network of

---

74   Anderson, Robert A.: *European Universities from the Enlightenment to 1914*. Oxford – New York 2004, p. 151 ff.

75   Mittelstraß, *Die unzeitgemäße Universität*, p. 31.

76   Paletschek, *Die permanente Erfindung*, p. 525.

77   vom Brocke, Bernhard: Wege aus der Krise: Universitätsseminar, Akademiekomission und Forschungsinstitut. Formen der Institutionalisierung in den Geistes– und Naturwisseschaften 1810–1900–1995. In: König, Christoph – Lämmert, Eberhard (Hg.): *Konkurrenten in der Fakultät. Kultur, Wissen und Universität um 1900*. Frankfurt am Main 1999, pp. 191–215, here 204–205.

78   Derwissis, Stergios Nikolaos: *Die Geschichte der griechischen Bildugswesens in neueren Zeit mit besonderer Berücksichtigung der Einflüsse der deutschen Pädadogik*. Frankfurt am Main 1976, esp. pp. 191, 194.

79   Langholm, Sivert: The new nationalism and the new universities. The case of Norway in the early 19th century, In: Norrback, Märtha – Ranki, Kristina (eds.): *University and nation: the university and the making of the nation in northern Europe in the 19th and 20th centuries*. Helsinki 1996, pp. 139–152.

80   Doležalová, Antonie: Ve vleku nemožného čechoslovakismu? Financování Univerzity Komenského v meziválečném období (skrze československý státní rozpočet). In: Slobodník, Martin – Glossová,

gymnasiums in the Habsburg empire from the 1880s produced a large number of students whose normal career course was the university. This was why Austrian governments were so hesitant about establishing more universities, even though there was a large number of candidates: Zadar, Terst, Ljubljana, Rovereto, Opava, Olomouc and Brno.[81]

However, mass education in the secondary and tertiary sectors produced a different type of scholar than in the past, who soon became far removed from the ideal of Kant, Humboldt and Fichte. The "new" students were much more pragmatic and saw money spent on their education as an investment. The costs of study were viewed as so exorbitant by families from the petit bourgeoisie and the peasantry that they were to be returned to the family as quickly as possible, either in a pecuniary form or at least in the form of heightened social status through prestigious employment.[82] As a result, values such as the search for truth and the cultivation of humanity as the general objectives of a university education were eroded under pressure from a general pragmatism and political and ideological particularism.

The pressure on the infrastructure and the lack of clarity concerning the future direction and mission of the university went hand in hand with doubts over being able to implement the Humboldtian vision of combining research and teaching for the greater good. The high number of poorly prepared students, hungry for a diploma more than an education, was more of a brake on research as it forced talented researchers to waste time on arduous mass education. The university began to be seen as an institution whose representatives failed to understand the challenges of accelerating technological and scientific research, indulging themselves in outdated philosophical idealism. There were cases in the humanities where it was not exceptional for a professor to work for decades on something which was intended only for a very small circle of specialists, and who was openly negative towards the wider reading community, which he ostentatiously ignored, veiled as

---

Marta: *95 rokov Filozofickej fakulty UK. Pohľad do dejín inštitúcie a jej akademickej obce.* Bratislava 2017, pp. 89–103; Garlicki, Andrzej et alii: *Dzieje Unywersytetu Warszawskiego.* Warszawa 1982, pp. 97–105; Grot, Zdisław (ed.): *Dzieje Uniwersytetu im. Adama Mickeiwicza 1919–1969.* Poznaň 1972, pp. 189–197.

81   Kostner, Maria: *Die Geschichte der italienischen Universitätsfrage in der Österreichisch–ungarischen Monarchie von 1864 bis 1914.* Diss. Innsbruck 1970; Otruba, Gustav: *Die Universitäten in der Hochschulorganisation der Donau–Monarchie: Nationale Erziehungsstätten im Vielvölkerreich 1850 bis 1914. Student und Hochschule im 19. Jahrhundert: Studie und Materialen.* Göttingen 1975, pp. 75–155; Anderson, Robert D.: *European Universities from the Enlightenment to 1914.* Oxford 2004, pp. 234–240; Gawrecki, Dan: Versuche um die Gründung einer Universität in Troppau im 19. und 20. Jahrhundert, In: Schübel, Elmar – Heppner, Harald (Hg.): *Universitäten in Zeiten des Umbruchs. Fallstudien über das mittlere und östliche Europa im 20. Jahrhundert.* Wien – Berlin 2011, pp. 59–68; Moklak, Jarosław: Lwów i Triest. Uniwersyteckie dążenia Ukraińców, Włochów, Chorwatów i Słoweńców (1908–1914). In: Pezda, Janusz – Pijaj, Stanisław (red.): *Europa środkowa, Bałkany i Polacy.* Kraków 2017, pp. 241–248.

82   Pokludová, Andrea: *Formování inteligence na Moravě a ve Slezsku 1857–1910.* Opava 2008, pp. 268–274.

he was in the cloak of "pure science".[83] The professor, who after many years of wallowing in the heuristic phase of his research, and despite amassing more and more sources and critiques, was unable to proceed to write even a short synthesis. Someone who in spite of the fact that the public knew little of his findings, held on tooth and nail to his post as a professor with a considerable salary from public sources; often maligning or getting rid of any (potential) competitors and pushing forward his own *famuli* – such a professor at the time would have been called a *"university mandarin"*, a favourite term often used by Tomáš Masaryk.[84]

The radical departure from "Humboldtian mandarinism"

During the interwar period, radical political forces were effective in recruiting sympathizers from amongst frustrated students and university graduates. The Nazis were particularly successful during the interwar period amongst the young research staff and the "eternal senior lecturers", waiting for a professor's chair to be made available.[85] However, the attacks by the radicals against university mandarinism were selective, though particularly effective against professors of Jewish origin or with Jewish partners, foreigners and strong opponents of fascist "völkisch" ideas. The far-left fought successfully against academics from a bourgeoise background and members of the academic community who stood in open opposition to them.

However, the majority of "mandarins" had no problem reaching a compromise with, or becoming fervent supporters of, politically radical regimes, whether Nazi or communist. Numerous professors quietly got rid of competitors and colleagues, while many simply did not have the courage to stand up for the persecuted or openly challenge the political authorities, preferring instead to hide behind the argument that their mission was academic, not political. Although some authors see the end of "Humboldtian mandarinism" with the destruction of the professors' tightly-knit bodies,[86] there is a misunderstanding here of the cultural context. The core of this social group with its specific culture remained intact despite the

---

83 Borovský, Tomáš (red.): *Historici na brněnské univerzitě. Devět portrétů.* Brno 2008, pp. 32–33, 78–82.

84 Ringer, Fritz K.: *Die Gelehrten. Der Niedergang der deutschen Mandarine 1890–1933.* Stuttgart 1983.

85 Grüttner, Michael: *Nationalsozialistische Wissenschaftler: ein Kollektivporträt.* In: Hachtmann, Rüdiger – Jarausch, Konrad – John, Jürgen – Middell, Michael (Hg.): Gebrochene Wissenschaftskulturen. Universität und Politik im 20. Jahrhundert. Göttingen 2010, pp. 149–166.

86 Friedländer, Saul: The Demise of the German Mandarins. The German University and the Jews. In: Jansen, Christian – Niethammer, Lutz – Weisbrod, Bernd: *Von der Aufgabe der Freiheit. Politische Verantwortung und bürgerliche Gesellschaft im 19. und 20. Jahrhundert. Festschrift Hans Mommsen.* Berlin 1995, pp. 69–82.

professors' lack of social credibility, and continued to insist on the classic ideals of university freedom and autonomy, at least in part.

Although the conditions at German universities under radical political pressure have been better explored than in other countries of Central Europe, it is clear that academic freedom and tolerance were not only in danger in Germany during the 20th century. Polish universities were hit by a wave of antisemitism from some sections of the student community which the professors were unable to counter effectively.[87] An anthology entitled *Za lepší svět* (For a Better World) from 1963 presents recollections of university life from the interwar period by Czechoslovak students from the far left. The memoirs contradict today's interpretation in the Czech Republic and Slovakia of students' lives as being an idyllic, politically indifferent time,[88] demonstrating as they do – albeit in a stylized, glorified and in places quite bombastic manner – the activities of politically radical groups of students in Czechoslovak universities. Although political indifference clearly prevailed in the student community, a large number of students were grouped in faculty societies of a professional character (The Lawyer, The Society of Philosophy Students, etc.), and there were fierce, sometimes even violent struggles over the leadership positions of students' political organizations. The radicalization of the public was also transferred to the university, dividing the academic community. This was manifested in German and Czech chauvinism and the eruption of conflicts in universities during the years of the "insignia wars" (1934–1935); the division of Polish academia in relation to Marshal Piłsudski's authoritarian reorganization; and the even starker divisions based on attitudes towards the Jewish question, Andrej Hlinka's Slovak nationalist movement, and the ultra-left radicalism of some sections of the student body.[89]

The metropolitan universities close to the centre of power were even more politicized.[90] The professors had their work cut out trying to maintain at least

87 Connelly, John: *Zotročená univerzita: Sovětizace vysokého školství ve východním Německu, v letech 1945–1956*. Prague 2008, pp. 140–143.

88 Grófová, Maria: „... a jako tretia vznikla filozofická fakulta". K počiatkom a prvým rokom FiF UK. In: *95 rokov Filozofickej fakulty UK. Pohľad do dejín inštitúcie a jej akademickej obce*. Bratislava 2017, pp. 40–72, pp. 44–61.

89 Domin, Karel – Vojtíšek, Václav – Hutter, Josef: *Karolinum statek národní*. Praha 1934; Domin, Karel: *Můj rektorský rok. Z bojů o Karolinum a za práva Karlovy univerzity*. Prague 1934; Goldstücker, Eduard (eds.): *Za lepší zítřek. Sborník a vzpomínek na studentské pokrokové hnutí třicátých let*. Prague 1963; *Dějiny UK IV.*, pp. 43–44; Friedländer, Saul: *The Demise of the German Mandarins. The German University and the Jews*. In: Jansen, Christian – Niethammer, Lutz – Weisbrod, Bernd: Von der Aufgabe der Freiheit. Politische Verantwortung und bürgerliche Gesellschaft im 19. und 20. Jahrhundert. Festschrift Hans Mommsen. Berlin 1995, pp. 69–82; Majewski, Piotr (ed.): *Dzieje Uniwersytetu Warszawskiego 1915–1945*. Warsaw 2016, pp. 251–295.

90 Kučera, Karel – Truc, Miroslav: *Poznámky k fašizaci Německé univerzity pražské*, Acta Universitatis Pragensis 1960, r. 1, sešit 1, pp. 203–223; Chlupová, Alena: *K volbě rektora a prvnímu otevřenému vystoupení nacistických studentů na Německé univerzitě v Praze roku 1922*, Acta Universitatis Pragensis,

some sense of cohesion and mutual respect, and there were several students who remembered strongly polarized political opinions, as well as a growing impoliteness and even vulgarity in behaviour. One Prague professor of philology refused to accept phonology in his department as it was the teachings of that "*Bolshevik Jew Jacobson*"[91]; his left-leaning colleagues then entered into the debate about the difference between Italian and German fascism with the words "*we're not going to argue about which shit smells worse*".[92] However, the erosion of political neutrality was also noticeable in the provincial universities in Bratislava, Poznaň and Brno. The activities of the communist students in Brno's universities were supported and even partially shielded by several professors, notably Jiří Kroha at the Technical University and Vladimír Helfert at Masaryk University. Otakar Vašek recalled the arguments between the radicals in 1932 in connection with a large political gathering of the academic community on the question of student social welfare and the controversial issue of the diplomatic recognition of the Soviet Union: "*At the medical faculty in particular, where the right-wingers were in a strong position, much propaganda was made of the slogan 'Kroha must not speak'. But Profesor Kroha did speak. In his speech he referred to the great example of the Soviet Union and the lives of its students now and in the future. His speech made a powerful impression and was a great success. However, the fascists at the medical faculty got their own back the next day when they beat bloody some students going into the faculty. They not only beat up students who had organised the meeting, but also Jews and foreigners, many of whom had nothing to do with yesterday's meeting.*"[93] Students were dragged into public life by the radicals through discussions and meetings in support of the Most strikes or the Spanish Republican regime; influenced by these debates, some of the socially vulnerable students became aware of class differences and their prospects in life. The radicals were very blunt concerning the differences between their political beliefs and those of their fellow students, as can be seen in one left-wing student's opinion of his colleagues: "*You can find good material* (for the chauvinist rebellions – author's

1978, r. 18, sešit 2, pp. 78–92; Psotová, Věra: *Fašizace německého studentstva a ohlas tohoto procesu mezi německými studenty v Československu*, Acta Universitatis Pragensis 1980, r. 20, sešit 1, pp. 31–60; Kindl, Vladimír: *Pokus o zařazení tzv. dělnického práva do výuky Právnické fakulty UK v období buržoazní ČSR*. Acta Universitatis Carolinae 1984, r. 24, sešit 1, pp. 45–66; Majewski, Piotr (ed.): *Dzieje Uniwersytetu Warszawskiego 1915–1945*. Warsaw 2016, pp. 251–295.

91   Roman Osipovič Jacobson (1896–1982), a Russian linguist considered to be one of the greatest linguists of the 20th century, during the interwar period he was one of the representatives of the Prague Linguistic Circle, an association promoting a structuralist revision of linguistic approaches.

92   Vávra, Jaroslav: *Zapomenutá doktorská disertace o Jaroslavu Haškovi. Ke vztahům mezi posluchači a profesory Karlovy univerzity za fašistického ohrožení ČSR*. Acta Universitatis Carolinae 1984, r. 24, sešit 2, pp. 55–68, here pp. 59, 61.

93   Žilka, Ladislav – Vašek, Otakar: *O brněnských vysokých školách*. In: Goldstücker, Eduard (eds.): *Za lepší zítřek. Sborník vzpomínek na studentské pokrokové hnutí třicátých let*. Prague 1963, pp. 177–184, here 183–184.

note) *at universities. The 'golden youth' were concentrated in universities – the sons of factory owners and businessmen in wholesale and the meat trade, green youths from the courts of estate owners and large farmers, as well as the sons of rich lawyers and doctors.*"[94]

In his analysis of the "Humboldt myth", Mitchell Ash states that its roots are obvious in the decades surrounding the year 1900. According to him, the reality of the Central European university started to be interpreted in a mythical way as a defence against impending changes. Ash terms the myth a neo-humanist code to defend the university from the influx of radically minded students from the petite bourgeois and the working class, and from the pressure from technical colleges and specialized research centres.[95] There were other threats on the horizon which motivated some professors to develop a neo-Humboldtian narrative – the unappealing idea of women entering academia and the greater influence of the socialists as the largest mass political party with an anti-elitist, international programme. There emerged a culturally pessimistic myth of the gradual disintegration of civilization as a result of the irreversible departure from the humanist tradition of the late Enlightenment.

In the eyes of German professors – the narrators of the myth – German civilization began to disintegrate around 1900. Externally, this was the result of being hemmed in by the demographic superiority of the Slavonic nations to the East, by the dynamic growth of the USA and its universities, and the rejection by the "old" European powers of Germany's political and colonial aspirations. Internally, it was threatened by the democratic pluralism of lifestyles and values, the decadency of consumerism, female emancipation undermining traditional concepts of masculinity, the international socialism of "comrades without nations", and the relativist values of the younger generation.

During this period the discourse of Czech and Polish professors was connected to the story of their nations and was optimistic as a result of the national-emancipation process and the emergence of their independent nations in 1918. It was the serious problems which the two new republics faced – chronic political instability in Czechoslovak democracy and the authoritarian regime under Józef Piłsudski in Poland, the economic crisis from 1929–1934, and the breakdown in the international position of both countries under pressure from Nazi Germany and Soviet Russia – which transformed Humboldt into a culturally pessimistic myth in Central Europe, requiring new solutions to be found.

The narrative of the Humboldtian myth had very ambivalent features under pressure from the Nazi and communist regimes. One common feature was a criti-

---

94 Borek, Zoltán – Lhotka, Jaroslav: *Studentské bouře.* Ibid, pp. 96–104, here p. 97.

95 Ash, Mitchell: Konstruierte Kontinuitäten und divergierende Neuanfänge nach 1945, In: Grüttner, Michael – Hachtmann, Rüdiger – Jarausch, Konrad – John, Jürgen – Middell, Michael (Hg.): *Gebrochene Wissenschaftskulturen. Universität und Politik im 20. Jahrhundert.* Göttingen 2010, pp. 215–245, here p. 243.

cal view of the myth as belonging to the historically discredited tradition of the bourgeois university which was to be eliminated when creating a new humanity. This critique focused on three problems of the late-Humboldtian university, clear even to the impartial observer:

a) The severe long-term lack of finance. The financial support was enough to keep universities operating at a minimal level with an emphasis on teaching, but not to concurrently develop pedagogical and research work at the pace of the top Western (private) universities. The Humboldtian ideal of combining research and teaching was just empty words.

b) The university's lack of capacity in research infrastructure and an inability and unwillingness to address the demands of applied science for top research products. Here the university failed in its role as an accumulator of knowledge for the benefit of all of society.

c) The individualism and exclusivity of university professors resulted in the failure of universities when faced with complex, transversal solutions to problems. Attempts at reform ran up against the closed nature of the professors who created, or ruled over, the universities' power structures, forming an image of overwhelming conservatism in the university committees which bordered on reactionary.

Ivan Málek, a biologist and Czechoslovak theoretician of management science, an admirer of the Soviet system and promoter of its application in the Czechoslovak Academy of Sciences,[96] was very critical of interwar university education in 1955, but made several pertinent points: *"We really only considered universities when we were looking at basic research issues. But what were the options? The subsidies were very small and were aimed at the work of the teachers, which they barely covered. The institutions were not scientific institutions in the true sense of the word, but rather teaching departments and were thus poorly equipped for scientific work. Scientists worked either on their own here or in small groups of scientific workers; but the majority did not work collectively, it was more or less every man for himself... And those individuals who worked scientifically, most of them only did so a little – in addition to their teaching or other routine work – basically in the evenings, during the holidays and only as an unpaid private matter. For many of them their scientific work was to aid their own careers, and so it was not uncommon that as soon as they had been awarded the title of senior lecturer or professor, their scientific work suddenly dried up... It is understandable that under these circumstances the ideal was "pure science", i.e. science unburdened by specific goals, because there was no other kind."*[97] By 1966 Málek had somewhat sobered up from his admiration of Soviet science, but still maintained his distance from the interwar situation: *"Science was always only done at universities, and then...only as an aside, a more or less*

---

96 Cf. Málek, Ivan: *Učíme se od sovětské vědy.* Prague 1953, p. 31.

97 Málek, Ivan: *Boj nového se starým v dnešní naší vědě.* Prague 1955, pp. 96–97.

private matter of individual scientists, which could not be made into a system... Due to the major teaching duties at universities and the essential structure being designed primarily for these responsibilities, it was impossible to have enough groups working on larger and more extensive tasks."[98]

In both cases the main area of criticism was the administrative character of the Humboldtian university, specifically the autonomous professorial committees – a symbol of their superiority. In 1954 the vice-chancellor of Brno's university, Theodor Martinec, stated that the interwar Humboldtian university tradition was incredibly elitist towards the students, and as such to be greatly condemned: "*When I was a student it was extremely difficult to speak to the dean or his assistant. Today you have the opportunity to talk to him. You are not allowed to regard the lecturers as superior beings. It is necessary to have a cordial relationship with them.*"[99] Ivan Málek was particularly scathing of the professors from the medical disciplines, whom he saw as having traditionally the highest level of superiority over the students and other university staff: "*The readings from the podium with the students sitting on benches, taking notes, created a barrier between teacher and pupil which could not be crossed with some kind of openness, not to mention criticism. A great many of us were aware of how badly any criticism was taken, though this even applied merely to questions. The teachers attempted to explain this superior relationship to the students by saying that it offered them "academic freedom", by which they meant absolute freedom in attendance at lectures and practical training. ...Students saw only too well at the clinics how their private practices were more important for them than teaching; they saw how the theoretical workers either trembled in their assistants' poverty, or they were forced to earn money in various ways; we can recall the habit whereby the professors stood the theoreticians in front of the dean in alphabetical order so that the gains from tax and promotion might substitute for what the clinicians had from their private practices.*"[100]

One of the first blows against the power of the professors came with the communist putsch in Czechoslovakia in 1948. There was a similar situation in other Central European countries within the communist bloc, where the new regime was attempting to deal with the problem that on the one hand, it did not believe that members of the post-coup professorial bodies would really lead their students towards socialism, on the other hand, they could not easily get rid of them due to their academic abilities.

Even prior to the legislative measures which either took away the decision-making powers from the committees or abolished them entirely,[101] the profes-

---

98   Málek, Ivan: *Otevřené otázky naší vědy*. Prague 1966, p. 35.

99   Archiv MU, Fond ČSM, k. 4, projev prorektora Martince ke studentům VŠ.

100 Málek, Ivan: *Přeměna lékařské výchovy*. In. Málek, Ivan – Gutwirth, Alois (ed.): O nového lékaře. Úvod do studia lékařství. Prague 1949, p. 97–116, here p. 101.

101 Connelly, *Zotročená*, p. 125

sorial body found itself under pressure from radicalized students and members of the youngest academic generation, whether they were Nazis or communists. John Connelly argues that only the Polish professorial bodies managed to act decisively and in unison against the pressure from the regime on universities, based on the tradition of professors' social exclusivity, bound together by Catholicism and their recognition of how they had preserved the nation's existence and identity during the Nazi occupation, which cost the lives of many academics.[102] In the other countries of the Eastern bloc, the communists managed to break up the professorial bodies – some of the anti-regime figures were removed from the universities, some were intimidated, while a large number collaborated.[103] Unlike in Poland, the identity of professorial bodies in Czechoslovakia and East Germany was much more unstable. In East Germany this was due to collaboration with the Nazis, while in Czechoslovakia this was largely because of the left-wing orientation of a large number of intellectuals, which linked the professorial bodies closely to the interwar regime and thus also to the shock of the failure of a Western-style democracy and the trauma of the Munich Agreement in 1938. The traditionally left-wing orientation of the secularized Czech public and the advantages of socialism in rebuilding the country after the devastation of war also played a large role – many Czechoslovak professors were certainly not ardent communists, but they were convinced that the communist regime would give them the opportunity to implement the left's traditional idea of social solidarity.[104] There were indeed many professors whose opinions did not substantially differ from those of the communists.[105]

For example, the assumption of power at Brno's Faculty of Arts by the "youth" in February 1948 had a very distinctive character. A group of young Communist Party members entered a meeting of the professorial body and told those present of the establishment of a new power centre in the form of the National Front Action Committee. Some professors were specifically named and warned: those now in power knew about their reactionary attitudes and recommended that they either stopped attending the meetings or refrained from voting. The seizure of power by the communists in Prague's university was somewhat less theatrical and

---

102 Jochen August: *Sonderaktion Krakau. Die Verhaftung der Krakauer Wissenschaftler am 6. November 1939*, Hamburg, 1997, esp. pp. 51–53; Szołdrska, Halszka: *Walka z kulturą polską. Uniwersytet Poznański podczas okupacji.* Poznań 1948, p. 5 ff.; Banasiewicz, Maria: *Polityka naukowa i oświatowa hitlerowskich Niemiec na ziemiach polskich „wcielonych" do Trzeciej Rzeszy w okresie okupacji (1939–1945).* Poznań 1980, p. 219–231; Gawęda, Stanisław (red.): *Straty wojenne Uniwersytetu Jagiellońskiego i stan powstały na wiosnę 1945 roku* red. Kraków 1974; *Reżimy totalitarne wobec ludzi nauki 1939–1945 : Uniwersytet Jagielloński: Sonderaktion Krakau, Zbrodnia Katyńska /* [tł. Philip Stoeckle], Warsaw 2007.

103 Connelly, *Zotročená*, pp. 125–130.

104 Urbášek, Pavel – Pulec, Jiří et al.: *Kapitoly z dějin univerzitního školství na Moravě v letech 1945–1990.* Olomouc 2003, p. 201.

105 Connelly, *Zotročená*, p. 131 ff.

there was more of an effort to gain legitimacy and express historical continuity. In March 1948 the Academic Senate proudly proclaimed that *"..for the first time in centuries, other members of the academic community can participate* (at the meeting – author's note) *as an equal part of the university."*

Academics interpreted the revolutionary act of the communist students in a historical way as *"renewing the tradition of the universitas magistrorum et scholari-um...as in the first decades of our university the academic community was as one: even students could be voted rector, only later did power transfer into the hands of the masters."*[106] However, the historical parallel was only an instrument and embellishment in the struggle for power. A short time later the Charles University Faculty of Medicine became embroiled in a dispute with a politically powerful student, and defended itself by referring to university tradition in the form of a court decree from 1791 and a 1904 ruling by the Supreme Court. However, there was an emphatic rebuttal to any *"appeals to decisions by the old rulers in the people's democratic republic"*.[107] The expulsion of several members of the professorial body for political reasons as a result of the Action Committee's influence in the Academic Senate was met with the banal sentence about *"painful intervention"* in the life of the university, and no other defence was needed.[108]

When the Protectorate of Bohemia and Moravia was first established, the Nazis also found many more supporters amongst the assistant and senior lecturers at university than amongst the professors, albeit that the months following the occupation in March 1939 brought disillusionment to their supporters amongst the younger academics.[109] They had originally hoped that the expulsion of Jews and political undesirables would result in career advancement, but this involved a protracted bureaucratic procedure which showed the central organs' lack of trust in people connected with the former Czechoslovakia, even if they were nationalists or pro-Nazi sympathizers. When the humanities were restructured in the German university in Prague, it was generally the case that the doors were open mainly to people with close links to universities in the Reich or people at the start of their academic careers, often new senior lecturers or associate professors. However, the personnel changes were overshadowed by the fact that a large section of the humanities in Prague was defined as either unimportant for the war or unimportant in general, and therefore destined to be downgraded, regardless of tradition

---

106 Archiv UK, Akademický senát UK, k. 38, zápis z jednání dne 12.3. 1948.

107 Ibid, k. 55, i.d. 666.

108 Archiv UK, Akademický senát UK, k. 38, zápis z jednání dne 12.3. 1948.

109 Míšková, Alena: *Německá (Karlova) univerzita*, Prague 2002, p. 64; Konrád, Ota: *Dějepisectví, germanistika a slavistika na Německé univerzitě v Praze 1918–1945*. Prague 2011, p.208.

or propaganda slogans about the blossoming of German science in the newly conquered territories.[110]

Both totalitarian regimes, therefore, challenged the Humboldtian principle of university autonomy and argued about the necessity of responding to the inflexible personnel conditions within the academic community with regard to ideological claims and the regime's strategic priorities. It was also relatively easy for them to attract young academics who were in the situation where the holder of the professorial chair was relatively young, while there were often many better-suited colleagues in front of them in the queue for this dream post.[111]

The instrumentalization of the Humboldt myth shows clear signs of it occasionally being "switched off" at moments when the narrative did not suit influential individuals within the academic community, usually with the support of a majority or at least a sizeable proportion of academics, and then reused in other contexts, often just a short time later. This arbitrary instrumentalization is the strongest admonition that in the 20th century we were no longer dealing with the real legacy of the humanist vision of Kant, Fichte and Humboldt, but only with a slogan used to defend various positions of power and interests within the university community. The rector of Brno's university, František Trávníček, a one-time supporter of Tomáš Masaryk and former legionnaire, who after 1945 gradually became the second most influential man in Czech science after Zdeněk Nejedlý, managed to move dramatically away from Humboldtian principles in his political-organizational attitudes and did not even attempt to disguise this in the relevant committees. Trávníček, ex-legionnaire and Masarykite, was appointed to the leadership of higher education and the Academy of Sciences in order to mercilessly crush bourgeoise traditions and bring Czechoslovak higher education and science in to line with the models of Stalin's Soviet Union. During the interwar period, however, Trávníček had been one of the most talented Czech linguists, a supporter of structuralism and received special recognition in the field of dialectology. His political U-turn, when he reassessed all of his interwar attitudes and set out in 1945 on a political course under the flag of the Czechoslovak Communist Party, was not entirely connected to his work as a Czech studies scholar. Even here, however, he attempted to apply Marxist-Leninist principles and did not deviate from the official line. In this regard, his behaviour towards some of his younger colleagues and the students was domineering, often to the point of being unbearable. But there were other cases where he was recognised for being willing to use his political authority to protect talented scholars, even though this was al-

---

110 Konrád, *Dějepisectví*, p. 215 ff.

111 Grüttner, Michael: Machtergreifung als Generationskonflikt. Die Krise der Hochschulen und der Aufstieg der Nationalsozialismus. In: vom Bruch, Rüdiger – Kaderas, Brigitte (Hg.): *Wissenschaften und Wissenschaftspolitik: Bestandsaufnahmen zu Formationen, Brüchen und Kontinuitäten im Deutschland des 20. Jahrhunderts*. Stuttgart 2002, pp. 339–353, esp. p. 352.

ways within the department or discipline and only to a certain extent.[112] Trávníček had more of an ad hoc approach to the Humboldtian love of scientific truth and was only lukewarm towards the humanist camp's ethos of *universitas*.

The shield of discipline continuity

The case of Trávníček is not that exceptional in Czech science. Josef Petráň places another two greats of Czech linguistics on the same level – the rector of Charles University, Jan Mukařovský, and the dean of Prague's Faculty of Arts, Bohuslav Havránek. *"Like so many other intellectuals after the liberation of 1945, they had to decide which side of the fence to sit on."* (...) These were cases of *"distinguished scientists who – despite not being communists before the war – joined the side of the 'progressive forces' because they understood the 'logic of history'."*[113] Petráň has a great deal of understanding for the difficult situation faced by these pro-regime academics and does not hide the fact that this is for personal reasons. He presents Mukařovský and Havránek as academics who were in the "thrall of the regime", and who destroyed the careers and lives of colleagues for ideological reasons, but who also tried to defend their subjects and the careers of other talented scientists from attacks by "apparatchiks", as Petráň calls those who evidently did not share the Humboldtian ethos of an academic.[114] They stood apart from the Humboldtian university culture, disrupting and threatening it. This category also contained a whole discipline – that of Marxism-Leninism and its related subjects, including the history of the international workers' movement and political economy.[115] Workers in these disciplines were quietly denied the position of insiders by the academic community, though the regime outside considered them as people who would oversee the correct ideological management of the university. This was despite the fact that many of those who worked in the ideological departments also taught subjects which were considered fundamental by the academic community, in particular history, philosophy and sociology. The Czechoslovak Communist Party tried repeatedly to break the isolation of the ideological departments from other academics, but without much success. Here the Humboldtian defence reflexes worked well.[116] In 1974, the apolitical character of "true science" was again singled out as the main failing at universities which the Czechoslovak Communist

---

112 Uhde, Milan: *Rozpomínky. Co na sebe vím.* Brno 2013, pp. 52–76; Šlosar, Jan: *Jaké hlavy, takový jazyk. Rozhovor o češtině a o životě vedli Jiří Trávníček a Jiří Voráč.* Brno 2008, pp. 37–38, 43 ff.

113 Petráň, *Filozofové*, pp. 208–221, here p. 217.

114 Ibid, pp. 244–245.

115 Urbášek, Pavel: *Vysokoškolský vzdělávací systém v letech tzv. normalizace.* Olomouc 2008, pp. 76–78.

116 Archiv UK, Ústav sociálně–politických věd, box V/53, i.d. 471, 475.

Party had been unable to tackle.[117] The distance between the "ideological" and "scientific" disciplines was apparent in the defence of the thesis, particularly with externals. They would usually not perceive any differences between the two kinds of disciplines, but during the defence of their thesis they would become all too well aware of whether they were entering a "temple of science" with their work, or if it was more on an ideological level.

One example of the defence a thesis in history at Brno University's Faculty of Arts in 1960 was that of Captain Josef Domaňský, a worker at the Department of the History of the Czechoslovak Communist Party at the Antonín Zapotocký Military Academy. His candidacy was supported by strong political arguments as Domaňský was an active communist who had done a great deal of teaching and propaganda work. The title of his work was "*The origin of the people's democracy of Czechoslovakia*" and the examination committee consisted mainly of pro-regime figures from the faculty (historian Bedřich Šindelář, professor of Marxism-Leninism Gustav Riedel, etc.), people who were considered by the academic community as borderline cases for political-ideological integration into the academic culture. The commission judged the objective of the thesis to be unacceptable – the author described it as "*strengthening the class education of our workers*"; and the commission also objected to the non-scientific character of the thesis, and that due to its "*sloganeering, it is a summary of lectures and propositions*". In some of their statements the examiners were acting within the spirit of university tradition, placing them as guardians of scientific purity and reliability. These people, though, were not top-class scientists – from the examination committee, only Šindelář was widely respected within his field at the time. And there were limits to this respect for tradition. In spite of the scathing professional assessments, the thesis was not entirely rejected – they only stated that it would be impossible to defend it in the discipline of history...but they recommended that the candidate ask for it to be recognised at the department of scientific communism.[118]

However, if we ignore the relatively small group of ideologically disciplines, the dividing line between the disciplines which collaborated with the totalitarian regimes and those which suffered under them is very unclear and had been artificially created in order to defend the interests of disciplines by using the Humboldtian myth of pure science. Several disciplines exist which would not have become established in universities had it not been for the help of a totalitarian regime, projecting its specific interests onto them. The discipline, therefore, served the regime, but the regime also served the discipline. Typical representatives of this group of disciplines were psychiatry, Eastern European history and Slavonic studies, atomic physics, aerodynamics, genetics and sports medicine. Some strongly

117 *Některé zkušenosti z práce SSM na vysokých školách.* Prague 1974, p. 28.
118 AMU, Fond A2, Filosofická fakulta, k. 1, CSc., i.d. 1/9.

ideological subjects simply changed their name – for example, the treatment of hereditary illnesses had been established during the Nazi era as racial hygiene. A large number of professors from this discipline did not even change the titles of their lectures during the period of political-ideological reversals.[119]

The shield of historical memory

"Humboldt" plays an important role when analysing the historical memory of the academic community. Its function is to act as a shield which deflects the many doubts about the dishonourable, inhumane or disloyal behaviour of academics confronted by the pressure of the regime. The myth immunizes the academic community against its own guilt, transferring it outside of the university walls. It presents an exalted vision where evil cannot coexist – it has to be brought there from the outside. Shortly after the arrival of the front in 1945, the senate of Göttingen University sent the representatives of the occupying forces an address: "... *the reasons for the recent disruption of scientific activities did not have their origins in the university grounds*" and so the professorial body "*is making every endeavour to follow the centuries-old tradition of the German university in the sense of idealism and universalism*", whose "*spirit can best thrive through the preservation of the university's autonomous administration*".[120]

Czech universities know a very similar story from 1989–1992 when they were coming to terms with the legacy of the communist regime. Special academic bodies – rehabilitation and ethical commissions – were set up for this very purpose at the universities in Prague and Brno. One key theme was how to compensate academics who had been expelled from university by the regime and whether – and how – to deal with those academics who collaborated with the regime or were directly involved in its repression. From the outset the atmosphere was tense, while the dramatic differences in the interpretation of historical memory greatly disturbed the post-revolution leadership of the universities and faculties. In the name of unity and calm within the academic community, academic dignitaries tried to transform that atmosphere as quickly as possible: "*The emotionally precarious contradiction, which I would term 'the worker on the inside – the worker waiting outside', has*

---

119 Walker, Mark: The Nazification and Denazification of Physics. In: Kertz, Walter (Hg.): *Hochschule im Nationalsozialismus*. Braunschweig 1994, pp. 79–91; von Knorre, Dietrich – Penzlin, Heinz – Hertel, Wieland: Der Lyssenkoismus und die Zoologie in Jena. In: Hoßfeld, Uwe – Kaiser, Tobias – Mestrup, Heinz (Hg.): *Hochschule in Sozialismus. Studien zur Geschichte der Friedrich–Schiller–Universität Jena (1945–1990)*, Band 2. Köln – Weimar – Wien 2007, pp. 1166–1180; Linnemann, Kai Arne: *Das Erbe der Ostforschung. Zur Rolle Göttingens in der Geschichtswissenschaft in der Nachrkriegszeit*. Marburg 2002.

120 Weisbrod, *Dem wandelbaren Geist*, p. 26.

to disappear as quickly as possible," wrote the vice-dean in terms of restructuring the management of Charles University's Faculty of Arts.[121]

Over time the activities of these commissions focused mainly on quelling passions, "*so that a wave of blind hatred did not sweep over the faculty*". Only a few of the commission members did not understand the strategy of the leadership of the two universities, led then by people from the anti-communist dissident movement, who, in the spirit of the "velvet" slogan from November 1989 "we are not like them", refused to intervene significantly against those from the academic community who had cooperated with the regime, preferring instead to pension off the main culprits. However, the Brno rector Milan Jelínek was in a more difficult position than the Prague rector, Radim Palouš, as he was criticized for his membership of the Czechoslovak Communist Party (1945–1969) and his prominent role at the university in the first twenty years of the communist regime – which was seen as the reason for his alleged excessive leniency towards the communists. It was said that Jelínek created an atmosphere at the university which was "*more conducive for the culprits than the victims.*" The rector indignantly defended himself, referring to the "*inquisitorial practices*" of some commissions. In the cases of both Prague and Brno, the situation was quickly brought under control, at least from an outside perspective. Those academics who demanded a radical break from the past found themselves isolated from the rest of the academic community in 1991–1992. Without the support of the students, who after the exertions of the revolutionary year of 1989–1990 began to lose interest in politics, it was impossible to establish a programme which would thoroughly reflect on historical memory. Although for the general public the issue of academics' participation in the evils of the communist regime was quietly set aside ad acta, and the academic community once again shielded itself under the cloak of dignified unity, this did not mean that historical memory ceased to influence internal university debates, though unfortunately more of the backstage intrigue variety.[122]

Prominent academics from within the structures of the communist regime often apologised for their behaviour by referring to the creation of "Humboldtian" space, where high-quality scientific research could be carried out freely during a challenging period by providing political cover for persecuted colleagues. A similar "sacrifice" for the maintenance of "academic freedom", at least within the limits of the department or discipline, was given by many an academic functionary from the time of the communist regime, as can be seen in more than one post-revolution laudation or obituary. Here "Humboldt" provides both an alibi and a feeling which is usually interpreted by the discipline as solidarity and pro-

---

121 Jareš, Jakub – Spurný, Matěj – Volná, Katka: *S minulostí zúčtujeme. Sebereflexe Filozofické fakulty UK v dokumentech sedmdesátých a devadesátých let 20. století.* Prague 2014, p. 586.

122 Ibid, pp. 604–606; Archiv Masarykovy univerzity, Fond A3 Lékařská fakulta, box. 2, sign. B.VI/2.

tection, which help to defend the freedom of research and teaching during times of repression.

Who was protected in this way and who was not? This protection could be enjoyed by individuals who did not get involved in politics and who anxiously avoided any direct confrontation with the regime. It required from them at least a minimal level of cooperation in the symbolic form of attending the regime's rallies, meetings, volunteer work, etc. It was also important for them to adapt their research themes, at least outwardly and formally, to ideological requirements – usually citing one or two classic Marxist-Leninist paragraphs would suffice, inserted before the main body of a work which otherwise had little in common with ideology. The researcher's private religious beliefs did not necessarily matter, nor did a petit-bourgeois or kulak background, nor did the fact that they were in contact with people who were openly opposed to the regime. However, "Humboldt" failed to defend the students, who were treated much more harshly in terms of ideology than university employees; there was no protection for political dissidents and rebels, or for solitary researchers straying off the beaten track of science without regard for the academic community or ideological regulations.

German historiography has demonstrated how unwilling universities were to deal with their Nazi past. Here historians talk about an asymmetric remembrance of the collaboration with the Nazis, which although affecting the aristocracy, the army and the industrial oligarchy, had nothing to do with universities (together with the church), which made the smooth transition to operating "normally", utilizing the moratorium granted by society thanks to the Humboldtians. This moratorium ended approximately twenty years after the fall of Hitler's regime and was linked to the generational change in the academic community.[123] Here the Humboldtian myth once again functioned as a selective means of defence. With the tacit approval of the Western Allied powers, the professorial bodies closed ranks around the Humboldtian principles of autonomy and politically independent science, claiming as one to have been the victims of Nazi despotism. After the war very few academics spoke out about the German universities' share in supporting the Nazi regime. One of them was the philosopher Karl Jaspers, who had been persecuted by the Nazis in the 1930s and 40s because of his outspoken views and his wife's Jewish background.[124]

It was only with political upheavals and the university crisis of the 1960s that another chapter was added to the lengthy appraisal by Central European academics of what "Humboldt" is and is not. The new social movements, in particular the politicized youth, demanded a comprehensive revision of the history of West German universities and the identification of those from the academic community

---

123 Weisbrod, *Dem wandelbaren Geist*, pp. 23–26.

124 Ash, *Konstruierte Kontinuitäten*, pp. 240–242.

who had been prominent in the Nazi regime. The students also came out strongly against the system of the "professorial university", demanding shared decision-making powers.[125] The student rebellion was targeted mainly at representatives of the humanities and social sciences, in particular the nationalist conservatives who had openly collaborated with the Nazis, and targeted the weakest point of the entire Humboldtian narrative – the fact that the humanities demonstrated the greatest willingness to collaborate with political authorities in order to strengthen their position within the university and with the public, a position which had been weakened by the gradual, general "farewell to Humboldt". The 1960s also saw attempts to establish in universities social-science disciplines which had previously been rejected by professorial committees, who referred to their overtly political foundations, normally based on US models (e.g. transcultural, gender and environmental studies). Their left or left-liberal ideological bases were supposed to be a guarantee of university equality in allegedly traditionally conservative disciplines and professorial committees.[126]

At this time in Czechoslovakia there was also tension within academia as a result of attempts to identify the political interference in universities during previous eras, specifically the Stalinist ideological deformation of academia, which in a certain sense brought an end to the debate which had briefly taken place in universities in 1956–1957. This was a revision of the communists' anti-Humboldtian programme in the late 1940s and early 1950s, and a return to the tradition of "pure science", restricting the influence of ideology on scientific research and relationships with countries from the capitalist bloc. As for the students, one notable phenomenon in the mid-1960s was the democratization of access to courses, which was similar to trends in the West. However, students did not face economic obstacles, as in Germany or the USA, but ideological obstacles which had previously sought to generate a new elite of the socialist intelligentsia. Unlike in the West, therefore, there was no anti-elitist conflict with the relics of professorial influence in universities, as this had already been destroyed with the communists' assumption of power in 1948–1949. In the long history of coming to terms with Humboldt, it is possible to see the Czechoslovak reforms of 1967–1969 as a very brief episode aimed at renewing the classic Humboldtian traditions, primarily in relation to scientific research, ideology and power. Naturally, the process of the Czechoslovak reforms was so short and chaotic and linked to the local character of the relationship between the university and the political powers that it had little influence on the future development of the theme in Central Europe. With one exception. Although the small gains in scientific independence were quashed by a resurgent Communist Party after 1969, the episodic liberalization in Czechoslo-

---

125 Ibid, pp. 240–242.

126 Menand, Louis: *The future of academic freedom*. Chicago – London 1996, pp. 4–5, 17.

vak science in the 1960s remained deeply etched in the memory of the academic community; first and foremost as an era of contrast compared to the ideological repression which came both before and after, rather than for developing ideals and concepts. Due to the haste of the reforms and the reformers' different interests, they never became part of the university tradition and were not referred to after the fall of communism.

Mitchell Ash noted that the continuity in handing over the Humboldtian narrative was always linked to people from the university or discipline who saw themselves as being affected less by political power than the academic dignitaries at the level of rector and dean.[127] It is also necessary to take into consideration that the staff purges carried out by the regime were always more extensive in the humanities than in the less politically orientated science and medical disciplines, which every regime needed to maintain in operation. The personnel changes in East German universities after 1945 were quite drastic, helped as they were by the voluntary departure of many academics to the western part of the country. Ralph Jessen shows that the turnover in staff in East German science was at 83%, albeit with large differences in the disciplines.[128] Although different authors give different figures, in comparison with Czechoslovakia and Poland, the continuity in personnel at East German universities saw the greatest disruption.[129] The personnel changes associated with both the rise and fall of the communist regimes in Czechoslovakia and Poland do not even come close to the aforementioned figures. Here the cohesion of the academic community was exceptionally high and the defence mechanisms worked well. One typical justification in the memoirs of actors from the revolution in 1989 would be a reference to the character of the people involved ("a nice person"), while their political affiliation and career within the regime's structures were marginalised. Ash points to a great amount of shielding, using strong words such as truth, freedom and democracy within these defence mechanisms.[130] In Czechoslovakia and Poland, unlike in Germany (for understandable reasons), there were many references to the nation: "national

---

127 Ash, Mitchell: Zum Abschluß: Bedeutet ein Abschied vom Mythos Humboldt eine „Amerikanisierung" der deutschen Universitäten?, In: also (Hg.): *Mythos Humboldt. Vergangenheit und Zukunft deutscher Universitäten*. Wien – Köln – Weimar 1999, pp. 253–266, here p. 257.

128 Jessen, Ralph: *Akademische Elite und kommunistische Diktatur. Die ostdeutsche Hochschullehrerschaft in der Ulbricht–Ära*. Göttingen 1999, p. 261 ff.

129 Ash, *Konstruirte Kontinuitäten*, p. 241; John, Jürgen: Der Mythos von „rein gebliebenen Geist": Denkmuster und Strategien des intelektuellen Neubeginns 1945. In: Hoßfeld Uwe – Kaiser, Tobias – Mestrup, Heinz (Hg.): *Hochschule im Sozialismus. Studien zur Geschichte der Friedrich–Schiller–Universität Jena (1945–1990)*. Band 1. Wien – Köln – Weimar 2007, pp. 19–70; Jeskow, Jan: Die Entnazifizierung des Lehrkörpers an der Universität Jena von 1945 bis 1948, In: *ibid*, pp. 71–95; Herrmann, Hans Peter: *Krisen. Arbeiten zur Universitätsgeschichte 1933–2010 am Beispiel Freiburgs i. Br.* Freiburg i. Br. – Berlin – Wien 2015, pp. 79–127.

130 Ash, *Konstruirte Kontinuitäten*, p. 243.

science", "bravery at a time of national oppression", "of the people, close to the wide strata of the nation", "a worker in national science".[131]

After 1989, membership of the Czechoslovak Communist Party was not one of the major issues in the staff purges – unlike the NSDAP, the Communist Party was not declared a criminal organization. Membership of the party amongst Czechoslovak professors and senior professors was commonplace, and it was hardly surprising that this community, under pressure from political changes, closed ranks around the principle of shared historical experience and their defence of Humboldtian academic freedom against ideology. This argument, understandably, did not apply to the so-called ideological departments which were more or less immediately thrown overboard by the academic community, marked as being those responsible for the university's decline. The academics symbolically listened to the calls from the students of the revolution, and expelled some of its members who had been too closely linked to the regime, while accepting several former dissidents as a symbol of purging and reconciliation.[132] However, there were no widespread personnel changes, despite the fact that some of the anti-communist forces within the academic community had called for them. After the political pressure from the radical students began to wane, the post-revolution university management applied a more conciliatory approach towards the subaltern members of the old regime. After all, a number of the new university dignitaries had personally known the prominent political professors, and some of them had also found it difficult to deal with their ties to communism. If we look at those who left university after the revolution in 1989, we see they were people who had abandoned the "Humboldtian traditions" by abusing the power structures, by showing a willingness to place ideology above science and by being too close to the political and ideological structures of the regime. In short, the boundary between those who suffered as a result of the revolution and those who came out unscathed, or who even improved their careers, was unclear and permeable.

At the forefront of the apologists' argument was someone who had sacrificed themselves for their discipline by accepting a political function and thus taking on the role of protector of more vulnerable colleagues. This was also backed up by ideological sources, where even high-standing academic functionaries were accused of trivializing the lack of class politics and Bolshevik toughness in strategic as well as personnel issues, hiding behind the concept of academic freedom and allegedly unbiased scientific positivism. In 1960 the Czechoslovak Ministry of Education stated that *"there has appeared in our universities a tendency to promote 'academic freedom' and an ambiguous attitude towards the teaching profession,"* and *"one of*

---

131 E.g. Archiv UK, Akademický senát 1882–1945, k. 17; Archiv MU, Fond B100, Otakar Borůvka, i.d. 818; Ibid fond A., RMU II, k., sign. 3357/49; k. 2, sign. XIV.

132 Archiv MU, fond Rektorát A II/2, k. 53, sig. 53/1; ibid. fond Lékařská fakulta A3, k. 9. sign. BVI/2.

the main dangers is the positivist interpretation of scientific and social-scientific issues."[133] After the fall of communism and Nazism it was possible to escape censure for having collaborated with the regime if you were able to call on a well-known opponent of the regime. Naturally, everything had to be embedded within the narrative of science suffering under a despotic regime.[134] Jaspers' reminder to his colleagues from Heidelberg University that their collaboration with the Nazi regime had not been as passive as they tried to make out, is considered to be one of three exceptions in the whole of Germany and Austria.[135] In a Czech context, only the memoirs of Václav Černý are similar in scale.[136] In other memoirs we tend to find only minor references where the author has the courage to touch on politically sensitive issues, or the memoirs might have been left with family members with the proviso that they were to be published thirty years after their death. Therefore, the real impetus for dealing with the impact of communism on universities has had to come from a younger generation of researchers.[137]

The shield of academic freedom

Let us move away from Central European university culture, which was so sorely tested by changes in ideology and regimes in the 20th century: Louis Menand used very similar language to speak about American universities and the instrumentalization of the Humboldtian contribution to academic freedom. He points to the elasticity of the concept when faced with the political pressure connected to the Cold War and the conservative wave of McCarthyism, which left American scientists in a similar dilemma to their Central European colleagues. Academic freedom came under further pressure at the end of the 1960s and the start of the 1970s, when according to many academics, the university's main mission was to fight against all types of inequality and racism, including all indications of democratic conservatism or American Republicanism. In 1996 – i.e. a long time before the anti-liberal revolt of American voters, labelled Trumpism by commentators – Menand stated that the majority of Americans thought that universities were hiding behind the shield of Humboldtian academic freedom in order to spread

133 Národní archiv, Fond MŠK, k. 27, zápisy z jednání kolegia ministra z 28.4. 1960 a 5.5. 1960.

134 vom Bruch, Rüdiger: Kommentar und Epilog, In: Weisbrodt, Bernd: *Akademische Vergangenheitspolitik. Beiträge zur Wissenschaftskultur der Nachkriegszeit.* Göttingen 2002, pp. 281–288, here p. 286.

135 Jaspers, Karl: *Erneuerung der Universität. Reden und Schriften 1945/1946.* Heidelberg 1986, p. 100; Ash, *Konstruirte Kontinutäten,* p. 243.

136 Černý, Václav: *Paměti III. 1945–1972.* Brno 1992.

137 Spurný, Matěj – Jareš, Jakub – Volná, Katka: *Náměstí Krasnoarmějců 2. 2: Učitelé a studenti na Filozofické fakultě UK v období normalizace.* Prague 2012.

the "*truth of multiculturalism and postmodernism*". Menand argues that universities alienate themselves from the rest of society with their stubbornly defended privileges, their existence paid for by public budgets, and by being out of touch with reality. Accordingly, this ideological concept has no hope of being generally accepted by Western societies.[138] The focus of criticism is the *Codes of Politically Correct Speech*, which in their extreme form caricature the ideal of academic freedom in a "colour-blind discussion" as the way towards an ideologically conceived vision of an absolutely equal society. Even the minorities who are supposed to be defended by these codes sometimes respond negatively to them. Kurt Shell presented the example of the Black Power Movement, celebrating everything black as beautiful (Africanization of names, afro hairstyles, etc.); including radical speeches, where all whites are labelled as racists and murderers.[139] The situation in British and European universities is not so different today, though unlike the USA the universities here share the dream of the Western European left about a liberal Islam and the possibility of completely integrating migrants into the secular model of Western society.[140]

In this light, the defence of a university's political independence using Humboldtian references would seem to be a very problematic area of debate. Humboldt's late-Enlightenment legacy did not survive the rise of democratizing movements at the end of the 19th century, in particular the "age of extremes", as historians have labelled the 20th century. At the start of the 21st century, academia has been unable to reach a consensus on how to update the old-fashioned Humboldtian arguments – at least their two main linchpins – which would stand up to the conditions of the 21st century. Today Humboldt has become a slogan where anything goes.

The debate has become all the more complex because the very concepts of democracy and political alignment have undergone a crisis in recent years, particularly in their liberal definitions, and thus it is difficult for a university to define its position within this turbulent landscape of public discourse. The university community likes to refer to Humboldt when setting itself up as the guardian of democracy, or as an island of absolute democracy from where it can criticize the rest of the world and set it to rights using democratic criteria, despite the fact that the public no longer sees it in this role. The public suspects academics of promoting their own economic and political interests and placing the academically defined natural law of "Good" above the positive-legal norms emerging from the deci-

---

138 Menand, *The Future*, pp. 4–5, 17.

139 Shell, Kurt L.: Die amerikanische Universität und die Herausforderung durch den Multikulturalismus. In: Steger, Hans–Albert – Hopfinger, Hans (Hg.): *Die Universität in der Welt, die Welt in der Universität*. Neustadt an der Aisch 1994, pp. 27–44, here p. 32 ff.

140 http://www.telegraph.co.uk/education/educationnews/12059161/Politically–correct–universities–are–killing–free–speech.ht (18.7. 2017)

sions of democratically elected parliaments. The fact that the majority of Western European universities appear to be left or liberal-left leaning is seen as evidence of the ideological character of universities and their disregard for the principle of objectivity, which academics like to refer to under the banner of Good and Truth. The uncertainty and defensiveness of left-wing forces in the West today has resulted in academics being charged with rewriting the results of democratic elections through their commitment to the left. In this light, the instrumentalization of the Humboldtian legacy appears as an attempt by academics to strengthen their position in a tumultuous public debate where radical opinions abound.

In comparison with their colleagues in the third world and even the USA, the mission of university communities in Central Europe is unclear. Although universities in places such as Indonesia, Thailand, India, Latin America and Africa, have accepted the principles from the classic European university model – i.e. its organisational structure, course system and titles, it is when it comes to political neutrality that the universities of the "third world" choose another path. From their foundation, these universities have grown from an ethos which was anti-colonial and on the political left, whether democratic (including Catholic) or radically revolutionary.[141] The nationalist-leftist orientation of universities in many third-world countries is reinterpreted according to the political situation, and is strongly present in university culture, albeit not explicitly expressed in official documents.

According to its conservative critics, the university mainstream openly talks about the university's mission as the fight against racism and all forms of inequality and discrimination – i.e. the highly political agenda of the liberal left.[142] However, this tends to be in a less overt form in official declarations concerning the mission of American public universities, where the specialist-organizational and efficient vision of academic capitalism is at the forefront. However, in places such as the University of Baltimore, the code still contains the declaration to "*continue to cultivate a community that values diversity, equity and inclusion*".[143] How that is subsequently implemented depends on the personal political affiliations of university dignitaries.

---

141 Shils, Edward – Roberts, John: *The Diffusionn of European Models outside Europe.* In: Rüegg, Walter: A History of the University in Europe. Volume IIII. Cambridge 2004, pp. 163–230.

142 Menand, *The future*, p. 17.

143 http://www.ubalt.edu/about–ub/docs/Strategic%20Plan_FINAL.pdf, p. 7 (16.8. 2017).

A shield against globalization

The declared mission of Central European universities usually treats the theme of political commitment with great care. The changes in regime and ideology in Central Europe throughout the 20th century provide a warning against political activism, and the academic community is very wary about ideological interference in science and teaching, albeit that even here there are differences amongst disciplines, and the social sciences in particular do not erect as many barriers as other disciplines. Overall, though, Central European universities are the most firmly rooted in Humboldtian traditions. As a result of their historical experiences, they place special emphasis on the vision of freedom of research and autonomous university administration. For example, as part of the definition of its mission, Poznaň University's central motto is *"In looking to the future we do not forget our traditions"*. It is tradition – the realization of the social good through science and teaching – which forms the central axis of that treatise. Another typical feature is an emphasis on regional and, to a lesser extent, national ties. This was strongly present in the original Humboldtian cultural context, though it was discredited by the Nazi regime in Germany, the heart of the Humboldtian university tradition. However, it is through these ties that the University of Poznaň has been a standard bearer of educational traditions in Poznaň and Greater Poland (Wielkopolska), though the national motif is used carefully and sensitively in the sense of being committed to creating a cultural legacy. The most politicized definition of its mission can be seen in a declaration on the values of democracy and pro-European ideas – though not explicitly the European Union – in the document *Magna Charta Universitatum* from 1988.[144] Comenius University in Bratislava has an even more "Humboldtian" mission, taking another step away from political interference. This is linked to service to the homeland and nation, and it even uses the title of *"national university"*, which in Western Europe, and Germany in particular, is usually viewed with scorn.[145] In the introduction to its mission, Ljubljana University defines its identity as being strongly linked to the national ideal, i.e. *"the consolidation of national identity with the development of specialist Slovenian terminology."*[146] The Ivan Franko University of Lviv uses "National" in its title, immediately declaring its position as a defender of Ukrainian national identity. The university museum is an interesting attempt to maintain high-quality courses and research after hundreds of years of terrible political conditions in this peripheral area of Europe – in the 20th century alone the dramatic changes in regime cost many lives, with the

---

144 https://amu.edu.pl/__data/assets/pdf_file/0004/239755/STRATEGIA-ROZWOJU-UAM_NOWELIZACJA.pdf, p. 10 ff. (15.8. 2017).

145 https://uniba.sk/o-univerzite/poslanie/(15.8.2017).

146 https://www.uni-lj.si/o_univerzi_v_ljubljani/poslanstvo__vrednote_in_vizija_ul/ (15.8. 2017).

university being renamed three times.[147] The mission of Brno's Masaryk University is introduced with the preamble *"Masaryk University's mission is to create and expand knowledge which will develop society's quality of life and culture. This comes from the values upon which the university was founded."* This also leaves us unclear as to what a university's mission might be in relation to political authority. What is again important here is the reference to rather idealized interwar conditions and values of democracy, interpreted carefully in a slightly liberal-left concept without being too specific: *From this emancipatory* (Czech national – author's note) *beginning then grew the democratic character of the First Republic Masaryk University, later supressed by the Protectorate and the communist regime. And it is from this initial direction that the values of the university are based today, evident in the accent on democratic values and humanity, an accent which can be seen in activities such as the inclusive nature of the education, strengthening the university's international links and supporting voluntary civic initiatives by the students.*[148] Therefore, the Humboldtian myth in the countries of Central-Eastern Europe has undergone a similar form of modernizing, though it is still firmly attached to the values of a regional and national identity. Within the political-cultural context of the countries of Central Eastern Europe, it is a theme which has been widely shared across society and the great majority of political camps. The viability of the Humboldtian narrative in the 21st century lies within the social acceptance of its moderately optimistic ethical vision.

There is a widening gap in Central European university culture between the missions of some German universities and those in Central Eastern Europe, as well as in the German provinces. In Germany, more so than in its eastern neighbours, the mission reflects the global aspect of competition which management is tied to. There is more political commitment and a progressive account of the Humboldtian myth, as well as a clear separation from the traditionalist-conservative aspects of Humboldtianism, in particular its national (Prussian and German) aspects. One of the most publicly committed schools from the Central European university tradition is the Freie Universität Berlin. At first sight its university motto of *Veritas, Iustitia, Libertas* seems to refer to Humboldtian ideals, but under the surface it is a substantial reinterpretation and modernization of the old vision. "Humboldt" is conceived of in such a modern way that it instils the feeling amongst traditionalists that it has been repudiated. However, a more accurate interpretation is that the Freie Universität, strongly rooted in the leftist traditions of the city of Berlin, is narrating the Humboldtian myth from a leftist-activist perspective. It extracts from an almost exhausted historical tradition some elements of Fichte's idealism and reinterprets them in the spirit of the liberal-socialist ideas

---

147 http://www.lnu.edu.ua/about/ (14.6. 2018).

148 http://www.muni.cz/media/docs/1110/Dlouhodoby_zamer_MU_2016_2020.pdf (15. 8. 2017), esp. p. 5.

of the 21st century. In Central European terms, the Freie Universität stands out due to the description of its mission as being socially committed, again in the spirit of the European liberal left: gender equality, dual career paths with ties to the family, ecological responsibility, inclusion and so on. Discursive elements emphasizing the example of American universities' efficiency are muted, the mission's regional link is absent, and unlike the universities in Central Eastern Europe, the national aspects are treated with great caution as a result of the Germans' historical experience with a nationally conceived polity.[149]

Conclusion

The example of the Freie Universität Berlin, as with other universities in Central Eastern Europe, goes against Ash's theory of the culturally pessimistic form of the Humboldtian myth, and points to the possibility of another life for this mythical narrative – though, of course, in a radically different form. This myth has not disappeared from universities in Central Europe, as there is still a strong demand for its role as a "shield". It may even shake off its defensive role and lose some of its culturally pessimistic features. There are two directions in which this narrative might develop – either in a moderately conservative form with links to national identity as a source of security and protection in the uncertain world of globalization, or it will be restricted to a leftist and left-liberal political subculture in a politically and ideologically polarized society, attached to the values of autonomous administration, academic freedom and democracy.

---

149 http://www.fu–berlin.de/universitaet/profil/gesellschaft/index.html (16. 8. 2017).

THE MYTH OF THE UNIFIED UNIVERSITY

In his famous treatise *On the Internal and External Organization of the Higher Scientific Institutions in Berlin* (1810), Wilhelm von Humboldt wrote: "*But if the principle of pursuing science finally becomes dominant in the higher scientific institutions, there is no longer a need to see to anything else in particular. There would then be no lack of either unity or completeness, the one seeks the other by itself and the two will put themselves – and this is the secret of every good scientific method – into the right reciprocal relationship.*"[150] According to some, the unity, the wholeness of knowledge and the synergetic character of the work of all the university's disciplines are the mainstays of their activities, and none of these attributes can be circumvented when searching for the university's meaning. According to others this is a chimera. Over the past decades the academic community has become so heterogenous that it is no longer possible to talk about its unity and, therefore, the idea of the academic community has also lost its meaning.[151] In a global comparison, American higher education appears as the most heterogenous, while in Scandinavia they continue to assert that each university and each of its disciplines are an integral part of the community.[152] "*We know the lion by his claw,*" said the ancient Romans: who adheres to the notion of a unified university in Central Europe today and why?

The idea of higher education being the accumulation of all human knowledge has ancient roots, stretching back to the Platonic Academy and to the universal

---

150 von Humboldt, Wilhelm: O vnitřní a vnější organizaci vyšších vědeckých ústavů v Berlíně, In: Jirsa, Jakub (ed.): *Idea university*. Prague 2015, pp. 31–39, here p. 34.

151 Prudký, Libor – Pabian, Petr – Šima, Karel: *České vysoké školství. Na cestě od elitního k univerzálnímu vzdělávání 1989–2009*. Prague 2010, p. 63.

152 Barr, Nicholas: Financování vysokého školství z hlediska ekonomické teorie, In: Simonová, Natalie (ed.): *České vysoké školství na křižovatce. Investiční přístup k financování studia na vysoké škole. v sociologické reflexi*. Prague 2005, pp. 19–39, here p. 20.

interpretation of Aristotle's works during the Middle Ages. Philosophy was given a key role here, something which members of the academic community still focus on today, particularly those who feel there is a lack of unity within the disciplines and the university in general. In 1899 the philosopher František Drtina wrote, "*In the Middle Ages, philosophy was the sum of all scientific work (including theology), during the Middle Ages the relationship between philosophy and theology was further shaped into a grand synthesis, during the Modern Age, philosophy had a strangely isolated status because the academic sciences which came from its womb began to function more and more independently, and opposite it stands theology, representing an older view of the world and life based on supernatural phenomena. Such is a brief outline of the intellectual development of European civilization during the Modern Age...*"[153] Drtina was worried by developments within philosophy. He criticized the German speculative (i.e. idealistic – author's note) philosophy of Georg Wilhelm Friedrich Hegel, whom he blamed for the focus on metaphysics, ontology, dogmatism and "*transcendental speculation*" in general. Philosophical inquiry had become overly analytical and had lost sight of the need for synthesis, thus losing contact with the increasingly confident exact sciences. These "*divided the universe according to scientific subjects carrying out their work individually, but the results of their work are transferred to philosophy to create a unified, conclusive world view.*"[154]

According to the mythical narrative, holistic knowledge is the link between the university and scientific truth, and provides the university's basis. This is what distinguishes universities from other higher-education institutes and is its main contribution and service to students and society. A discipline structure worthy of its name in a traditional university – labelled a "bricks and mortar university" in the Czech context – should be comprehensive and the disciplines should show some synergy. The construction of a unified university has been supported by quotations from famous people, where there is no lack of pathos or authority from antiquity. The philosopher František Drtina (1861–1925), a leading Czech expert on higher education, was obviously strongly influenced by a passage from a lecture by Professor Gundling to the professorial corps at Halle in 1711: "*The truth is laid out in the centre, let he who can, approach it, let he who dares, grasp it – and we will applaud him!*"[155] There was no shortage of similarly bombastic speeches during a debate on the governance of Masaryk University in Brno on 28 January 1919. One member of parliament, Otakar Srdínko, was no less histrionic when in the name of higher-educational teaching he formulated a vision for the university. For understandable reasons, the references here were more to Masaryk than to the German university visionaries Kant and Humboldt: "*Masaryk University, never*

---

153 Cited from Drtina, František: *Universita a učitelstvo. Soubor statí.* Prague 1932, p. 1.

154 Ibid, p. 5.

155 Ibid, p. 244.

be unfaithful to the principles of your founder, our liberator, spread the love of the truth, defend the truth, preach honesty everywhere and teach pure humanity!"[156]

The myth of comprehensiveness and unity is a historical phenomenon which has been engraved into the identity of the university: during its medieval origins, theology guaranteed generality and contact with the truth, which all the university disciplines were directed towards. With the growth of religious particularism in the 16th century, the position of theology became weakened and with it the unified interpretation of the world, and then in the 18th century, theology passed the torch on to the royal disciplines of philosophy and law. The last third of the 19th century is considered the start of a new era of university development, when the influence of philosophy and the humanities markedly weakened in favour of the exact sciences.[157]

The beginning of the natural sciences' emancipation from the "domination" of philosophy and the arts in Central Europe dates back to the establishment of a separate science and mathematics institute in 1869 at the university in Tübingen, which was followed by other universities: Strasbourg (1872), Heidelberg (1890) and Frankfurt (1914), until subject particularism became widespread during the interwar period.[158] The fragmentation of the disciplines in "bourgeois" universities was the focus of reforms carried out by the communists in the Soviet Union (from 1930) and by the Nazis (from 1933), which in both cases tried to use ideology as a bond to unite the differentiated disciplines.[159]

These experiments came to an end with the collapse of communism in 1989. Influenced by neoliberalism, misinterpreted models adopted from the USA and the development of technology, discipline particularism in universities began to take on a form which is considered a threat to the continued notion of the university itself.

The myth of unity and universalism is today seen in the historicizing, almost nostalgic idea of the possibility of converting all inquiries into either a single or a few formulas. This task is most often assigned by the university academic community to philosophy as the alleged guardian of a pure form of rational thinking and universal knowledge that every university worthy of the name should have. In this sense, philosophy is the most important science. Naturally, in its claims to be universal it competes with other sciences which stylize themselves in the role of the most important science, though without raising this claim in a universal form.

---

156 http://www.psp.cz/eknih/1918ns/ps/stenprot/022schuz/s022008.htm (7.1. 2018).

157 Rüegg, Walter (ed.): *A History of the University in Europe. Volume III. Universities in the nineteenth and early twentieth Centuries (1800–1945)*. Cambridge 2004, pp. 16–20.

158 Ibid, p. 19.

159 Connely, *Zotročená*, pp. 331–355; Wróblewska, Teresa: *Die Reichsuniversitäten Posen, Prag und Strassburg als Modelle nationalsozialistischer Hochschulen in den von Deutschland besetzten Gebieten.* Toruń 2000, pp. 39–52.

This attempt to become the "first of all sciences" is most often connected with molecular biology, neurology and sociology.[160] Philosophers in the postmodern era usually respond to universalist expectations by extending their research work into the methodology and ethics of science, i.e. disciplines which are expected to have the most universal applicability. Within a developed university, these types of bonding activities are most often found in academic training in PhD courses. These tend to be quite successful and well-attended series of seminars examining the methods of inquiry of different sciences. It is with the education of young academics and their introduction to comprehensive scientific inquiry that the troublesome feeling arises that only a few experts are capable of stepping outside their own enclosed discipline to look holistically at science, the university, or even the faculty. This narrow specialization is most frequent in the natural sciences, but also in the humanities which are under pressure from systems for evaluating science and academic capitalism, where there is the strong presence of a "fortress mentality" and the defensive withdrawal behind historically proven inquiry and the methods of their own subject, regardless of developments in other disciplines.

The mission of the Central European university

Analysing the myth of the unity of the university is impossible without looking at the roles of those who commission work from universities – i.e. uncovering the motives of the founders and the financial providers. Their objectives are initially projected into the formal symbols of the university's existence, such as foundation memoranda, statutes and the organizational structure, and secondly into the institutional culture of the university. Therefore, who did the university "serve" and who does it "serve" today?

This is a very difficult question to answer. The oldest higher education was the result of an agreement between the Holy See and the sovereign, usually to varying degrees of good will from both sides. The Reformation weakened the influence of Rome and increased the power of the rulers who aimed at absolute control over their territory, including the universities. The university's connection to the ruler began to weaken with the awakening of the national movements in the 19th century, which in many countries separated the national interest from that of the ruler or dynasty, or even placed it against it. With the breakup of the multinational empires at the start of the 20th century, the university strengthened its connections to the nation and the nation state, albeit that for political-ideological reasons this emphasis on the nation was more disguised in successor states to the Habsburg

---

160 Hagner, Michael: Ansichten der Wissenschaftsgeschichte, In: also (Hg.): *Ansichten der Wissenschaftsgeschichte*. Franfurt am Main 2001, pp. 7–39, here p. 18.

empire which had diverse ethnicities. This connection of the university to the nation was to be strengthened enormously with the German Nazis' concept of nationalism, which subordinated German-language universities to the ideological vision of a world-conquering German nation. Non-German universities in Central Europe were interpreted simply as oppositional and hostile to German interests, and attempts were made to restrict their activities, though for tactical reasons their approach in the Protectorate of Bohemia and Moravia was different than in the occupied territories of Poland and Yugoslavia. The postwar university in Central Europe also kept its links to state power and the nation, but in a different form. This was either determined by the communist plan to build a new society, or the liberal-democratic idea of assigning the university the role as a school of liberal democracy and plurality. In the first case, the initial enthusiasm of the "cultural revolution" gradually waned and the university became increasingly defined as an institution supporting the development of a socialist national economy. In the second case, the role of the university gradually became interpreted as meaning support for the capitalist economy, which was considered the West's main calling card and the central argument for the success of liberal democracy as opposed to other political-economic systems.

After 1989 in Central Europe it became unclear as to the actual purpose and objectives of the university. Historical answers to similar questions were either rejected outright, as in the case of building a communist society, while other conceptual answers were looked at with a certain reserve, as was the case for the definitions associated with national, provincial or regional interests. The arguments linking the university to the European ideal were also rejected as they were seen by the majority of society as too abstract, concealing the specific political interests of some European countries and the power of the Brussels bureaucracy. With increasing globalization, several prestigious Anglo-Saxon universities formed the centre of the international university network, and as a result, the relationship between the university and the interests of global capitalism came to the forefront.

In this setup, which is often described as the "ever closer integration" of states, nations and universities, it is difficult to predict what fate has in store for the historically defined Central European university communities and the different justifications for their existence. This is not merely the result of the dramatic political turmoil that has engulfed Europe since 2005 (France's rejection of a European constitution in a referendum, the economic crisis, the crisis of the Eurozone, the migration crisis, etc.). Therefore, with events still so fresh, a clear and straightforward answer to the question *"who does the university serve today?"* is practically impossible. In Central Europe the enormous political turmoil has resulted in a confusing tangled web, where the university tradition has been in the service of the nation, the region, socialism, capitalism, Europeanness, liberal democracy and neoliberal ideology. It might appear that with such a complicated mixture of traditions, the Central European university has a particularly difficult role, but it is not the case. We might recall the fates of other parts of the global university network on the periphery and undergoing profound reforms, such as in South Africa. The local universities emerged as ambassadors for the British empire with liberal-humanist subtexts, and gradually this identity overlapped with Afrikaans nationalism and racism, then later with the visions of a liberated black Africa, black racism, and in recent decades with the ideas of neoliberal capitalism.[161]

The vision of completeness and university organisation

Looking at the issue from a historical perspective, we might ask ourselves the question whether the organisational structure of a university is reflected in the vision of completeness over time. The oldest universities were understood as an association of masters and students seeking general knowledge. The unified organizational structure of the oldest European universities was mainly connected with the University of Paris, which was founded in 1150. General knowledge was the remit of the arts faculty, which was understood as the stage before a professionally oriented education from the theological, legal and medical faculties. After obtaining a bachelor's title, a graduate from the arts faculty could then continue their studies in the professionally oriented faculties or they could remain at the arts faculty and focus on the highest level of education – the master's artium liberalium. The arts faculty, the predecessor to the philosophical faculty, was the largest organizational element and often had more students than all of the other faculties combined. However, a general knowledge was not only provided in universities by arts faculties, which were often considered to be less important than the vocationally oriented faculties, but rather as the result of the predominance of philosophical-theological teaching at medieval universities in general. The size and influence of the arts faculties was magnified by the widespread influence of theological education, which in many respects also maintained a universal character, reaching into every discipline and guaranteeing a unified interpretation of the world. We may recall that the medieval university created its organizational regulations based on monasteries, and to a large degree the community of students and masters was seen as a spiritual community, similar to that of a monastic society.[162]

The organizational structure taken from the traditions of medieval universities did not even undergo significant changes during the Early Modern Age. Under pressure from sovereigns, the increasing power of states and the decline in the

---

161 Wolhuter, Charl C. – Mushaandja, John: *Contesting Ideas of a University: The Case of South Africa.* Humanities 2015, 4, pp. 212–223.

162 Rüegg, Walter (Hg.): *Geschichte der Universität in Europa*, I., München 1993, pp. 68–69.

influence of papal universalism in large parts of Europe, universities lost their universal character. The newly established universities in Central Europe were clearly defined by their founders as "provincial" (Gießen/1607, Kiel/1665, Göttingen/1734, Bonn/1818 etc.), though this trend was more evident in the university culture than in its organizational structure, which usually remained the same. Firstly, there was an increased emphasis on vocational education focusing on the needs of the state, linked in particular to the legal and medical faculties. Even theological courses in Protestant countries had to respect the absolutist rulers' demands for the intellectual disciplining of their subjects. And secondly, there was a rise in the confidence of the natural-science disciplines, committed to a "scientific" path which *"has no connection with divinity, metaphysics, morality and politics"* as the Royal Society stated in 1662.[163]

The development of science in the 18th century brought significant changes to the respected hierarchy of faculties and disciplines, and to the general provision of knowledge. This was reflected in Central Europe with the Humboldtian reforms of higher education in German countries (and to a lesser extent in the Habsburg Monarchy), and the reforming work of John Henry Newman in an Anglo-Saxon context. With regard to the issue of a universal knowledge, both reformers of higher education were on a similar wavelength and aimed at the scientization of all disciplines taught at university. The university teacher was first and foremost a researcher, and all researchers, regardless of discipline, had to guarantee objectivity in their relationship with the public. Regarding university teaching, both of these towering figures put forward a claim for the integrity of education, as Immanuel Kant had done some time earlier in his work *Der Streit der Fakultäten* from 1798,[164] and Friedrich Daniel Ernst Schleiermacher in his treatise *Gelegentliche Gedanken über Universitäten in deutschem Sinn* from 1808. The discourse of the Humboldt-Newman followers contained many statements such as *"love of truth"* and *"the superiority of science over the state"* in the sense of the ancient ideals of the Platonic Academy for selecting statesmen through education from a mass of candidates.[165] However, the implementation of these lofty ideals for humanity was carried out by the Prussian bureaucracy in accordance with a state doctrine characterized by a strained hierarchism, legendary discipline, nationalism and militarism, and thus the Prussian university founded in Berlin in 1810 had features from these two intellectual worlds.

---

163 Hüther, Otto – Krücken, Georg: *Hochschulen. Fragestellungen, Ergebnisse, und Perspektiven des sozialwissenschaftlichen Hochschulforschung.* Wiesbaden 2016, p. 25.

164 Kant, Immanuel: *Der Streit der Facultäten in drei Abschnitten.* Leipzig 1880, p. 71 ff.

165 Langewiesche, Dieter: *Die „Humboldtsche Universität" als nationaler Mythos. Zum Selbstbildt der deutschen Universität in ihren Rektoratreden im Kaiserreich und in der Weimarer Republik,* Historische Zeitschrift 2010, 1, 290, pp. 53–91, here p. 58.

The new flourishing of universities was connected to service to the nation, meaning *"to the nation found within the family of civilized nations in Europe,"*[166] bringing to an end the previous two phases in the history of the university – firstly the medieval phase, formed by religious universalism, and afterwards the phase of early modern age states, characterized by religious and territorial particularism and the absolutism of sovereigns.[167] According to the Humboldtian school of thought, the nation was superior to partisanship, while the service of science and the university to the nation was seen as apolitical, removed from all conflicts in public life, and in this sense the only comprehensive one. The university was called upon to accumulate comprehensive and objective knowledge in the service of the nation, despite the fact that the practical use of this knowledge was not a pressing issue. The decision concerning what was and what was not useful was transferred to the abstract "nation". This large degree of independence gave university representatives the mandate to look at social phenomena in a balanced manner and formulate appropriate recommendations for the correct actions. The fact that in the world of science the concept of timeless knowledge is very problematic as it constantly leads to formulating, defending or rebutting new theses, was not reflected on in the relationship towards the nation. Therefore, the scientific debate was not perceived as a social and political phenomenon, as the indication of particularistic interests, but as the rivalry between representatives of national science. From the perspective of foreign observers of German Humboldtian education, the legendary Prussian discipline and order, together with fervent nationalism, were evident here because through *"regulations and customary laws the nation shows its will."*[168]

In the multinational conservative Habsburg empire, statism and the disciplining of the population did not reach the same levels as in Germany. National antagonisms were not imperialist in nature, aimed at vying with the old superpowers for global control, instead they were directed inwardly at trying to secure the best possible deal for their own nation within the empire. The university was, therefore, viewed as proof of a nation's maturity, and acquiring one was seen primarily as furthering the cause of national emancipation rather than as a progressive step for all of mankind. National antagonisms were also in evidence due to the fact that the foundation of universities which were not German-speaking undermined the hitherto predominant German culture in the Habsburg empire. The relatively calm Austrian Germans accepted the Polonization of the universities in Krakow and Lvov due to the fact there were few German inhabitants living in Galicia. However, the success of the Czechs with the establishment of the Charles-

---

166 Ibid.

167 Ibid, p. 72.

168 Ibid, p. 59.

Ferdinand University (1882) was seen by the Germans as at their expense, and was part of a growing trend towards the Czechization of Prague and Bohemia, where there was a large German population.[169] The university became a weapon in the national struggle, and although there was one exception to this in the small Austrian university in Bukovina's Chernivtsi, where the teachers and students from many different nationalities managed to coexist, this did nothing to change this pattern.[170]

However, the interests of the nation were not only promoted through the use of its own language in the university, but also through the comprehensive academic excellence of all the university's disciplines. The standard of academic work in the countries of Central and Central Eastern Europe was traditionally benchmarked against the top research institutes in Germany, which were global leaders in the 19th century and the first three decades of the 20th. Matching the new methodologies emerging from Germany and developing a specific Czech response to them became a question of national honour.[171] However, not every discipline was able to easily adapt to the measurements of objectivity in the service of the national interest. Some of the arts disciplines were generally regarded as having been weakened by their unscientific nature and lack of practical application. The emancipation of the natural-science disciplines from the domination of the humanities, hamstrung by metaphysics and speculation, was perceived by the left in particular as the path to progress.[172] The humanities had been left behind in terms of methodology, which had been a very strong part of German science during the 19th century. For a long period in Czech humanities research, the dividing line had been unclear between a rational-scientific approach and an emotionally charged, fanciful, national-historical narrative. There followed unsatisfactory responses concerning the practical dimension of the humanities and their usefulness in general. This opened the door to doubts about the meaning of the entire university – in comparison to the previously integrated system of teaching, research and interpretation of the world, there was now a conspicuous gap caused by the fragility of the humanities. Speeches made by three consecutive rectors at Leipzig University reflected on this contempt for the humanities. In 1891 the traditional philologist Justus Lipsius spoke about the tasks for the future from a defensive position, protecting his and related disciplines against the idea that

---

169 Cf. Seibt, Ferdinand (Hg.): *Die Teilung der Prager Universität 1882 und die intellektuelle Desintegration in den böhmischen Ländern*. München 1984.

170 Turczynski, Emanuel: Czernowitz als Beispiel einer integrativen Universität, In: Seibt, Ferdinand (Hg.), *Die Teilung der Prager Universität 1882 und die intellektuelle Desintegration in den böhmischen Ländern*. München 1984), pp. 25–36.

171 Havránek, Jan (red.): *Dějiny Univerzity Karlovy III. (1802–1918)*, Prague 1997, pp. 260–267.

172 *Die Naturwissenschaften als Grundlage der Schule*, Volksfreund 10.3. 1887, year 7, no. 5, p. 2; *Die Clerikalen und die Naturwissenschaften*, Volksfreund 13.6. 1889, year 9, no. 11, p. 1.

they were merely subjects to be taught and were not research disciplines. In 1893 the chemist Johann Wiscelinus did not ask for support for his own discipline – he did not deem it necessary to have to explain its scientific character and social necessity to his listeners – but support for other disciplines, mainly the humanities, which he argued were important for a comprehensive education. *"Can chemistry address the final principles of matter? No, chemistry alone cannot definitively answer such questions."*[173] For Wiscelinus, the university was an institution whose internal unity was not allowed to be destroyed by research development in disciplines or increased specialization, as it would then lose its way in scientifically explaining the world in its entirety. In 1910 the historian Karl Lamprecht formulated a position which was common within the humanities and social sciences – that as a result of pressure from the global economy and the ever-closer communication links between continents, the university would have to respond to *"an unusual number of new stimuli, gain a complete understanding of them and build on their foundation a world of shared ideas and moral ideals."* Allegedly these developments mercilessly targeted outdated and unreformable institutions. Lamprecht, as a leading figure in historical science, called for changes in the approaches in the humanities, which were to focus more on themes which were considered as relevant from the perspective of the exact sciences and were suitable for wider cultural-historical-comparative analyses, which would bring the university together again.[174]

Wilhelm von Humboldt himself saw the humanities as an important part of the *universitas*, as its bond in the scientific search for an integrated interpretation of the world. At the same time, as a linguist, he also contributed significantly towards raising the academic standards in both his own discipline and in the humanities as a whole.[175] In a lecture from 1852, the reformer of English higher education, John Henry Newman, considered the role of the humanities in a similar way: *"..all branches of knowledge are connected together, because the subject-matter of knowledge is intimately united in itself, as being the acts and the work of the Creator. Hence it is that the Sciences, into which our knowledge may be said to be cast, have multiplied bearings one on another, and an internal sympathy, and admit, or rather demand, comparison and adjustment. They complete, correct, balance each other... Let me make use of an illustration. In the combination of colours, very different effects are produced by a difference in their selection and juxtaposition; red, green, and white, change their shades, according to the contrast to which they are submitted. And, in like manner, the drift and meaning of a branch of knowledge varies with the company in which it is introduced to the student."*[176]

---

173 Langewiesche, *Die „Humboldtsche Universität"*, p. 71.

174 Ibid, pp. 75–77.

175 von Humboldt, *O vnitřní a vnější organizaci*, p. 34.

176 Newman, Henry John: Idea university. In: Jirsa, Jakub (ed.): *Idea university*. Prague 2015, pp. 40–51, here pp. 40–41.

However, the emphasis on the scientific character of the discipline implied the search for disciplines' specific characteristics and – supported by the personal ambitions of the researcher, the rivalry between universities and their supporting political-economic interest groups – brought with it a dramatic growth in the number of professorships. At that time, the social contribution of the exact sciences was seen as incontrovertible by the public and taxpayers. This was reinforced by the continuous flow of discoveries changing people's everyday lives. In contrast to the "usefulness" of the exact sciences, the humanities were in a weak position and their social prestige came under threat. The secularization of European society in the 19th century had earlier eroded the position of theological courses which had at one point been the most important member of the university's family of disciplines, and the re-division of the university hierarchy of prestige continued, practically always at the expense of the humanities. By 1900 the arts were being accused in Germany and Austria of producing too many "academic proletarians" or people who had a general education but who were practically unemployable due to their lack of specialization and practical knowledge.

Berhard vom Brocke attempted to account for the surge in professorial chairs for the humanities that were established in German-language areas. The development of the portfolio of disciplines in German universities was to a significant degree determined by developments in higher education in the Habsburg monarchy. The main wave which established specialized disciplines was in German states from 1766–1829, while in the Habsburg empire it was markedly slower, with disciplines typically being established after 1850, usually first at the University of Vienna.[177] There was a growth here from the mid-19th century in the number of lectures given in languages other than German; during the second half of the 19th century some universities declared themselves as non-German language (the Jagellonian University in the 1870s, Charles University in 1882). In particular, the arts faculties in the Habsburg empire were incubators for subjects which had not yet developed into fully fledged scientific disciplines, and which did not acquire their own professorships until the 1890s, and then later entirely separate faculties. In 1885 the arts faculty at Graz University represented 42% of the university's capacity, and this was only slightly less in other schools.[178] There were even jibes aimed at arts faculties in German-Austrian areas which spoke of the "*Universitätsrumpelkammer*" or the dumping grounds for the university's flotsam and jetsam, meaning disciplines which were to be avoided by the other faculties.[179]

---

177 vom Brocke, Berhard: Die Entstehung der deutschen Forschungsuniversität. Ihr Blüte und Krise um 1900. In: von Schwinges, Rainer Christoph (Hg.): *Humboldt International. Der Export der deutschen Universitätsmodells im 19. und 20. Jahrhundert*. Basel 2001, pp. 367–401, here p. 376.

178 Engelbrecht, *Geschichte*, p. 235.

179 Langewiesche, *Die „Humboldtsche Universität"*, p. 54.

Prague's faculty of arts become significantly more heterogenous in the mid-18th century. 1761 saw the establishment of a professorship of higher mathematics, in 1766 a professorship of political and cameralist sciences, and the third phase from 1774–1792 saw the development of several key professorships for the humanities. Some endeavours at the faculty had more of an experimental character, and a professorship of agricultural sciences was in existence there from 1775 to 1781. After 1803 the foundation of the technical university meant the ambitions to establish the technical disciplines outside of the faculty of arts had been realized, nevertheless, Prague's faculty of arts continued to be very diverse in terms of its disciplines. In the 1880s the number of regular and associate professorships was between 42 and 48, in the school year of 1899/1900 it reached a maximum number of 65 professors divided into the natural-science and social-science sections, which were informally considered at the faculty to be more prestigious and usually demonstrated better scientific results due to better equipment.[180] New professorships were added to physics, geography, anthropology and zoology, while the humanities quickly differentiated between the history and art-history disciplines, which in Central Eastern Europe was a reaction to the boom in German historical science represented by the methodological and organizational work of Leopold von Ranke (1775–1886).[181]

In the mid-19th century the Jagellonian University in Krakow, another of the top research institutes in Central Eastern Europe which was attractive to the Czech lands, had fourteen disciplines in its faculty of arts which had the statute of an independent professorship: philosophy, general history, Polish literature, German studies, two professorships for classical philology and another two professorships for mathematics, one professorship for mineralogy and zoology, and then astronomy, physics, chemistry, botany and geography. The number of specialized philological disciplines increased and we can also see here the rapid division of the history disciplines: three departments existed in 1869 and by the start of the 20th century there were eight professorships in total for history including auxiliary historical sciences and the history of music and art. There was an exponential growth in professorships for the natural-science disciplines from the 1890s, particularly in Earth science.[182] As a result, in the twilight years of the Habsburg empire, Krakow's faculty of arts had 50 professorships, 28 divisions and nine seminaries.[183]

---

180 Petráň, *Nástin,* p. 227.

181 Ibid, pp. 267–270.

182 Schmidt, Peter: *Zum 100. Todestag von Ernst Ludwig August von Rebeur–Paschwitz.* Nachrichtenblatt zur Geschichte der Geowissenschaften, No. 5, pp. 58 – 59, 1995.

183 Stinia, Maria: *Uniwersytet Jagielloński w latach 1871–1914. Modernizacja procesu nauczania.* Kraków 2014, pp. 98–125.

The conflict between universal and professional education

The concept of "Humboldtian" university unity began to break apart around 1900 due to two issues which had been part of the idea of the university since its very inception: the relationship between the professionally oriented disciplines and the general-education disciplines, and how disciplines should respond to current political, economic or cultural challenges in order to gain social legitimacy. The potential for conflict in the first issue lay in the fact that professors of professionally oriented disciplines often did not carry out any relevant research and, closed within their narrow discipline specialization, did not engage in the debates and issues of other disciplines. However, the importance of professional education for society and the state was not, and in view of the public financing of the university, could not be doubted. However, this led to numerous important disciplines being torn away from the vision of the "Humboldtian" university, in particular the medical and law faculties which created their own autonomous culture. Therefore, the unity and comprehensiveness of traditional higher education was only an illusion.

The second issue then created lines of conflict between disciplines as well as inside them. In their dominant position, the natural sciences courageously allied themselves to a vision of their contribution towards "dominating the world" through scientific discovery for the greater glory of the nation. Some in the humanities shared this "national commitment", while some stubbornly defended the idea of pure science standing above political interests and refused to be drawn into the public debate. The conflict often involved personal fights between professors. While the Prague historian Jaroslav Goll (1846–1929) was a leading figure in the strict rejection of submitting science to social-political demands to prioritize research, and refused to update his own work in medieval research,[184] his colleague, a historian of the Early Modern Age, Antonín Rezek (1853–1909), attempted to popularize scientific knowledge through his many publications and activity in public life, which even led to him gaining a ministerial post in the Austrian government.[185] Tomáš Masaryk's involvement in the Hilsner affair was an extreme example of a university professor stepping into public life and led to dramatic conflicts within academia as well as the general public – Masaryk was loved by some, hated by others. Even if we ignore the extremists' views in the whole dispute and are aware of the fact that Masaryk had had previous experience dealing with the public, it is clear that the activism of one of its professors was a severe test for the position of the university and the culture of solidarity within

---

184 Petráň, *Nástin*, p. 215.

185 Kučera, Martin: *K politické činnosti historika Antonína Rezka*. Východočeské listy historické, 11–12, 1997, pp. 11–33.

academia.[186] There was another test for the apolitical vision of the university in the Czech setting with the conflict over establishing a university in Brno, culminating in the events of 1905. In Germany, meanwhile, there was the political involvement of universities on the side of the nationalist radicals in the dispute over the Baden language reforms from 1895–1899, and the so-called Wahrmund affair in 1908 at Innsbruck University, relating to sharp criticism of the Catholic Church.[187]

In relation to the vision of a united university, we can see three basic strategies adopted by the Central European universities in the twentieth century which were founded on the basis of the Humboldtian concept. These were strategies filled with contradictions, each of which brought at least some short-term positives as well as numerous negatives. The first of these was the even more fiercely defended idea of maintaining university unity through grand social projects, whether this was through nationalism, liberal democracy, socialism or racism. It was more or less the repeated claim of the humanities having a leading status in the university and an attempt to subordinate both specialized disciplines and narrowly professionally orientated disciplines to the higher concept of university service to the public. From the perspective of the thousand-year history of the *universitas*, the benefits of this approach for the humanities were more of a short- to medium-term character. The negatives were obvious: in the turbulent twentieth century with its incredibly fast turnover of regimes and ideologies, it was easy to discredit and even liquidate people and disciplines which were too closely linked to some of these ideological concepts. As a result, any similar politicization of the humanities and social sciences was interpreted as evidence of their unscientific character which could lead to doubts as to whether they had the right to exist in the university's community of disciplines – not to mention any claims about its leadership or ability to unite.

The second strategy lay in the refusal to accept the role of the academic worker in public life. The objective was to focus fully on the role of the apolitical civil servant following state-defined scientific tasks, particularly in teaching, where any activities that could be labelled as political would be avoided. It was about modifying the old vision of the university as an accumulator of pure knowledge through the coexistence of the university with a strong state. At the very least, there was to be limited engagement in the education of the public, which was seen as a necessary evil, as a tax on the apolitical scientific and educational activities at the university. The university's declaration of loyalty to the state in all circumstances proved to be an important legitimizing strategy for the unity of the university, which allowed it to bridge periods of growing pressure from political ideologies, and the very dangerous period when their influence was changing. This was an attractive strat-

---

186 Rys, Jan: *Hilsneriáda a TGM*. Prague 2016.
187 Trauner, Karl–Reinhart: *Die Wahrmund–Affäre*. Vienna 1992.

egy for the Central European academic faced with political turmoil. It allowed for some basic moral consistency based on the simple apolitical acceptance of state orders, where the task was to carry them out, not to question them. It made it easier to transfer the blame away from yourself if an old political concept collapsed or if it was rejected by society, because someone who was only following orders from their superiors could not be guilty. This strategy of a very close link to the state, inspired by French or Russian/Soviet universities, made the university into a united and internally highly cohesive community, whose culture was very similar to that of the state bureaucracy's priorities. Only the façade remained of Fichte and Humboldt's vision of a struggle for a better person and new humanity; the university had lost its intellectual ethos and become a bureaucratic tool. However, it was able to very effectively defend individual members of the professorial corps from persecution, as well as disciplines that were allegedly socially redundant or politically dangerous, as it was able to respond with a high degree of unity, following the example of bureaucracy. An attack on one member of this community was perceived as an attack on the whole community. The strategy was also compatible with the integration of certain figures who were more prominent in political projects as a result of having accepted academic functions; the first and second strategies therefore had the potential to coexist. The role of academics at the intersection of politics and pure science was interpreted as a personal sacrifice made to maintain the basic apolitical character of a discipline and its scientific activities. The defence of the allegedly largely positive role of these people was part of legitimizing the discipline in times of political change.

In Central Europe the third strategy was most common in Austria and West Germany. It was aimed at a fundamental revision of the concept of the university as an institution which provides education and scientific training in *all* scientific disciplines (universitas litterarum). In a certain sense it meant defending the remains of the conservatively conceived notion of the university by being resigned to grouping some disciplines together which were not supposedly compatible with the university and transferring them to specialist colleges or research institutes. The concept of a fully-fledged university was revised in those areas which brought most tension to the traditional hierarchy – the narrowly vocationally focused disciplines were removed from the university (to specialist colleges) as were the technical and scientific disciplines which had the greatest potential of working with the industrial and commercial sectors (to specialist research centres). There was an erosion of the influence of the humanities and the social sciences within the university community, and they demonstrated their inability to maintain their legitimacy when faced with specific demands from doctors, lawyers, technologists and some scientists. The movement of the technical disciplines to technical universities was a precursor to the next development in higher education in German "Humboldtian" circles, and there followed a debate on the expediency of establishing special colleges for the pedagogical, art and medical disciplines. Then there were deliberations which went straight to the heart of the idea of the university – whether to systematically differentiate academic disciplines characterized by their exact nature on the one hand, and those disciplines which tended to analyse interpretations of reality. It was then easy to see a dividing line between the science and arts disciplines as representing these two fields. The debates on how difficult it was to incorporate all of the traditional areas of the Humboldtian university were mainly connected with how certain aspects of the Soviet and American higher-education system were received. These developments reflected the fact that in the 20th century the culture in Central European universities had been shaped by the Cold War and the pressure from a different political and economic environment which altered university habits.

The Soviet influence on the Central European university

The Soviet model for higher education was based on disciplines cooperating to achieve a common goal – communism – and in this sense could be seen as reintroducing unity to the university. In order to achieve this the communists used similar measures to those which the Nazis had introduced to Central European universities. The model National Socialist universities included the universities in Prague and Poznaň (Reichsuniversität).[188] The Reich university had been designed to replace the old "Humboldtian" university tradition in the name of ideologically committed unified science, which served to educate the "new man", and also specifically applied science – the Reich universities helped to develop some of the Nazi's plans for the final solution of Europe following victory in war in terms of racial cleansing, Germanization and incorporation into the greater economy of the Third Reich.[189]

In the countries lying in the Soviet sphere of influence, after the Second World War the conflict lines and ideological pressure were familiar to universities from the Nazi period. The formal role of universities in communist-bloc countries was also subordinate to the goal of building a socialist society and educating the "new

---

188 Wróblewska, *Die Reichsuniversitäten*, s. 17–52; Nagel, Anne Ch.: Anspruch und Wirklichkeit in der nationalsozialistischen Hochschul– und Wissenschaftspolitik. In: Reulecke, Jürgen – Roelcke, Volker (Hg.): *Wissenschaften im 20. Jahrhundert: Universitäten in der modernen Wissenschaftsgesellschaft.* Stuttgart 2008, pp. 245–262; Konrád, Ota: *Dějepisectví, germanistika a slavistika na Německé univerzitě v Praze 1918–1945.* Prague 2011, p. 202 ff.

189 Konrád, *Dějepisectví*, pp. 227–230.

man".[190] The ideological departments helped to inscribe the "cultural revolution" into the identity of every university in the communist era, particularly in smaller and more modern schools, rather than in the case of the large, traditional Charles University. For example, the goal of Olomouc's Palacký University (re-established in 1946) was described as the struggle against clericalism, agrarianism and the relics of bourgeois thinking in the catchment areas of Eastern Moravia, Těšín and Western Slovakia.[191] The regime's favoured disciplines (Marxist-Leninist philosophy, the history of the international workers' movement and political economy)[192] were used as instruments to carry out the "cultural revolution" across disciplines and the entire university community, therefore, *"to educate the masses to creatively master the scientific world view and the continuous struggle against bourgeois ideologies whose actions hinder the pace of constructing socialism."*[193]

At the end of the 1940s Zdeněk Nejedlý, the leading ideologist of communist science, described Czechoslovak universities as a bastion of conservatism, as an example of the inability and unwillingness to adapt their work to the new society and political conditions, and to strive to build a socialist society. Nejedly's rhetoric was quickly adopted by Communists and the Czechoslovak Youth Associations operating in the universities, who called for the dismantling of the differences in the disciplines and the integration of the university on an ideological basis: *"You only see strict faces in the faculties. Paper, books, bad individualism, academia. Noses held high and intellectual smart alecs. One sighs over 'old English', another over 'yer', the third over Czech grammar. As though several hundred creatures were enclosed within their shells. The conglomerate of these shells has created a hermetically sealed faculty/fortress. The second year of the Five-Year-Plan is everywhere in motion, yet the faculties act as though they knew nothing about them."*[194] The principles of the Humboldtian university were treated by the communists as the remnants of a capitalist society which had to be overcome and destroyed. Alongside the empty ideological phrases of the cultural revolution which were in such evidence in the 1950s, the role of the university in the development of the socialist economy was emphasized by communist governments in Czechoslovakia over successive decades: *"The bourgeoisie created a form of education and appropriate educational institutions for its own needs. Communism can never come to terms with them. It will find its own new revolutionary paths and methods, institutions and forms of education, a mass education disproportionately greater than*

---

190 Connelly, John: *Zotročená univerzita: sovětizace vysokého školství ve východním Německu, v českých zemích a v Polsku v letech 1945–1956*. Prague 2008, p. 166 ff.

191 Ibid.

192 Archiv UK Praha, Ústav sociálně politických věd, i.d. 471, 474.

193 Zemský archiv Opava, pobočka Olomouc, KV KSČ, schůze byra, k. 54, zápis z jednání dne 14.11. 1955.

194 Archiv MU, Spolek posluchačů filosofie G1, kart. 1 Jak jsme začínali – vzpomínky na školní rok 1949–1950, příloha k zápisu ze schůze ze dne 5. 3. 1951.

that of capitalism – the mass march towards education and a new, hitherto unknown increase in production and productivity based on the expansion of mechanization and automation."[195]

Although in ideological terms the contribution of the individual disciplines and groups of disciplines was defined similarly as building a socialist society, in practical terms there were significant differences. While the humanities and social sciences were systematically treated as being in the service of propaganda-educational work, the science and medical disciplines were spared the worst aspects of ideological pressure due to the practical interests of the regime in industrial production and the health of its population: *"We laugh when a reactionary philosopher or historian emigrates* (to West Germany – author's note). *However, it is a different case with a physicist, mathematician or technologist for whom we have no replacements."*[196] Amongst East German scientists there was the fitting comparison of their discipline to *"a golden tooth in the reactionary muzzle,"* which was used by one of the leaders of the communist regime.[197]

However, during particularly turbulent times for the regime, professional education and the interests of industry were subordinate to ideological education, and in this sense the ideological pressure of the communist regimes covered all departmental differences, strengthened the unity of the university, and in so doing led university education out of a crisis. However, this was only temporary, as the costs for this policy of ideologically supporting the unity of the university were considerable. On the one hand, disciplines (mainly from the arts and social sciences) were selected on the basis of being ideologically suitable or ideologically tainted, suspicious or unnecessary; while some scientific and informatics disciplines were ideologically disparaged for being bourgeois and unsuited to the process of building a socialist society – with a subsequent catastrophic impact on the economic performance of communist countries.

The regime's ideological pressure on the whole *universitas* in the countries of the communist bloc thus papered over the dispute concerning the social contribution of disciplines when this aspect was redefined according to their own criteria. Entire groups of disciplines (theology) might be rejected. Elsewhere the regime was more moderate in the selection process, where only a few disciplines or subdisciplines were cut back (classic philology, ecclesiastical history, genetics, sociology). In the communist university, the economic criterion of efficiency was

---

195 Archiv UK, Fond Vědecká rada UK, zápis ze dne 31.3. 1960, p. 37.

196 Connelly, John: *Zotročená univerzita: sovětizace vysokého školství ve východním Německu, v českých zemích a v Polsku v letech 1945–1956.* Prague 2008, pp. 125–126.

197 Jessen, Ralph: *Von den Vorzügen des Sozialismus und der deutschen Teilung. Kollaborationsverhältnisse im ostdeutschen Wissenschaftssystem der fünfzigen Jahre.* In: Weisbord, Bernd: Akademische Vergangenheitspolitik, pp. 39–52, here p. 48.

subordinated to the ideological mission and thus lost its strict, pragmatic and dangerous character to the integrity of the university.

The American influence on the Central European university

During the Second World War and the Cold War, American, British and many other smaller Western European countries combined their resources in order to maintain and increase the West's technological superiority over the fascist and then communist blocs. Understandably, this did not apply to all disciplines, but only to a select few. The humanities and social sciences were also part of the efforts by the USA and its allies to defeat fascism and hold back communism, but only to a limited degree, without the generous funding and support in personnel which the scientific and technical disciplines could enjoy. In the 1950s there also began to appear in Western universities well-financed, ideologically tinged disciplines (such as Sovietology, which was strongly represented by émigré professors from the Eastern bloc).[198] The communists' "cultural revolution" and attempts to enforce their ideology upon universities even had its counterpart in the social disturbances which rocked American and Western European universities in the 1960s, when social-science disciplines were formed which pushed universities towards a more left-liberal, even neo-Marxist, political discourse (Black Studies, Gender Studies, Intercultural Studies, etc.). However, in comparison with the "cultural revolution" in the universities of the Eastern bloc, pressure on colleagues, whether politically indifferent or critical, usually came from "below", i.e. without the support of the university leaders or the regime's security forces. On the other hand, in their fanaticism and aggressiveness, these methods were similar to those used by the activist and avant-garde elements of the communist regime. Overall, it would be wrong to suggest that these political-ideological developments in the academic communities of the USA and Western Europe fundamentally threatened the viability of disciplines or entire universities which rejected the pressure from the left, or remained apolitical. Marc Taylor talks unreservedly about an ongoing cultural war with its main front centred on American universities.[199] Remaining outside the main left-liberal discourse for changing society was possible – this was one of the advantages of the strong democratic institutions of Western universities which had not been weakened by the aforementioned left-wing pressure "from below". The price for remaining outside of the mainstream was to be

---

198 Isaac, Joel: *The Human Sciences in Cold War America*. The Historical Journal, 50, 3 (2007), pp. 725–746.

199 Taylor, Marc C.: *Crisis on Campus. A Bold Plan for Reforming Our Colleges and Universities*. New York 2010, p. 34.

involved in heated debates and numerous minor inconveniences, but this position was and remains tenable.

In 1981 the American cultural historian Jackson Lears termed the clash over the meaning of the university in the USA as *"an ideological war raging between the politically correct left within the universities and the neoconservative misanthropes outside of it."*[200] The first of these, who gradually began to dominate in American universities in the 20th century, argue that the curricula and research priorities which are linked to social demand, and the educational role of the university which is aimed at overcoming racism and discrimination of all kinds, are more diverse, open and viable. The second group see the meaning of the university as being threatened by the activities of *"politicized professors with their uptight standards of expression, who had long since rejected the principle of scientific objectivity."* It might have appeared as though the unity of Western universities had been restored with the firm transfer of the torch to a left-liberal ideology. And this is despite the criticism from outside the university which often perceives the university as a ghetto of left-liberal activism. But Lears believes that this argument concerning the role of the university is a dead end. Despite the fact that the tyranny of all ideologies and their associated activism is stifling, in his opinion the real danger for the unity of the university comes from academic capitalism or *"the application of a market-dictated managerial approach which tends to subordinate universities to quantitative standards of efficiency and productivity, treats education as a commodity, and transforms centres of open investigation into research laboratories for massive corporations and training centres for employees."*[201] Some disciplines are unable to withstand such challenges and their weakened position or even closure destroys the integrity and unity of the university. With this observation, Lears is, interestingly, in agreement with the critique of American universities from the communist bloc in the 20th century.[202]

What is meant by academic capitalism? It is a way of defining the university in terms of the values of managerial capitalism, such as the quantification of performance, excellence in research, operational efficiency, measurable work productivity, demonstrable social usefulness, quality of management; naturally with an emphasis on the university's visibility as measured by the "Shanghai Ranking" (Academic Ranking of World Universities).[203] The managerial style of viewing universities first appeared in the USA within a narrow group of elite private universities (Harvard, Princeton, Yale, etc.), but it fitted in well with the American public's demand for a clear definition of a university as an institute financed by public

---

200 Lears, *No place*, p. 107.

201 Lears, *No place*, p. 107.

202 Macháček, Jaroslav: *Výzkum na vysokých školách v USA a jiných kapitalistických státech*. Prague 1966; Kocevová, Marie: *Přehled o aplikovaném výzkumu na univerzitách v USA*. Prague 1978; Cipro, Miroslav: *Idea vysoké školy. Studie o vysokém školství ve světě socialismu a kapitalismu*. Prague 1981, pp. 50–57.

203 http://www.shanghairanking.com/ARWU–Methodology–2016.html (15.6. 2017).

money and which, therefore, has to respond to the needs of society and the tax-payer. In the cultural context of traditional American pragmatism, the preference for the principle *winner takes all* and the anti-intellectualism of a significant part of the American public shifted the debate about the meaning of the university back in the 19th century towards searching for criteria on which to base a hierarchy of quality and prestige amongst the universities as well as within each of them, naturally with an impact on those departments which for various reasons are unable to survive this competition.

In spite of the ideological rivalry within the academic community, economic pragmatism became the most important threat to university unity first of all in the USA and then later also in Western Europe. It was not the ideological spats between disciplines, nor the squabbling between activist professors and supporters of "pure science", but the relentless pressure of the market that determined which disciplines in the university were viable and which were not. Characteristically, the demands of the market do not include an overarching grasp of reality, and the priority is the usefulness of a university's work in relation to the labour market or applied research. The managerial interpretation of the university's role directly contradicts the conservative understanding of the humanities, and it is striking how incompatible this is with a university which is defined in this sense. Back in 1907, William James (1842–1910), a famous psychologist and philosopher, pointed to the damage which the practical and economic underestimation of the humanities could do to university research: *"You can add the humanities to almost any material if you teach it historically. Geology, economics, even mechanics can become an arts science if you teach it with reference to the successes of their genius founders. If you do not teach it that way, then literature remains grammar, art a catalogue, history a list of dates and science a set of formulas, weights and measurements."*[204]

Historically, European and especially Central European "Humboldtian" university culture has been shown to be the least able to absorb the elements of a managerial interpretation of the university's role. The main reason has been the tradition of very close ties to the state budget and perceptions of economic realities which are different to those of private American universities, which have now become the benchmark for university quality. The way in which Central European universities that were established after 1989 reacted defensively to the challenge of academic capitalism referred slightly nostalgically to the Humboldtian ideal of university unity in the fundamental character of the work carried out by disciplines. The humanities have been particularly active in defending the myth of university unity as they are the ones most threatened by a movement towards "Americanization".

---

204 Lears, Jackson T. J.: *No place of grace: antimodernism and the transformation of American culture, 1880 – 1920*, New York 1981, p. 110.

Why did Central European universities look so stubbornly for models in the elite American universities? What happened to their former self-confidence? Innovative tendencies in the 20th century were not an outstanding characteristic of Central European universities, which slowly began to lose out in terms of their high quality and prestige during the interwar period, and even more rapidly post-1945, to the American universities, where a handful of institutions enjoyed exceptional prestige and influence on the global interpretation of the *universitas*. European universities were discredited for indulging in politics and accused of failing to understand the real needs of society; the setbacks for the university mandarins in their ivory towers had significant political potential for conflict in the two decades after the war. One particularly drastic example of crossing the limits in the tradition of the university was that of the German universities and their relationship towards Nazism, including their woefully inadequate response to their own part in Nazi rule, which only began to improve in the 1960s. After 1945, the demise of universities which had once been considered the elite of the "Humboldtian" cultural circle was so evident that the Americanization or westernization of West German higher education was often seen as a liberation from decades of crisis and floundering on the part of Central European universities. One symbolic expression of American influence on German higher education was the establishment of the Berlin Freie Universität in 1948, which was to be the counterpart to the "old" Humboldt university located in the Soviet-occupied zone of the city.[205] Implementing this programme to transform Germany – defined as a *"powerful influence for freedom and democracy in German higher education"* – was the logical result of Hitlerism and an attempt to deal with its causes and consequences; at the same time, it was viewed a priori as suspicious by the entire German university culture.

In public debates about the state of universities, the American example of academic capitalism has thus become something which, from an ahistorical interpretation of the development and achievements of only a handful of American universities, is viewed as the model for the future development of universities in the distinctly different cultural, political and economic environment of Central European educational systems. It is certainly possible to agree with Louis Menand who in 2009 entirely rejected the concept of the "European university", believing that the university today is a global concept with its centre in the USA.[206] However, this view should not be confused with a rejection of plurality in the interpretation of the university's role in society and therefore its holistic work. Putting forward American models is more of a way to disguise an unwillingness to provide universities with adequate funding from public budgets, and to apply neoliberally

205 Paulus, Stefan: *Vorbild USA? Amerikanisierung von Universitäten und Wissenschaft in Westdeutschland 1946–1976.* München 2010, pp. 171–203.

206 Menand, Louis: *Marketplace of Ideas: Reform and Resistance in the American Universities.* Norton 2009, p. 96.

inspired political-economic pressure on universities to introduce methods of academic capitalism. In practice this means cutting back the arts and social-science disciplines which are incapable of meeting the demands of open, or more often, concealed academic capitalism. Those disciplines which are connected to industry are adored, while the social importance of the humanities, as well as some scientific disciplines such as biology and physics, is underestimated or hidden. Due to their strong orientation towards basic rather than applied research, they are often held up in Europe as the suffering Cinderella, even though they are a firmly respected part of all the prestigious American schools. Naturally, the American elite universities also have excellent arts and social-science departments, whose work is an important contribution to the school's global renown and attracts the interest of sponsors and patrons.[207]

Even in Germany, which has had the longest experience of the Americanization of its universities, the symbolic images of "German Harvards" appear in the discourse on the future of universities; the largest step carried out in this direction was the attempt to combine the Ludwig-Maxmilians Universität and Technische Universität in Munich into one large school, bringing together the best of research to compete with the stars overseas. There were some confused responses, *"A few Harvards, Stanfords and Yales aren't going to help the present higher-education crisis. Rather than magical words, our Oldenburgs* (an allusion to one of the few respected German universities – author's note) *need more freedom and, above all, a more reliable state."*[208] Less common were nostalgic voices recalling that Baltimore's Johns-Hopkins-University had at one time presented itself as the *"Göttingen of Baltimore"*. At the same time, it is recalled that in the 19th century the famous north-German university was known mainly for its excellent work in the humanities, in particular philology, whose most famous representatives were the brothers Jacob and Wilhelm Grimm. Pragmatic voices are also to be heard, warning of the large differences in the standards between the top private American universities on the one hand, and many of the public universities on the other, as well as the risks inherent within the utilitarian transfer of university cultural models.[209]

These risks apply to the integrity of the university and the importance of the unity of university education and research for the very meaning of the university. The reductive transfer of the traditional Humboldtian university across the ocean, its adaptation to American conditions and then its ahistorical return appears to threaten the very existence of the university; it raises questions, but so far no satisfactory answers have been forthcoming. The Central European *universitas*

---

207 Paulus, *Vorbild*, p. 549.

208 Rubner, Jeanne: *Die Märchen–Universität*, Süddeutsche Zeitung 6.1. 2004, https://archiv.szarchiv.de/Portal/restricted/Start.act.

209 Paulus, *Vorbild*, pp. 545–550.

has to contend with public demands for the effective use of resources on the one hand, while respecting academic freedom on the other. The fact that there is relatively little private finance in universities means that the key issue for the successful operation of a university in Central Europe is its visibility amongst political representatives. The tax-payer and voter are not particularly interested in the importance of a holistic education at university, instead preferring a vocational education, and similarly, neither are they interested in basic research or any type of research which fails to present clear results which can immediately be put into practice.

Two anecdotes might serve to illustrate this contradiction. The first is an answer which a British professor apparently gave to a student in the 1960s when asked why he used Icelandic in his research work. The student wondered what the point of all that time and money was when it was only spoken by a handful of people. The professor's reply was apparently somewhat surprising and certainly concise: "*But we are at university here.*" The teacher characteristically did not think it necessary to refer to the richness of Icelandic literature or the democratic traditions of Icelandic culture, but simply and solely to the fact that at university the professor can research whatever he wants, and so the question had no meaning. The second is a paraphrase of writer Gilbert K. Chesterton's famous remark about attending balls – they would probably be more interesting if you didn't have to dance at them...but then they would no longer be balls. In the same way, the university would be interesting for many people "*without the pedantic criticism of colleagues, without the primacy of truth over particular interests and profit, but then it wouldn't be a university.*"[210]

The special characteristics of the Czech university

Traditionally, the Czech notion of higher education has been strongly tied to the university due to the fact that this type of school traditionally dominates the education system in smaller countries, while the proportion of specialist higher-education facilities is very small compared to Europe.[211] Czech universities, perceived as unified organisations without taking into account their internal differences, have failed to produce a coordinated response to developments in university culture and the relationship with the public, and continue to stress the criterion of measurement above all others. Some clear advantages – such as attempts at university ranking abroad – are enjoyed by universities which are old, large, met-

---

210 Machula, Tomáš – Machulová, Helena: Hodnoty na univerzitě, In: Hanuš, Jiří et al.: *Jak mohou přežít hodnoty?* Brno 2017, pp. 59–69, here p. 68

211 Vlčková, Irena: *Reforma vysokoškolského studia v kontextu evropské vzdělávací politiky.* Liberec 2010, p. 50.

ropolitan and have a historically defined socially exclusive position. They usually have no doubts as to whether it is necessary to develop or maintain a comprehensive discipline structure. In the Czech Republic, Charles University is undoubtedly a complete university in the historical sense of the word, which has had all of the traditional disciplines over a long period of time. The Czech university rankings obviously place Charles University into a different group from the university in Brno (established 1919) and Olomouc (restored in 1946), which are part of the group of universities registered in the Shanghai Rankings, albeit with different rankings. The question, therefore, arises of whether these are comprehensive universities.

Olomouc university's portfolio of disciplines has been exposed to more tests and trials than in the case of Prague's university. The university did not take on its comprehensive character until the start of the 1990s. The university was founded in 1573 as a Jesuit academy with graduation rights. The university was closed for a short time in the 17th century and heavily damaged during the Thirty Years' War. Its position within the university system was then greatly weakened by the abolition of the Jesuit Order in 1773, and the state's takeover of the university was evident in its structure and location – from 1778 to 1782 the university was moved to Brno. Olomouc university was closed completely in 1860 with only the Theological Faculty remaining, which was incorporated into the newly established Palacký University in 1946. Although the Theological Faculty provided continuity for the university with its early modern traditions, this was also juxtaposed against the school's left-nationalist postwar character, which was determined by Zdeněk Nejedlý, a communist exponent of transforming higher education along Soviet lines in the so-called national-progressive tradition.

The university in Brno was founded following the emergence of the Czechoslovak state and victory in the long-running Czech-German struggle over the establishment of a Czech-language university in Moravia. The fervent republicanism of the triumphant Czech national movement in 1918–1919 prevented the integration of Catholicism into an imagined Czech (Czechoslovak) national identity. In the spirit of the progressive-left traditions of the latter period of Habsburg empire, the church was seen as an unstable foreign element and even as treacherous, and voices called on cutting ties to the papacy which was viewed as an institution that was against the national interest. The attempt to settle scores with the traditional Austrian alliance of throne and alter was reflected in the effort to construct the university in Brno as a bastion of secularization and even anti-Catholicism. Therefore, unlike the universities in Bratislava, Cluj (the Romanian university in Cluj), Ljubljana and Poznaň, which were founded in the same year, in Brno the incorporation of a Catholic theological faculty was unthinkable. Its place in the historical hierarchy of faculties was taken by the law faculty. While the Czech national movement considered this a triumph in the struggle against Roman Catholicism, other so-called republican universities were less strict in implementing French secular models, and theological faculties were established, albeit occasionally after long periods of uncertainty (Ljubljana 1919, Cluj 1924, Bratislava 1936, Poznań 1974).

During the interwar years, Masaryk University suffered from state-imposed economic cutbacks which prevented the expansion of certain disciplines to the level known in the universities in Prague and Bratislava, which enjoyed political privileges in interwar Czechoslovakia. Although the university managed to prevent dramatic reductions in the number of disciplines and faculties, after the restoration of the university in Olomouc – only 100 kilometres from Brno – the issue of cutbacks or merging the two universities appeared again. Aside from the absence of theological studies, the structure of the disciplines at Masaryk University was affected most by the closure of the law faculty from 1950 to 1969, while other organizational changes were less significant for the integrity of disciplines. No theological faculty was established in Brno even after 1989, despite several debates on this issue in the 1990s. The main obstacle was the uncertainty over the viability of theological studies in a strongly secularized Czech society, particularly with competition from theological faculties in Prague and Olomouc, and more recently in České Budějovice.[212]

For various reasons the other universities, which usually emerged from the transformation of separate faculties of education in the 1990s, do not have a realistic chance of challenging the elite trio, and usually do not even attempt to offer a comprehensive range of disciplines. The criterion of visibility shows that their ambitions are still long-term, despite the fact that some of the schools have excellent research teams and the quality of teaching is not far behind that of the leading trio of universities, albeit greater differences exist within the disciplines. The newer universities have to pay for the state's decision in the 1990s to facilitate an enormous boom in the establishment of universities in the regions. In particular for the fact that the regional focus was on building university-style schools instead of specialist higher-education facilities, which are relatively rare in the Czech Republic in comparison with abroad, and whose position in the system of education and research alongside universities and science academies is unclear.[213]

From a strategic point of view and in light of the experiences in German and Western Europe, it must have been foreseeable that the newly established universities would not be granted the time, opportunity or state support to comprehensively develop a wide spectrum of university disciplines. In the best case scenario, academic capitalism would allow for the establishment of just a few disciplines around some researchers with a special reputation in their field or in the interna-

---

212 https://www.online.muni.cz/udalosti/382-v-brne-zacina-teologicke-studium-na-akademicke-pude (11.5. 2018)

213 Vlčková, Reforma, p. 50.

tional academic community. Therefore, from a historical perspective it was impossible to avoid this uneven development in disciplines in the new universities, and it has proven to be very dangerous for the development of university culture and the whole direction of the debate on the *universitas* as an instrument for the holistic improvement of mankind. Therefore, the experience of the public and politicians was not formed by a view of the overall consistency and comprehensiveness of the academic community in Prague, Brno and Olomouc, where in spite of complicated historical developments and the differing interests of disciplines there still exists cooperation and a vision of integrity. Instead, it was formed by a view of universities with fragmented disciplines, emerging from the momentary demands of the market, where some might occasionally stand out from the ordinary, but in no way does this shift exhibit any formative results for the vision of a university as an instrument for the holistic development of mankind.

The chaotic development of the Czech *universitas* can be illustrated through the stories of two newer schools. The university in Pardubice, created in 1994 around the Institute of Chemistry that was founded in 1950, has gone through its own specific phase of development. The narrowly focused vocational education in chemistry was held in high regard due to the high quality of both the teaching and the research, but the new disciplines added in the 1990s failed to reach those standards. The school was unable to reach the level of a comprehensive university due to the absence of a law faculty and the limited portfolio of science disciplines. There was a similar situation at the Tomáš Baťa University in Zlín, where in 2001 a university was added to the Faculty of Technology (1969).

In terms of the unity and comprehensiveness of the university in the Czech Republic, over the past twenty-five years, as in other countries, the humanities have suffered as a result of the demands for a scientific character which is identifiable with precision and can therefore be subject to measurement. It was symptomatic for Czech university and scientific culture that this had been carried out stealthily over the years without any public discussion or debate between academia, the country's political leadership and various groups of external stakeholders in the educational and scientific process.

Over the years, measures were introduced by the ministry of education and the administrative bodies of Czech science which gradually shifted the concept of science in favour of the technical and scientific disciplines to the extent that the humanities found themselves as an encumbrance, usually portrayed in the discourse as an incompetent or infirm person, an invalid, a discipline on the edge of extinction due to its lack of social usefulness, and even how damaging it could be with regard to the coveted technocratic approaches used in dealing with serious problems.[214]

---

214 von Erdmann, Eisabeth: *Imagination und Reflexion. Zur Gefangenschaft der Geisteswissenschaften im Nutzen– und Leistungsdenken*, In: Gauger, Jörg – Rüther, Günther (Hg.): *Warum die Geisteswissenschaften Zukunft haben!*, Freiburg – Basel – Wien 2007, pp. 180–191, p. 181.

The science disciplines – viewed by the university's external stakeholders and later by themselves as the university's benchmark for the validity and visibility of academic activities – believed that the humanities had been deviating from scientific standards for a long period. However, one fact is hidden in the debate – the fact that the natural disciplines achieved precise standards long before the humanities. Whereas people such as Galileo Galilei, Isaac Newton and René Descartes had been defining natural inquiry as a science back in the 17th century, the humanities had to wait until the mid-19th century, when their scientization is associated with the names of Johann Winckelman, Leopold von Ranke, Wilhelm von Humboldt and Ferdinand de Saussure.[215] Above all, the linguistic revolution in science together with the work of Ludwig Wittgenstein, interpreting language as a certain type of behaviour, brought phenomena into the arts and social sciences which were viewed with suspicion by the exact sciences. In place of the values of *truth, justice* or *balance,* notions such as *interpretation* came to the forefront, which critics saw as only faintly obscuring the values of nihilism and political opportunism in the humanities and social sciences.[216] In 2002 at Masaryk University it was also stated that *"the situation in the natural sciences is relatively clear, where evaluations by quantitative parameters have great weight and are respected to a large degree. But this is the opposite case in other sciences. This is a weakness, according to natural scientists, and there is sometimes the suspicion of low quality and objectivity. From the perspective of social scientists, the reason lies in the relatively simple subject examined by the natural sciences and a lack of respect for the characteristics of other disciplines."*[217]

The perspectives of the humanities

The gulf between the interests of the natural-science disciplines on the one hand, and the arts disciplines on the other, is seen as the most serious threat to the unity of the *universitas* today. Other disciplines and groups of disciplines then look for their place on this scale with its two extreme poles. This is based on their ability to respond to the demands of scientometrics (established primarily to suit the needs of the technical and scientific disciplines), in their scientific inquiry and methodology: the problem the subjects of the faculty of arts have in terms of scientific legitimacy are to a significant degree also shared by the didactic disciplines

215 Gauger, Jörg – Rüther, Günther: *Die Geisteswissenschaften als selbstverständliches Element moderner Kultur. Zur Einführung in die aktuelle Debatte,* In: also (Hg.): *Warum,* p. 13–65, here p. 15.

216 Schütt, Hans–Peter: Der „Geist" der Geisteswissenschaften, In: Arnswald, Ulrich – Nida–Rümelin, Julian (Hg.): *Die Zukunft der Geisteswissenschaften.* Heidelberg 2005, pp. 63–76, here p. 71.

217 *Hodnocení a etika vědecké práce,* Universitas (Brno), 2/2002, pp. 40–48, here p. 41.

at faculties of education,[218] legal-science disciplines and theological disciplines. Disciplines from the social-science and economics faculties have a higher degree of compatibility with scientometrics, even though the aforementioned gulf often appears here within faculties and individual disciplines in relation to the different approaches of each researcher.

In the everyday operation of the university, this leads to serious flaws in the thesis of the comprehensiveness of university science and education, and the crisis of the unity of the *universitas* is an important feature in the general debate on the university crisis.[219] This is not a new phenomenon, not even in the Czech Republic, which is very poor when it comes to the theoretical debates on the direction of the humanities. At the start of the 20th century, František Drtina promised to clarify the conditions in the humanities following the establishment of an autonomous teacher-training institute in a separate faculty.[220] Following the separation of the teacher-training institute, the faculty of arts was to become *"an institute focusing all the theoretical work of science, which would be the basis for all the other specialist faculties maintaining an organic relationship with it."*[221] Unfortunately, education faculties today normally experience their own complicated search for a position in research-orientated universities, without the problems of the legitimacy of the arts disciplines as a whole being overcome.

The humanities cannot even hope to extricate themselves from their precarious and undignified position by going down the route of emphasizing vocational qualifications, which provides legitimacy for the medical and law faculties at the university. The existing attempts to focus education in the humanities on specific professions such as media advisor or literary critic, have been unconvincing and are difficult for many arts disciplines to accept. The path for the humanities is universal knowledge, which its legitimacy is based upon. However, this universality attracts students who are unsure about their future career direction, who are not highly motivated to study one specific discipline, who are not committed to their studies and are thus often less successful than those in medical or legal science. Within the first two semesters, 60% or more of students drop out of their courses in the humanities, and the Czech situation is similar to that of abroad.[222] The humanities often respond to this in ways which further weaken their position

---

218 Seichter, Sabine: *Erziehungswissenschaft zwischen Einfalt und Vielfalt*, Vierteljahrsschrift für wissenschaftliche Pädagogik, 91 (2015) 2, pp. 171–181.

219 Taylor, Mark C.: *Crisis on Campus. A Bold Plan for Reforming Our Colleges and Universities*. New York 2010, p. 48 ff.

220 Drtina, *Universita*, p. 254–255.

221 Ibid, pp. 258–259.

222 Frankenberger, Peter: Die Rolle der Geisteswissenschaften zwischen Spezialisierung und Interdisciplinarität, In: Arnswald, Ulrich – Nida-Rümelin, Julian (Hg.): *Die Zukunft der Geisteswissenschaften*. Heidelberg 2005, pp. 77–92, p. 85.

in the university – by lowering the requirements in the entrance exams and in the courses themselves in order to maintain students as a source of finance.

The attempt to overcome the significant differences between the interests of the faculties and groups of disciplines leads to the elaboration of the myth of university integrity, particularly by representatives of the humanities and their representatives amongst the university dignitaries. In the Czech Republic there are three basic responses to the myth of university integrity available to the representatives of other disciplines. Undoubtedly the most common response, very often outside of the humanities, is to see the humanities as a historical warning about the erstwhile status of the *universitas*, seen in the best case scenario as an interesting diversification of the historical image of one's own narrowly defined discipline, in the worst case as a period of excessive moaning by those who feel unappreciated. The second response appears less frequently, which asks more profound questions about the identity of the discipline and its position in the university; and although unsystematically and usually superficially, it still looks abroad to the discussions on a similar theme. The third response is rare outside of the arts disciplines. This is how the debate on the role of the humanities in modern society and within the university is received – at times consciously and theoretically grounded, at other times intuitively so. This has been the response to the German philosopher Odo Marquard, who introduced the "compensatory interpretation" for the role of the humanities.[223] Its task is to help people as both individuals and within societies to bear *"the burden of modernization"*.[224] It is a thesis which attempts to bridge a gulf, where on one side stands the confidence of the natural and technical sciences, which contribute fundamentally to dynamic economic and social development. However, even though they *"change the world"*, they are not focused on the future and fail to consider it properly. On the other side of the gulf are the humanities which have not participated in the changes of the modern age, which stand apart from it as observers and critics whose task it is to ask provocative and often unpleasant questions.[225] In their defensive reaction, the humanities indulge in the idea of two cultures of science, of the isolated poles of the natural sciences and the arts, which have never been, and never will be,

---

223 Marquard, Odo: Einheit und Vielheit. In: also. (Hg.): *Zukunft braucht Herkunft*. Stuttgart 2003, pp. 205–219; Marquard, Odo: Über die Unvermeidlichkeit der Geisteswissenschaften. In: also (Hg.): *Zukunft braucht Herkunft*. Stuttgart 2003, pp. 169–187.

224 Summary of the debates, see Arnswald, Ulrich: *Die Geisteswissenschaften – unterschätzte Transmissionsriemen des gesellschaftlichen Wandels und der Innovation*, In: also – Nida–Rümelin, Julian (Hg.): Die Zukunft der Geisteswissenschaften. Heidelberg 2005, pp. 111–162, esp. pp. 123–124; Kuhnle, Till: Die ungeliebten Kernfächer – eine Streitschaft zum Ethos der Geisteswissenschaften. In: Malinowski, Bernadette (Hg.): *Im Gespräch: Probleme und Perspektiven*. München 2006, pp. 127–146, here p. 131.

225 Arnswald, *Die Geisteswissenschaften*, pp. 127–128.

compatible.[226] Through consequential thinking and an application of the reality of events at universities and grant agencies, Marquard's famous thesis places the humanities into a subordinate or servile position in relation to the natural and technical disciplines, as they are the ones who will set the areas of inquiry and themes whose secondary effect will clearly increase the tension between the humanities and modern culture.

Only very rarely, and practically never outside of the humanities in the countries of Central Europe, has there been greater reflection on the role of the humanities than in Marquard's penetrating and lucid thesis. Apart from a lack of interest on the part of numerous important stakeholders at universities and who form the national policy of academic management, the reason for this lies with those who frequently intervene in the debate over the future of the humanities, i.e. academics working in the humanities. In their contributions they are too strongly attached to the particular issues of their own sciences, they fail to take into account the diverse complex issue of the management of universities and science, in particular the financial consequences. One common viewpoint – as is traditional in the humanities – is the historicizing interpretation of the humanities within the *universitas*, with reference to the medieval *universitas magistrorum et scholarium*, Wilhelm Humboldt, and other defenders of the humanities within the university, regardless of financial and managerial aspects. This attitude often adopts an aggrieved tone and occasionally a confrontational one.

The aggrieved responses include the attempt, aided by the mythical narrative of the history of the *universitas*, to turn away from the current problems of the university's standing in society, its financing, etc, and to build or develop a mythical narrative on only one aspect of the university's existence which gives political weight to the humanities' claims. The absence of some important, mainly managerial and economic elements in this mythical narrative about the integrity of the university, is surmounted by an attempt to manipulate the public's emotions in the hope of mobilizing them in the political struggle to maintain the identity of the *universitas*. This mythical narrative does not usually effectively mobilize the entire university community, but it is impossible to overlook its significance for the faculty communities of the disciplines which are affected, where it becomes part of the reflections on their own identity. This often has a distinctly defensive character, sometimes even lamenting their own unfortunate fate in their besieged faculty. But there also exist more combative, or at least optimistic, interpretations. Eberhard Lämmert accepts Marquard's thesis about the compensatory role of the humanities, but *within it* he rejects any kind of emotional lamenting – he prefers an active approach based on sharing the responsibility for dealing with social

---

226 Snow, Charles Percy: *Die zwei Kulturen*, In: Kreuzer, Helmut (Hg.): *Die zwei Kulturen. Literarische und naturwissenschaftliche Intelligenz.* München 1987, pp. 19–58, here p. 35 ff.

problems as part of the entire portfolio of sciences. For example, he sees the humanities as having an essential role in post-industrial societies in non-repressive solutions to social conflicts, in work relating to historical conscience and above all in supervising and humanizing technological projects.[227] The German historian Eva Matthes set out eight points to be fought for using a common approach by the humanities and related disciplines, which would renew the confidence of the humanities and provide the opportunity to go on the offensive:[228]

a) The humanities must ask for the university's activities to be guaranteed by the state and firmly reject any forms of economism, whether it comes under the label of the entrepreneurial university, academic capitalism or the concept of optimization, as is so popular in bureaucratic jargon.

b) Request the unconditional interdisciplinarity of research.

c) Request room for plurality in scientific approaches.

d) Request the effective combination of work in research teams with solitary research.

e) Look for the historical contexts in all areas of science.

f) The humanities are not to be viewed as a prescription for society's ills.

g) Create motivational mechanisms to loosen the humanities' territorial ties and aim towards a more continental or global approach.

h) Strengthen the ties to practical work.

Dissatisfied representatives of the humanities train their barbed criticism not on representatives from the science disciplines, but on the state and university administration. According to them, they had *"broken the chain"*, as Ingeborg Gabriel described the conditions at the University of Vienna. The university administration began to see itself as the management of the university, transferring rules from the top private American universities without any knowledge of their context, while ignoring the historically shared ideal of the university when applying them, particularly in those areas concerning the ideal of the integrity of the *universitas* and the ideal of academic freedom.[229]

Based on attitudes towards economic aspects, it is possible to divide the arguments within the humanities on the need to maintain the integrity of the *universitas* into two different types. Some of the participants in the debate believe that

---

227 Lämmert, Eberhard: Geisteswissenschaften in einer industriellen Kultur. Referat anläßlich der Jahresversammlung der Westdeutschen Rektorenkonferenz 1985 in Bamberg, In: *Anspruch und Herausforderung der Geisteswissenschaften*. Bonn 1985, p. 83 ff., 127 ff., 135 ff.

228 Matthes, Eva: Geisteswissenschaften in die Offensive! Historisch–systematische Reflexionen über Stellenwert ud Relevanz der Geisteswisseschaften, In: Malinowski (Hg.), *Im Gespräch*, pp. 147–157, here pp. 155–156.

229 Gabriel, Ingeborg: Im Spannungsfeld zwischen Universitärer Freiheit und kirchlicher Bindung. In: Grochlewski, Zenon – Bechina, Friedrich – Müller, Ludger – Krutzler, Martin (Hg.): *Katholisch–theologische Fakultäten zwischen „Autonomie" der Universität ud kirchlicher Bindung*. Heligenkreuz 2013, pp. 101–105, here p. 103.

complete financing by the state is required to preserve the university's autonomous character, and that it is necessary to renew the social contract which allegedly worked so well during the golden age of the "Humboldtian" university in the 19th century. For this to work, political representatives and the taxpayer have to recognise the social contribution of the university and provide sufficient resources to the university without asking questions about the relevancy and efficiency of the work of its departments or even individuals from the academic community. From this perspective, politicians and the public have to rely on the academic's own moral code to prevent any long-term neglect of educational or research work or the abuse of generous financial resources. Naturally, some academics will only do the bare minimum of work, but they are supposedly only a small minority of academics. The argument tries to convince the public of the irreplaceable role of the humanities either as a mediator between the narrow scientific view of the world,[230] or as a cultural forum aiding cooperation.[231] On the other hand, they are usually sceptical about interdisciplinary cooperation due to the subordinate position of the humanities in research teams,[232] and are in a quandary when searching for an answer to whether the confident, rich and powerful scientific and technological disciplines would be prepared to cooperate with humanities scholars on an equal basis.[233] This scepticism is based on several very enterprising concepts, one example of which is a text by Konrad Liessmann who presents the humanities as a "*monastery*", and an "*island of the spirit*" inside the university, which continues in the reading and understanding of text despite encroaching subject specialization, digitalization and economization of the university, which will be further separated into specialized research centres and professionally oriented academies.[234]

The second type of argument is heard more often in debates and is more pragmatic, though whether it has the support of the majority of academics in the relevant arts faculties is uncertain. It does not shy away from openly talking about the current profound crisis of legitimacy that the arts and social sciences find themselves in.[235] The ideal of the stability of the "Humboldtian" university in the 19th century is not discussed here; the argument is less historicizing and responds

230 Breidbach, Olaf: Brauchen die Naturwissenschaften die Geisteswissenschaften?, In: Gauger, Jörg – Rüther, Günther (Hg.): *Warum die Geisteswissenschaften Zukunft haben!*, Freiburg – Basel – Wien 2007, pp. 136–179, here pp. 149–150.

231 Brandt, Reinhard: Zustand und Zukunft der Geisteswissenschaften, In: Arnswald, Ulrich – Nida-Rümelin, Julian (Hg.): *Die Zukunft der Geisteswissenschaften*. Heidelberg 2005, pp. 29–61, here 61 ff.

232 Honecker, Martin: Welche Zukunft steht den Gesisteswissenschaften bevor?, In: Gauger, Jörg – Rüther, Günther (Hg.): *Warum die Geisteswissenschaften Zukunft haben!*, Freiburg – Basel – Wien 2007, pp. 358–372, here p. 370.

233 Breidbach, *Brauchen die Naturwissenschaften*, p. 149.

234 Liessmann, Konrad Paul: Das Kloster. Über die Zukunft der Universität, In: Kovce, Philip – Priddat, Birger (Hg.): *Die Aufgabe der Bildung. Aussichten der Universität*. Marburg 2015, pp. 103–114.

235 Menand, *The Marketplace*, p. 13.

more to other situations than just those of the humanities. Peter Frankenberger aptly compares the role of humanities in the university to that of a lawyer who takes on a very difficult, practically hopeless case, and so opts for a strategy of minor concessions, defending the viability of its position in at least the fundamental points, which should protect it from being completely cast off by inscrutable political elites and supporters of academic capitalism.[236]

It does not hesitate to openly discuss the deficits in the work of the humanities, above all the low level of communication with the other disciplines in the university, the overly tight territorial bonds and the lack of international cooperation. On the other hand, narrow vocational training is seen as an uncrossable line, which the humanities consider to be fundamentally unacceptable, while the importance of the Humboldtian ideal of connecting teaching and (basic) research, which is the university's most important code, is held up as sacrosanct, and the guardian of which is the humanities. This line of argument states that it has to be accepted that those who finance the running of the university – i.e. political representatives of the taxpayer – have the final say. It also accepts the thesis that in a rapidly changing world with numerous calls for modernization, the state is the purchaser of services from the university, and that these orders must be clear and understandable as they may also change over a relatively short period of time. The humanities have to try to adapt to this and hope that any accommodation will not be at the expense of the identity of the humanities, and will not place it into a service role for the scientific and technical disciplines of the university community. The vision of interdisciplinarity plays an important role here, and an important element of this argument is progressivism which draws on its support from recent changes in the relationship between disciplines and interdisciplinarity, and the cooperation between the humanities and science, medicine and technology – for example, the increased cooperation between archaeology and botany and anthropology, or the development in computer linguistics.[237]

Interdisciplinarity as a scientific concept is approximately one hundred years old. It is a natural response to the fact that the structure and range of a discipline's inquiry does not correspond to the structure and range of the issue under examination. The testing ground was mainly in the arts and social sciences where attempts to link disciplines appeared in the works of Gustav von Schmoller (history and economics), Werner Sombart (economics, sociology, history) and Karl Lamprecht (history, psychology). Today they are considered to be from the prehistory of interdisciplinarity as they were not based on a balanced and deep understanding of one or more disciplines, but rather attempts which were eclectic and unsystematic. The true pioneers are seen as those from the American debates of

236 Frankenberger, *Die Rolle*, p. 78.
237 Ibid, pp. 85–89.

the 1920s and 1930s (John Dewey and George Mead, etc.), and for Central Europe the advocates of the concept of "Vollksgeschichte" as part of the nationalist school of German and Austrian science. They promoted a comprehensive interpretation of German-settled territories with a sense for the interdisciplinary interpretation of family and settlement structures, geography, history, folk culture and language. Due to its association with the goals of Nazi science it was largely discredited, but it can also be seen as an expression of the untenable situation for narrowly specialized scientific analyses, rather than just an opportunistic response to a political request. There were similar trends amongst liberal- and left-oriented humanities scholars, but which they were prevented from developing.[238] The present calls for interdisciplinarity are seen by Jürgen Kocka as a challenge to bring research and practical work closer together. If the affinity here is far from complete, interdisciplinary-based research still opens up non-academic expectations and initiatives which help to increase science's acceptance by society. The new trend is not seen as weakening academics' resistance to political and commercial pressure, instead *"the crossing of disciplinary borders implies that those involved clearly define and profoundly understand them."*[239]

Interdisciplinarity is not an obstacle to academic learning, rather it pushes it forward to analyse issues in the real world of today.[240] Naturally, a successful transdisciplinary researcher has to be acquainted in detail with at least two disciplines, with their techniques, methodologies and organizational work in order to develop an interdisciplinary culture of research, thereby defending the integrated nature of university science. Kocka proposes that a hybrid approach be used more often which draws on two academic methodologies.[241] In 2000, Patricia J. Gumport suggested that the issue of maintaining the comprehensive character of the university would become an area over the coming decades which would undergo the most changes.[242] She presented four possible scenarios for future developments:

a) Optimistic (and obviously unrealistic – author's note.) – as a consequence of attempts to rationalize problem-solving in society, there is a sharp rise in the demand for expert analyses of a comprehensive character which can

238 Klein, Julia T.: *Interdisciplinarity. History, Theory and Practice.* Detroit 1990, p. 24 f.f.; Oberkrome, Willi: *Methodische Innovation und völkische Ideologisierung i der deutschen Geschichtswissenschaft 1918–1945.* Göttingen 1993.

239 Kocka, Jürgen: Disziplinen und Interdisziplinarität. In: Reulecke, Jürgen – Roelcke, Volker (Hg.): *Wissenschaften im 20. Jahrhundert: Universitäten in der modernen Wissenschaftsgesellschaft.* Stuttgart 2008, pp. 107–117, here pp. 116–117.

240 Bammer, Gabriele: *The Relationship of Integrative Applied Research and I2S to Multidisciplinarity and Transdisciplinarity*; retrieved from : http://www.jstor.org/stable/j.ctt2jbkj5.37 (25.9. 2017).

241 Bammer, *The Relationship*, p. 217; also Tuunainen, Juha: *Hybrid Practices? Contributions to the Debate on the Mutation of Science and University.* Higher Education, Vol. 50, No. 2 (Sep., 2005), pp. 275–298.

242 Gumport, Patricia J.: *Academic restructuring: Organizational change and institutional imperatives.* Higher Education 2000, Volume 39, Issue 1, pp. 67–91.

only be provided to customers by the university, thereby increasing their prestige.

b) Pessimistic – the university community transfers its expertise into the hands of managers and bureaucracies, leading to a loss of social prestige for universities and professors; academics become disillusioned with their mission in society and there is a subsequent loss in the traditional values and standards which form the foundation of a university's identity. This trend destroys the unity of the university as it creates dramatic differences between those disciplines which are able to respond to the challenges of the commercial sector and those which are not.

c) Catastrophic – universities will become marginalized in their role in society and their respect dramatically reduced, some of their work will be transferred to other institutions (vocationally oriented academies, non-university research centres, social networks, etc.).

d) Realistic – the traditional role of the university will undergo fundamental changes related to the demands of a post-industrial digital society. Academics will no longer cultivate the fundamental cultural features of the university, above all they will give up on the notion of a holistic interpretation of the world. Teaching and research will be very specialized, applicational, transdisciplinary and non-hierarchical in character, the criterion of the discipline's usefulness will increase dramatically as will its ability to respond to specific demands from external, commercial partners. This will lead to an erosion in traditional, authoritative science in favour of relativism and multiprofessionality.[243]

Conclusion

What remains at the start of the 21st century of the calls for the completeness and unity of the university? Our understanding of the complexity of the issue in front of us has certainly increased and is much greater than in the time of Kant, Humboldt and Newman. Understanding a complex and chaotic world through an integrated concept of science is a challenge of exceptional significance and is an undertaking first and foremost for universities. The narrators of the myth of the unity and comprehensiveness of the university see the solution to the issue as a *conditio sine qua non* for the future of the university as a form of higher education, thereby attracting the attention of the academic community which is otherwise engrossed in its own particular interests whether professional, politi-

---

243 This thesis is applied to Central European universities in Melosik, Zbyszko: Uniwersytet i komercjalizacja. Rekonstrukcja zachodniej debaty. In: Drozdowicz, Zbigniew (red.): *Uniwersytety. Tradicje – dzień dzisiejszy – przyszłość.* Poznań 2009, pp. 97–109, esp. pp. 107–109.

cal or personal. In this light, the mythical narrative about the completeness of the university is an ambitious attempt to overcome the chaotic concepts of state higher-education and research policy, as well as the ever-present particularism of academia, and once again place the university at the heart of the debate on solving the most pressing problems faced by society today – and thereby rescuing the university as an institution and a distinctive culture.[244] However, the mobilizing potential of the mythical narrative has been critically limited by the fact that the centre of the narration has moved markedly towards the arts and social sciences. There is little interest in this subject from the medical, scientific, economics or informatics disciplines. Therefore, the arts and social sciences find it difficult to find partners and opponents amongst the university community who would, on the one hand, temper the pomposity of their interpretations, their professional limitations, typical historicism, mistrust of modernity and frustration at their long-standing retreat from a golden age within the academic world, and on the other hand, provide an honestly shared concern about the cardinal issue of the complexity of scientific inquiry, in truth the foundation stone of the identity of the *universitas*.

---

244 Elkana, Yehuda – Klöpper, Hannes: *Die Universität im 21. Jahrhundert. Für eine neue Einheit von Lehre, Forschung und Gesellschaft*. Hamburg 2012, pp. 112–113.

THE MYTH OF INDISPUTABLE FOUNDATIONS

In the modern age, stakeholders in university and higher education often turn to values which at a specific time have seemed indisputable, fundamental and determining. Even here, however, we can speak of myths, as the four examples chosen demonstrate that although the foundations were often very well respected, this was only within a given time period. We will gradually examine all four of them: religion, national interests, social discipline and liberal education.

Religion

In the pre-modern age, religion created a cohesive foundation for society and the state, which was also reflected in the teaching and training of younger generations.[245] It is possible to look at developments towards secularization in this social segment using the development of universities in the USA. This example is also useful as it was in the USA (and parts of the British Isles) where certain forms of religious culture appeared and have shown themselves to be very resilient, unlike in Europe. A legitimate question, therefore, is which of these "two worlds" is the exception?[246]

During the 17th and 18th centuries, the higher level of education in English settlements was directly related to religion. The Puritans who settled in the Massachusetts Bay Colony in the 1730s set up a college to promote "scholarship" and preserve it for their descendants. Harvard college was established in 1636 and regular teaching began there in 1640. As in the colleges from Oxbridge, which it

---

245 Berger, Peter: *Posvátný baldachýn. Základy sociologické teorie náboženství.* Brno 2018.

246 Davie, Grace: *Výjimečný příklad Evropa. Podoby víry v dnešním světě.* Brno 2009.

sought to emulate, it tried to provide a liberal education but with a religious direction: the majority of its graduates continued in their studies designed for religious vocations. Doctrinal conformity was ensured by a group of influential judges and clergymen who supervised the college. The 18th century continued a certain synthesis of liberalism and theology. This trend was strengthened at Harvard college with the creation of a professorship of theology. The professors at this department argued for a more rational and tolerant interpretation of Christianity. By this time Harvard was already a respected educational institute, when William and Mary College in Virginia (established in 1693) and Yale college in Connecticut (established in 1701) were still in their infancy.[247]

Roger Geiger explained it is important to realize that the American colonies were basically provincial outposts of European, mainly English, culture: throughout the first half of the 18th century the college was heavily influenced by the culture of Calvinism. The greatest intellectual upheaval during this period was the Great Awakening of the Evangelical movement in the 1740s, radiating mainly from England and Scotland. Yale was built in an attempt to counter this threat to a unified education and religious orthodoxy. This demonstrates that the intellectual environment at that time was still marked by religious disputes and that it was religion which determined education programmes. However, by the middle of the century, the college was staring to absorb the most important intellectual movements of the age, which, as in Europe, also included the Enlightenment. The influence of the Enlightenment played an important role in establishing the new colleges in New York (1754) and Philadelphia (1755). However, we should not overlook the fact that the self-educated Benjamin Franklin was also a representative American intellectual, who as a young man had nothing but scorn for colleges. In New England, however, the majority of educated people still sought careers in the clergy. Following a long term of service, they could then continue in educational institutes. This was the case for Samuel Johnson, who was appointed rector of the new Royal College (1754–1763), and Jonathan Edwards who accepted a post at New Jersey College (1757–1758). Colleges outside of New England relied mainly on migrants who had been educated in England or Scotland. This applied to for the College of William and Mary, the College of Philadelphia College and the College of New Jersey (now Princeton University).

The College of New Jersey made a significant contribution towards the intellectual life of the colony, when a Scottish Presbyterian minister, John Witherspoon, took over as rector (1768–1794). Geiger mentions that in his inauguration address entitled "The unity of piety and science", he declared the union of enlightened rationalism with Evangelical piety in the so-called moral philosophy of common

---

247 The interpretation of this section is based on Roger L. Geiger's apt characterization of American university culture in the book Cayton, Mary Kupies (ed.): Encyclopedia of American cultural and intellectual history. NY 2001, pp. 267–268.

sense. Not only did Witherspoon expand the teaching of science at the college, but he also imparted values to the students which became the basis of the battle for American independence. He was also a clergyman who signed the Declaration of Independence and his college trained generations of political leaders for the new nation. The intellectual synthesis of reason, revelation and morality was in accordance with the religious and political ideas held by gentlemen of that era. These new ideas also helped shape the convictions of the founding fathers.[248]

The years following the American Revolution until the start of the nineteenth century were a time when organised religion found itself in an ambivalent position in universities and colleges. Despite their status as Christian institutions, the colleges became more secular and nonconfessional in spirit. Some campuses were even presided over by people who were not members of the clergy. Well-known themes from the Enlightenment became part of the curricula: a greater integration of science, efforts to include professional specialists, the teaching of modern languages including English, and instruction in civic education which was to mould the citizens of the new republic. These concepts relatively quickly led Americans to think of a new form of higher education – the idea of the republican university. These institutions were conceived of basically as public institutions. The college in Philadelphia and the College of William and Mary were taken over by their respective states at the start of the American Revolution. Harvard was reconstituted as a university institution by the state of Massachusetts in 1870 and even added a medical faculty. Columbia University was restored as part of the University of New York State. North Carolina, Georgie, Maryland and Vermont all included a university within the structure of the state.[249] Columbia University came closest to the republican ideal when a state grant allowed it to appoint professors to four new disciplines (law, chemistry, Hebrew and French). Although this development was accompanied by failures, the trend was already clear.

Religious disputes were commonplace, but they began to have wider resonance. Enlightenment ideas were appropriated by the revolutionaries in France and their radical sympathisers in America – such as the political pamphleteer Thomas Paine, whose *Age of Reason* (1794) contained a caustic attack on the Bible.[250] The opposite extreme was the emotional Evangelicalism of the Second Great Awakening, which also threatened the liberal Calvinism of the Presbyterian and Congregationalist colleges. The most accessible defence against both these fronts was in the philosophy of common sense which had rationalized and refined

---

248 Ibid, p. 268.

249 Cf. Frederick, Rudolph: *The American College and University. A History*. University of Georgia Press, 1990.

250 Cf. Paine, Thomas: *The Age of Reason*. Peterborough 2011.

the natural order revealed by science, the moral order experienced by human consciousness, and the theological order advocated by Calvinism.

But these developments were not straightforward. The most noteworthy feature of religious progress in academia in the first quarter of the nineteenth century was the establishment of theological faculties and seminaries which were either connected to the colleges or were independent of them. The first of these schools was founded as a result of teaching being refused in the colleges. The orthodox Calvinists reacted to Harvard's liberalism by establishing a Theological Seminary in Andover in 1807. The Presbyterians were then faced with the apparent decline of religiosity at the College in New York with the creation of the Princeton Theological Seminary, which appeared next to the college but was not part of it. Soon afterwards, Yale and Harvard (1819 and 1822) opened their own departments of theology. More than twenty theological seminaries had been founded by 1825. Geiger considers them to be the first real postgraduate schools. In reality, at least for their professors, they allowed for a certain type of serious intellectual activity which the colleges had basically excluded. For the students, however, they were the main place where they could acquire professional skills. They prepared thousands of students for the clergy. In addition, most of the pre-war professors working outside of the natural sciences studied for a period in these seminaries. These institutions might be an example of both American and European developments – theological seminaries, faculties as well as ecclesiastical universities also emerged in Europe during the 19th century. However, unlike in America, they were associated more with the specifically European "cultural struggles" connected with building individual national identities or opposing them.

Around the mid-19th century, higher education in the USA still offered the world view of the moderate Evangelical Protestants, which was shared by the majority of Americans. As a direct descendant of the moral philosophy of common sense, this world view assumed the unity of the realms of the mind, nature and spirit. As was stated in the most widely read book used in the advanced courses of moral philosophy, "the truths revealed by religion are in perfect harmony with the truths of natural religion".[251] These truths were not only academic – they were presented repeatedly to the adult community in sermons, lectures, pamphlets and other popular works by college and university educators. However, in the last thirty years of the 19th century, the moral and religious support of American higher education collapsed. Developments in academic disciplines transformed the knowledge base of higher education and ushered in an academic revolution of immense scope. The unified world view of the philosophy of common sense and natural theology found itself on the defensive due to inconvenient geological discoveries as well as criticisms of the Bible based on philology and archaeology.

---

251 Geiger, Roger, L., *cd*, p. 269.

The matter became critical both symbolically and substantially with the work *On the Origin of Species* (1859) by the English naturalist Charles Darwin and other such studies. Academic opinion was divided between scientific supporters of evolution, those who rejected it on the basis of Biblical arguments, and a large number of academics who tried to arrive at an increasingly distant means of reconciliation.[252] A form of consensus was eventually found: within their own spheres, science and religion would represent separate routes to different forms of truth. But in this scheme it would be difficult for religious truth to be represented by the many dogmas of different denominations. This was to be found more within an academic approach to religion. However, such an approach did not offer much comfort to believers and was more or less irrelevant to those seeking scientific truth. The education historian Julie A. Reuben states that by the end of the century no support remained in academic education for the moral and religious basis of knowledge.[253] However, this intellectual development was only one facet of a wider academic revolution. This involved attempts to imitate European university culture (primarily German), being aware of the importance of "useful knowledge", the professionalization of many disciplines resulting in professional research, and the establishment of new institutions and academic journals, contacts between universities, curricular changes, etc.

In the twentieth century, American universities became part of the system of production and the transfer of specialized knowledge and an inexhaustible source of expertise which inspired Europe. However, when carrying out these roles they were accompanied by problems that were no longer religious in nature. In the USA, though, the religious foundation of university and higher education remains a subject of discussion which can be seen in the public sphere even today (the ongoing disputes between evolutionists and creationists, while at many American universities there are "clashes" between representatives of Christianity and atheism, etc.).

Europe experienced stronger secularist waves and different patterns of development, particularly at the turn of the 20th century and then again after the Second World War. Religion was often expressly banned from higher education as well as from public debate. The exodus from the church and ecclesiastical societies, the loss of their influence on society, the decline in interest in the priesthood, the movement away from religious morality – these are all phenomena which determined the character of the university on the European continent. The British historian Hugh McLeod provides a very fitting description of the situation in Western Europe when he characterized the typical state of conflict between the

---

252 Cf. Johnson, Phillip: *Spor o Darwina.* Prague 1996.

253 Cf. Reuben, Julie A.: *The Making of the Modern University: Intellectual Transformation and the Marginalization of Morality.* University of Chicago Press, 1997.

clergy and the medical profession in the 1970s in Europe as: "*The conflict between the clergy and the medical profession (...) was most visible in France, where there was probably no other profession as anti-clerical and anti-Catholic as the doctors, and where the students of medicine stood at the head of anti-clerical demonstrations, masked processions and riots. Since the 1970s some of the most prominent figures in the medical profession have come out openly as libertarians (...). Two of the most passionate anti-clerical politicians of the Third Republic, Georges Clemenceau and Émile Combes, were originally doctors, as was Alfred Naquet, who proposed the law legalizing divorce (...) In Germany at the end of the nineteenth century, doctors as a profession supported political liberalism, gaining the reputation for being Unkirchlichkeit.*"[254]

However, the most appropriate example of this modern trend is the establishment of the university in Brno in 1919 without a faculty of theology, which was seen as "old fashioned", a matter for the church to look after itself, and also as an institution which did not suit the new republican ideology. It is easy to assert that the old university tradition was turned on its head here. During the founding era of universities, theology was considered the queen of all the disciplines which united all strands of knowledge. In Central Europe the split between "science" and "religion" was presented by regimes based on a Marxist-Leninist ideology, which radicalized European secularization, leading to utter conceptual confusion. It is possible to view the Marxist-Leninist ideology as a dogmatic system far more rigid than all of the religious systems put together. Paradoxically, Christianity, Christian science and philosophy have become representatives of a far freer and more tolerant world view than ossified Marxism-Leninism. Naturally, this does not mean that the idea has returned to society that religion could be its bond, not even after 1989. This idea seems to contradict the pluralist character of society and the principle of the freedom of religion and belief.

National interests

The nineteenth century is sometimes referred to as the "century of nations" or of "nationalism". We need only look at Central Europe to realize the extent and parameters of this phenomenon, as well as its impact on education and university teaching. The nineteenth century saw the development of "revivalist movements". To begin with, this involved mainly cultural objectives such as protecting the language, promoting the national literature and history, and – of course – various types of primary schools. Meanwhile, the Austrian empire ruled over nations (or ethnic groups) which had different pasts that they referred to in different ways.

---

254 Hundreds of publications describe the development of European secularization, cited from McLeod, Hugh: *Sekularizace v západní Evropě (1848–1914)*. Brno 2008, p. 130.

Later there were attempts to form various patriotic organizations and associations, some of which had academic interests. Even the situation within Austria was quite diverse; for example, Hungary prevented the national and political development of the Slovaks and Croats. The position of the Catholic, Protestant and Orthodox churches is also interesting as they played greater or lesser roles in forming modern nations – in several cases they contributed towards the preservation of the language and a historical consciousness. In Central Europe, unlike in the West, we can talk about the prominent formative role of the bourgeoisie and the rural intelligentsia in "creating the nation" from below – nations and later states began to emerge thanks to the cultural elites, the priests and teachers. Differences appear here: whilst the Czechs had lost their original elites over the preceding centuries (the renewal was, therefore, mainly led by rural and urban intellectuals inspired by the spirit of romanticism), in Hungary and Poland this continuity had never been completely broken – however, even in these countries with a local aristocracy it was romanticism which forged the national identity. One consequence of these national aspirations was disturbances caused by secret societies and the activity of political émigrés. The Hungarians, though, had been basically pacified by the Austro-Hungarian Compromise, which guaranteed them complete internal autonomy, even though outwardly they were not independent. The Czechs had already been living in constitutional 'Cisleithania' and could – even with the support of the court – strive to create a modern cultural nation, a horizontally and vertically integrated society. Of these three nations the worst off was Poland as Poles were living in both Prussia and Russia – and in both states (particularly in Russia) there were attacks on their language, traditions and Catholicism. It is also important for educational institutions how the so-called horizontal national identity develops – in Bohemia it defined itself in opposition to German domination, the German language and the strong representation of Germans on Czech ethnic territory. One instrument later became the division of Czech and German institutions, even at the price of a rupture between the two communities. It is possible to observe separatist tendencies amongst the Poles and the Hungarians and the nations which lived in-between them: in the case of Hungary this applied to the Transylvanian Romanians, the Slovaks and the Croats, in the case of Poland – the Ruthenians, Ukrainians, Belarusians and Lithuanians. Unlike the Czechs and Hungarians, horizontal integration in Poland was only a success after the war, when Poland had also gained its independence.

For Central Europe the development of a commonly shared culture was, to a certain extent, essential, as culture was created and maintained in the large cities, and one of those was Vienna, the capital city of the monarchy. The metropolis set the tone. Vienna's influence reached beyond Austria to Germany and other countries in Eastern Europe. Viennese music, architecture and art radiated across the whole of Europe. Krzyzstof Pomian was correct when he wrote that: "*In the individual national cultures, the European dimension is maintained thanks to the similarity of the cultural institutions in all of the countries of the ancient Latin territory, to which are added even more countries from the ancient Greek territory. The goal of these institutions is to transfer, reproduce and spread the national culture. Firstly, this involves the educational institutions – the lyceums and gymnasiums whose curriculum was basically the same everywhere apart from national history and literature, and the universities which in the mid-19th century were modernized by the state according to the Berlin model, sometimes even against their own will.*"[255] Other tendencies described elsewhere can also be attributed to this trend: the importance of religion declines even with this common cultural endeavour while the importance of science increases: biology, geology, physics and so on.

If we look at the situation in Central Europe in terms of establishing universities and institutes of higher education during this period, then we can see that universities, lyceums and institutes of higher education (including technical ones) were influenced by the aforementioned cultural trends. Naturally, this also applied to the "old" universities (Prague, Krakow, Vienna, Graz, Lemberg and Innsbruck), but above all to the newly established ones. These included the university in Chernivtsi (1875) as well as several new technical schools (Graz, Vienna, Brno, Lemberg, Příbram and others); in Hungary there were new universities in Klausenburg (Cluj, 1872), Agram (Zagreb, 1874), Debrecen and Pressburg (Bratislava). The final one mentioned was opened after the war but was founded prior to it – new universities were also opened in Pécs and Szeged as "substitutes" for Bratislava and Cluj. Before the former Polish territory was divided, it was possible to study in Krakow and Lemberg (Lviv), even though many Poles (and Czechs) studied in Vienna. Naturally the situation was tense as the university in Warsaw had been closed (due to the uprising in 1830) and Poles from the former "kingdom" often studied in Kiev or St Petersburg. In 1964 the university in Warsaw was entirely Russified – for this reason many Poles chose exile and universities in Western Europe, particularly in France. To this list could also be added new universities from the margins of Central Europe in the new states of Romania, Bulgaria and Greece, even if these universities did not always have all the faculties (Iaşi, Bucharest, Sofie, Athens).[256]

One common denominator for all of these institutions was that they were based on German (in some cases with a hint of French) models and were influenced by both universal cultural influences as well as the aforementioned national movements and their demands: cultural, linguistic, social and later political.

255 Pomian, Krzysztof: *Evropa a její národy. Ve znamení jednoty a různosti.* Prague 2001, p. 177.

256 Cf. Rüegg, Walter: *Geschichte der Universität in Europa. Band III: vom 19. Jahrhundert zum zweiten Weltkrieg 1800–1900.* München 2004, chapter by Christophe Charle, pp. 49–51.

A good example is the division of the university in Prague into its German and Czech parts in 1882, which might be considered a specific type of modern "foundation". A leading Czech historian, Otto Urban, described this event as follows: "*It was impossible to justifiably prevent the development of a university style of Czech higher education, all the more so as a separate Czech technical university had existed in Prague since 1869. The heart of the matter lay in whether – and to what extent – existing universities should be split up or whether new ones should be established alongside them. The Czechs explicitly rejected proposals to establish an entirely new university which was not historically or legally linked to the ancient teaching at Charles University, and also initially fought against any comprehensive division – i.e. they wanted to preserve certain common bodies, including the rector as the main representative of the university. The resulting solution, which took into account economic, financial and other practical matters, was a certain compromise. Based on an imperial decree from 10 April 1881, it was decided to divide the university into two schools with German and Czech teaching and entirely separate administrations, whilst both universities adopted, in a historical and legal sense, all the features of the Charles-Ferdinand University, including its name. (...) The implementation of the law then required some time: teaching at the law faculty and the faculty of arts began in 1882/1883, 1883/1884 at the medical faculty and not until 1891/1892 at the theological faculty.*"[257]

Czech and German nationalism could be seen its rawest form in the activities of the students. Even though they were in daily contact, they were becoming increasingly estranged. This was also undoubtedly due to the fact that German teachers came to Prague with their academic and organizational preconceptions, and were often exceptionally intelligent individuals (Konstantin Höfler – František Palacký's rival – and Ernst Mach). The division of the university was not only meant to shackle intellectual Moravia to Bohemia, but it was to expand the national plurality of academic institutions. Up until the First World War the university was criticized as a place which lacked enough prominent academic figures, but by the 1890s it had already managed to overcome its greatest problems. As the historian Jaroslav Marek pointed out, the Czech university emerged during the middle of political disputes and was constantly being drawn into them: "*Its teachers entered into politics, responsible behaviour was required from them and importance was attached to their voice. The flipside to this connection with national life was that its representatives were taken out of their departments and given work which would normally have been carried out by professionals and trained politicians. Political commitment grew when younger people came to the university and became professors. The philosopher and sociologist Tomáš G. Masaryk came from Vienna and joined local prominent figures such*

---

257 Urban, Otto: *Česká společnost 1848–1918*. Prague 1982, p. 358.

as the historians Jaroslav Goll and Antonín Rezek, the aesthetician Otakar Hostinský and the classical philologist Josef Král. Jan Gebauer represented the older generation."[258]

As can be seen in the previous example, "national interests" could even be addressed inside a multi-ethnic empire, particularly those which tended towards internal plurality and more liberal forms of government (constitutionalism). The Czechs had much better conditions in constitutional Austria than other smaller nations or ethnic groups within the Russian or Ottoman empires. This began to eventually dawn on nations in South Eastern Europe for whom Slavonic Prague was the closest in terms of geography and emotion. This was aided by the fact that there were not only experts among university teachers, but also people with wider cultural interests.[259]

National interests, therefore, contributed greatly towards the foundation of modern universities, even when they were established within a multi-ethnic empire. However, these interests often represented a "disruptive element" to the ideal of the universality of higher-education institutes. Instead we see here the promotion of particularism and specific national (ethnic) objectives.

Disciplining the youth

There is a common belief that universities and colleges provide young people not only with an education but also an overview of the world, a calming environment and the appetite to work for society. This idea, which is typical for parents and optimistic teachers, is contradictory and sometimes even naïve. Students have always represented a relatively turbulent element, and on two levels in particular.

Firstly, it is necessary to mention their sensitive, critical view of the state of society. This occurred in Europe and elsewhere in both the 19th and 20th centuries during student protests and riots, with the students' involvement in the great revolutions, both national and European wide. Here we can provide a few events and names from the 19th and first half of the 20th century. The modern, and at the same time, ambivalent participation of students in revolutionary politics probably dates back to the Polish support of Napoleon and, on the contrary, the restoration of the Prussian state and the pan-German national uprising. This crucial period is often referred to in the literature as the students' fight for freedom (1800–1834), and radical romantics and "nationalists" are mentioned in England, Poland, France and Germany – the students' Burschenschaften were particularly

---

258 Marek, Jaroslav: *Česká moderní kultura*. Prague 1998, p. 200.
259 Cf. ibid, p. 201.

famous in many German universities, especially in Jena.[260] This was followed by the students' involvement in the revolutions of 1848–1849 across the whole of Europe – students who would later emerge as professional revolutionaries. Academic legions are also known from revolutionary Prague. The students' political commitment was not only evident in their radical liberalism, but also in their nationalism and sometimes even conservatism. In terms of ideology, from the mid-19th century a crucial role here was played by the various associations with their national or European objectives – one university could house all of the offshoots of organised ideas and their supporters. In the last twenty-five years of the 19th century, Holland, Belgium, Sweden, France, England, Germany and even Russia were famous in this regard. Russia is often associated with the case from the 1870s when university students left the lecture halls to "go out among the people" in the naïve belief in the power of the word to spread ideas about a just, modern world. It is also well known what happened to the students: "*The peasants continued in their unwavering belief in God and the Tsar and saw nothing wrong in the fact that the Tsar exploited people if he alone was the exploiter. But this fact did not convince the committed radicals to change their minds; instead it spurred them on to violence. In 1879 around 30 members of the intelligentsia formed a secret terrorist organisation called the "People's Will", with the aim of assassinating Tsar Alexander II. It was the first organisation in history dedicated exclusively to political terror.*"[261] With the rise of extreme nationalism and modern ideologies: fascism, racism, communism and national socialism, the student involvement in these movements naturally increased – not least because the supporters and promoters of mass political movements were happy to have the radical youth amongst their ranks. On the other hand, the events of the First World War were to be of key significance as they rent asunder the "old world" with all of its certainties. It is also well known that the impetus for the war came from the Bosnian-Serbian student Gavrilo Princip (1895–1918), who murdered the Austrian successor to the throne. Meanwhile, the French student section of Action francaise demonstrates that the radical commitment of students was not confined to countries affected by Italian or German fascism.

In Central Europe the pre-war and postwar destruction of the old world did not only usher in political ideas. Of equal if not greater importance to the intellectual world of students were the new theories, the most important of which came from the psychiatrist and founder of psychoanalysis, Sigmund Freud (1856–1939), who was born in Příbor in Moravia, and who not only influenced the world of university lecture halls, but practically all areas where students and other intellectuals were to be found. Most important of all were Central Europe's cafes, the most fa-

---

260 Cf. Rüegg, Walter: *Geschichte der Universität in Europa. Band III: vom 19. Jahrhundert zum zweiten Weltkrieg 1800–1900.*, chapter by Lieve Gevers and Louis Vos, pp. 227–299.

261 Pipes, Richard: *Dějiny ruské revoluce.* Prague 1998, p. 38.

mous of which was Vienna's Griensteidel, a favourite haunt of Europe's foremost intellectuals (A. Schnitzler, H. Baahr, H. von Hofmannstahl, J. Brahms, M. Buber and G. Lukács).[262] The traditional idea of "Bildung" collapsed from within as well as from without. This was helped by the transfer of evolutionary theory from biology to the social sciences (social Darwinism), the critique of the old concepts of ethics, and the influence of decadence, aestheticism, new avant-garde styles in literature and art, as well as the aforementioned psychological theories. The assault on young minds was considerable, and it is little wonder that it created ever newer forms of polarization.[263]

The second half of the 20th century did not fare much better – the student revolts in Western and Eastern Europe in the 1960s have received the most attention, but it is possible to offer dozens of other examples. These are also interesting for showing the transformation the younger generation was going through (maturing intellectually, a tendency towards radicalism, attempts to change the "old world"). The philosopher Paul Ricoeur described the student revolts in the late 1960s which he experienced in Nanterre, where he had gone to from the Sorbonne, as he himself said, "to try something where I would have real contact with the students". He described the students' revolt thus: *"It started in Nanterre because of things which were not related to the teaching, for example, the right of the boys to visit the girls in their dorms; the primer was in fact the 'sexual revolution'. Nanterre suffered two handicaps: on the one hand, the faculty of arts and the law and economics faculties were all under one roof. The students of the arts faculty were a strong left-wing group, while the lawyers were right-wing activists, and so a clash was inevitable. The second handicap arose from the catchment areas for the students: some of them came from the middle-class residential quarter of Neuilly XVI and XVII, and others from proletarian Nanterre and other poorer suburbs. The sons and daughters of the middle-class families were left-wing. For the others, the communists, it was important that the institution operated properly: for them the university was a traditional environment providing knowledge and the prospect of social achievement. The middle class began to feel that the university had ceased to be an elevator to the social heights for them: their parents already occupied those positions and so the young middle class joined with those who did not have a realistic chance of completing their studies and began to dream of destroying an institution which they no longer saw as a unique way to future success. When I became rector in March 1969 I was ideologically supported by both sides: by the anti-left communists and by the socially committed Catholics; paradoxically, my opponents were the traditional middle class and the left-wing middle class."*[264] Ricoeur's other observations are also interesting and at the same

---

262 Cf. Veber, Václav et al: *Dějiny Rakouska*. Prague 2009, pp. 498–499.

263 A concise characterization of the turn of the 20th century, which had such an influence on intellectual and, therefore, university life, is provided by J. W. Burrow in his book *The Crisis of Reason. European Thought 1848–1914*. (*Krize rozumu. Evropské myšlení 1848–1914*, Czech edition, Brno 2003).

264 Azouvi, Francois – Launnay, Marc de: *Ricoeur, Paul. Myslet a věřit (rozhovor)*. Prague 2000, p. 58.

time accurate: for example, he talks about how difficult it was to evaluate that year in France. Was it just a "great playful dream" or something much more important which had "cultural significance", a form of "social eruption"? He presents common element's – for both Western Europe and the university campuses in the USA – a sharp and uncontrollable demographic growth, the elitism of university representatives, changes in the youth's morals, a desire for emancipation and the important role of the unions.[265] Ricoeur sees the rise of de Gaulle to power as specific to the French experience, which deepened the ideological rift and radicalized the students who in 1969 "rejected knowledge" and began to identify knowledge with power and power with violence.[266] However, the student movement developed under different circumstances in Central Europe in the 1960s: the objective of the student movement was to obtain greater freedom within a totalitarian communist regime rather than a democracy. This contradiction was once more apparent in Czechoslovakia and other Central European countries at the end of the 1980s as part of the students' "anti-communist" revolutions.[267]

Secondly, there were intergenerational transformations. University students in the modern era not only often protested against the state of the society in which they lived, but they also rebelled against the older generation, against their fathers and grandfathers who had lived under the assumption that the younger generation would follow in their footsteps and share the same values. Social and generational critiques would often merge. This was related to a different understanding of employment, free time, values in life, the growth in individualism and transformations in society. Related to this is also the loosening of traditional family ties and the search for new moral criteria. This was captured very succinctly by the British historian Eric Hobsbawm: *"There were perhaps even more serious consequences to come from the loosening of traditional family ties as the family not only stopped being what it had always been – a tool for its own reproduction – but it stopped being a tool for cooperation. The family had been essential in this last role for the maintenance of the agrarian and early-industrial economy, both local and global. (...) The old moral vocabulary of rights and duties, mutual obligations, sin and virtue, reward and punishments, could no longer be translated into the new language of desired gratification. Once such practices and institutions were no longer accepted as part of a way of ordering society that linked people to each other and ensured social cooperation and reproduction, most of their capacity to structure human social life vanished..."*[268]

---

265 Ibid.

266 Cf. ibid, p. 60.

267 For the example of Czechoslovakia, see Otáhal, Milan: *Studenti a komunistická moc v českých zemích 1968–1989*. Prague 2003.

268 Hobsbawm, Eric: *Věk extrémů. Krátké dvacáté století 1914–1991*. Prague 1998, pp. 348–349.

There were some very valuable observations of university life from the Czechs who emigrated in 1948 and 1969. Those who were able to find a position in Western universities all talk about the left-wing boom in the 1960s, albeit with different assessments depending on their ideological preferences. It is interesting to read about their lives either through interviews or biographies. Post-August-1969 émigrés offered some inspiring observations, in particular from Jaroslav Krejčí, an economist and historian (a Czech Arnold Toynbee), in his memoirs on his university life in Lancaster, England; and in the USA,[269] Rio Preisner, a German-studies scholar and philosopher working in Pennsylvania.[270] The testaments of the "Forty-Eighters" have been preserved thanks to an anthology entitled "Separation 1948", edited by P. Hrubý, P. Kosatík and Z. Pousta. The witnesses not only described their diverse fates, but also the conditions in different Western universities. One good example is the Czech German-studies scholar, Antonín Hrubý, who worked at Washington University from 1961 to 1990. He described the 1960s, a period of change, thus: *"These were years when illusions were lost and a period when I came to better understand how American democracy worked. Naturally, I was in a daze during the first few months. Never before had I had so much free space around me, both in a literal and figurative sense. No obstacles – the college, my colleagues and the community welcomed us with open arms. They welcomed us to the wagon rack with music and gifts. But of course Vietnam, marches against segregation, riots in the ghettos and student demonstrations, presidents murdered, corruption and political scandals – that was the other side of America which was difficult to come to terms with. However, time taught me to trust the American system of checks and balances."*[271] In his memoirs the author also described the American university system and how it differed from that in Western Europe (universities as "business enterprises", the importance of the administrative councils, the independence and activity of the senior lecturers and professors, universities as umbrella organisations for all types of activities, etc.). Another author, the historian and philosopher Zdeněk Dietrich, a professor at the University of Utrecht, compared the situation in Western Europe with his former native country, specifically the example of the university in Brno in the 1960s: *"I picked up signals that something new and important was happening. I had left behind an old friend in Czechoslovakia, the historian Jaroslav Kudrna, who had a career at the Brno university. He became a professor there before I did at Utrecht, and wrote dreadful things about the West European bourgeoisie and putrefying capitalism. It was awful to read, especially from someone who used to be incredibly intelligent and had wonderful ideas. In addition to being an expert on Marxism, which everyone there was buried in, he was also interested*

---

269 Krejčí, Jaroslav: *Mezi demokracií a diktaturou. Domov a exil.* Olomouc 1998.

270 Preisner, Rio: *Americana I. a II.* Brno 1992–1993.

271 Českým germanistou v Seattlu. Antonín hrubý a Šárka Hrubá. In: *Rozchod 1948. Rozhovory s českými poúnorovými exulanty.* Interview by Petr Hrubý, Pavel Kosatík and Zdeněk Pousta. Prague 2006, p. 107.

in Spanish mysticism. I remember how he used to go around the university arguing that St Tereza of Avila was a greater materialist than Vladimir Ilyich Lenin. So this Kudrna was making a living there and then suddenly in the 1960s I received a parcel in the post from him with Kundera's The Joke. So I read The Joke and I was amazed. This was such a strong satire on that whole situation..."[272]

Therefore, even the idea of social discipline through university study can be considered more of an ideal than reality. Students have often been volatile elements, rebelling or even being directly revolutionary, and the commonly shared school often intensified this radicalness. In the 20th century, certain types of radical behaviour were promoted by the great ideological systems which the universities greatly influenced, as well as by changes in the social climate and generational conflicts.

The weaknesses of a liberal education

Recently the American political scientist and commentator Fareed Zakaria (1964) came to the defence of liberal education, referring to the situation both in the USA and in Central Europe, where issues surrounding "liberalism" are not completely clear and can also be very sensitive. What did Zakaria understand by "liberal" education? It is a certain type of university education (corresponding to the European Bachelor's course), whose ideal is not specialization but universality. As the author Andrew Lass wrote in the introduction to Zakaria's book: "*To successfully learn about medicine it is without question necessary to acquire an education in the natural sciences. However, our specialization does not only define us as a general practitioner. We will be better doctors (and better members of society) if we have the opportunity to acquire a solid grounding in other disciplines (such as philosophy, sociology and sculpture). It is necessary to distinguish professionality and education, which mutually complement each other, and therefore overlap.*"[273]

As is clear from this assessment, liberal education means a certain idea about the importance of universality and the dangers of narrow specialization, which is connected to an understanding of the mental development of young people around twenty years of age, as well as a specific concept of the role of education in society. This stands in opposition to the older traditions, which in the eyes of the liberal defenders express "obedience" and "discipline" and whose goal is a mature person with good behaviour and a set of skills and knowledge "*symbolized*

---

272 Il Divino Boemo: Zdeněk Dittrich. In: *Rozchod 1948. Rozhovory s českými poúnorovými exulanty,* p. 134.

273 Zakaria, Fareed: *Obrana liberálního vzdělání.* Prague 2017, p. 15 (introduction).

in the well-dressed businessman or a cadet in an elegant uniform."[274] The outcome of the liberal approach should not be *"responsible bees acting within a hierarchy of orders and regulations, but a thoughtful and creative individual who has a personal awareness of their citizenship and their rights and responsibilities."*[275] Such an evaluation resonates within Central Europe, where there already exist many stereotypes as part of the critique of the Austrian empire and its "traditional" system of education.

Zakaria describes liberal history as dating back to the time of antiquity, which is a contentious point. On the other hand, it is true that since time immemorial scholars have wondered what education should look like and what should be given priority. Zakaria rightly points out that the emergence of colleges was of more fundamental importance than the construction of continental universities. Unlike them, the colleges became more important with their internal structure: *"Unlike universities, which often did not have a coherent form, the college was already defined by the character of its buildings. The imposing stone buildings usually had an open courtyard and the student's dormitories were in the side wings. There was a common room inside where the students could meet, a chapel where they could pray, and a library where they could read. This English model of a residential college spread to the whole Anglo-American world and is still the typical environment today where undergraduate students live and study."*[276] According to Zakaria, this form of college gave Harvard and Yale their liberal character, as these universities combined the idea of the college and the research institute (a combination of study and living). Even the advancement of secularization did little to change this: living together no longer meant praying together but rather playing sports together or watching films together. Although the traditional curriculum also contained specialist subjects, its basic objective was to develop students' abilities in order to maintain their attention, focus their thoughts, awaken their imagination, lead a debate and thus develop their own talents. Zakaria believes that a good example of the struggle for a liberal education was the numerous transformational changes which were difficult to implement: he considers the most important of these to be the work of Charles Eliot, who he believes changed Harvard at the end of the 19th century and with it the whole of America. He did this by introducing more freedom for the students in choosing their curricular programme, which was frowned upon by influential educators at the time. This dispute is still in evidence in the USA today and Zakaria prioritizes a system which emphasizes a "common, broad foundation", which creates shared intellectual experiences and thus has a unifying character. He is a supporter of student motivation, which according to him occurs when the student has input into the choice and structure of the educational programme. He also prefers

---

274 Ibid.

275 Ibid, p. 16.

276 Ibid, pp. 39–40.

moves away from the strict evaluation of students, even though he conservatively emphasizes the "reading of books" as one of the surest paths to true knowledge.

The liberal system of education is supposedly an open experiment, equipping graduates with "the ability to connect thinking with writing" (it teaches to think through writing), it links with modern technology and leads to the creation of a natural aristocracy based on ability and talent. The liberal system allegedly allows for the "progress" which medicine and science alone cannot bring and requires the humanities: "*The basic cause of the growth of the non-Western remainder of the world – developing countries have been developing much more rapidly than in previous decades – is the spread of knowledge. When I visit a developing country, I discover practically everywhere that they are governed much more efficiently today than in previous decades. At the helm of the economic policies are usually graduates from some of the Western universities. They might have studied at Chicago or Georgetown or the London School of Economics and then returned to their central banks or ministries of finance to put in place something from what they learned. Health-care systems are also far more sophisticated, based on ideas which have been tried and tested elsewhere. This approach to the organisation of society is behind the ever-wider interlinking of cultures and knowledge through conferences, meetings, publication activities and telecommunications.*"[277]

Zakaria, in the final analysis, does not see any meaningful alternative to the liberal system of education, even though he does admit that it has minor flaws and imperfections. A liberal education has a global perspective. In his book, the author's concept about defending a liberal education is very seductive through its optimism, even in Central Europe. However, it is possible to raise a number of fundamental issues with Zakaria's thesis from a Central European perspective. There is no doubting the fact that American higher education has been enormously efficient and successful. However, it is debatable whether this efficiency can be related exclusively to a liberal education in Zakaria's narrow meaning of the liberal arts. Modern education, particularly in America, has been created from a combination of universal education and academic research, but it is connected just as importantly to the development of American capitalism and its priorities, and also to the system of privately supported universities which is unparalleled in Europe. This support was created on a basic pluralistic (liberal) framework, which was unthinkable in continental Europe, as it had been too closely linked with the state since the Enlightenment and with various ideological concepts in the 19th and 20th centuries. It would, therefore, appear there is a certain problem in the definition of a "liberal education". Liberal in the sense of universal is certainly only one aspect of the whole thing and it is debatable whether it is the key to solving the main problems affecting higher education. It is also no secret that in the

---

277 Ibid, pp. 93–94.

American higher-education tradition the liberal arts also have a high standing due to the weaker level of the high schools that it more or less replaces.

On the one hand, Zakaria's optimism is endearing, but on the other, it is necessary to ask whether it might not be misleading in some cases. The idea of openness, interdisciplinarity, cultural exchanges and knocking down stereotypes and prejudices sounds positive, but everything could be completely different in reality. In Zakaria's celebration of university alternatives it is necessary to wait for the new projects to operate for twenty years to see any long-term trends. Based on his experience in India, Zakaria overgeneralizes the possibility of a conflict-free mingling of world cultures which are fundamentally different in their essence. The promoters of liberalism do not seem to take into consideration the various cultural wars and conflicts, which according to all reports are occurring in American universities – and which to a certain degree determine the cultural conflicts in Western and Central Europe. This applies mainly to the influence of political correctness, wrongly understood as multiculturalism and gender philosophy, which appears to be changing the atmosphere in American universities, creating "battle fronts" between progressives and conservatives, and destroying generational bonds. Of course, these ideological positions are related to technological changes. For example, Zakaria does not take into account the fact that technological changes contain within them possible risks and dangers for any generational understanding between teachers and students.

However, from a Central European perspective, like over-specialization, there is a destructive tendency towards constantly introducing reforms favouring different alternatives and ill-considered ideas – all at the expense of the educational theory and practice in the traditions of individual countries and cultural regions. In other words, the transferability of the "American liberal model" to Europe and Central Europe is open to question here. Some caution is required because the transference of "cultural models", as well as educational ones, comes up against problems which the majority do not take into account during the enthusiastic period of the transference. In the 1990s there were also Zakaria-style experiments in the Czech Republic (one good example was the Charles University Faculty of Humanities or some "project" departments), and it is necessary to decide whether the implementation of only one model is needed for further positive development. The fact that "colleges" correspond to the Anglo-Saxon model and social-cultural traditions is self-evident: everyone knows this who has seen or read Harry Potter. After experiments with upper-secondary schools in Central Europe, which were often not granted the right to award Bachelor's degrees and desperately fought for their place in the sun, the whole affair has to be viewed as problematic.

The "liberal arts" as a counterweight to over-specialization is perhaps necessary where specialization is in fact a threat. But is this really the case in Central Europe? In terms of Czech higher education, in the majority of the humanities disciplines, students acquire a wider overview as part of a dual-discipline programme, which corresponds to a new product in the system – the major and minor programmes. It is also necessary to challenge proposals to replace the traditional disciplines in the curricula. Is it not a part of European academic knowledge that the entirety is, in its way, present in partial understanding? Suggestions to introduce various methodological disciplines in place of factualism may also be misleading. It is also necessary to consider the changes associated with how students and young people mature mentally, i.e. with regard to the results from biological, anthropological and in particular, psychological studies, which suggest that today's young people mature mentally later, and therefore it is difficult to expect qualified decision-making from them regarding their own future.

The Zakaria-style liberal concept undoubtedly has its supporters in Central Europe and the Czech Republic, and it seems that some of them hold positions of influence. It will soon become apparent the extent to which replicating American models will influence Czech and Central European higher education.

Conclusion

These four examples show how the modern age challenges foundations which were originally regarded as permanent and indisputable. Religion has ceased to be a social bond and basis for educational policy – even in societies where religion has remained visible and is publicly active (as in the USA). The national interests which were alive until the mid-20th century are giving way to more universal concepts in both politics and education, irrespective of the fact that universities have always had a certain "international character" and have resisted strong nationalist pressure. Neither was this pressure entirely resisted by the "preservation" regimes of the USSR's Central European communist satellites, which petrified a certain type of nationalism. The notion of disciplining young people by incorporating them into the educational structures was also shown to be spurious in the modern age – it is as easy to talk about disciplining as it is about a potentially revolutionary character which occasionally surfaces. The present debate about the "liberal basis" also shows how problematic it is to transfer different concepts from one cultural environment to another, and how difficult it can be to search for a "middle way" between the old stereotypes and untried alternatives.

THE MYTH OF CONTRIBUTING
TO SOCIETY

In 1963 the president of the University of Berkeley, Clark Kerr, wrote: "*A univer-sity anywhere can aim no higher than to be as British as possible for the sake of the under-graduates, as German as possible for the sake of the graduates and the research personnel, as American as possible for the sake of the public at large....*"[278] Kerr also showed a sense of humour when presenting one of his serious books, mischievously stating that: "*I find that the three major administrative problems on campus are sex for the students, athletics for the alumni and parking for the faculty.*"[279]

What does the university in fact contribute to society? Is it the provision of a comprehensive education, prioritizing interdisciplinarity and general critical thought, or is it on a narrower, occupational basis? Is it the education of scientists who are led step by step through basic research, adapting themselves to the work-ing conditions of the academic community? Is it about the university's ability to be at the forefront of technological developments in close cooperation with the commercial sector, contributing to the expansion of the economy? Or should the university be a forum which debates complex social problems and looks for ra-tional solutions? All of these and more are possible answers to the question posed. The narrative on the benefits of universities is motivated by the need to legitimize the social and political position of the university in a form which suits the differ-ent internal and external interest groups. Under their direction, therefore, it is a myth which serves to mobilize students to attain specific objectives, principally the rearrangement of economic priorities and power relationships in tertiary edu-cation, in the competitive environment of the university network and within the framework of the specific university. With regard to the global character of the

278 Kerr, Clark: "*The Uses of the University*". Harvard 2001, p. 14.
279 Rorabaugh, Wiliam Joseph: *Berkeley at War: The 1960s.* New York 1989, p. 12.

university, there are international examples and related arguments for practically every area of social benefit relating to Kerr's thesis.

Historically, four responses have appeared relating to the usefulness of the university:

a) The university is a "temple of science and education", maintaining a critical distance from society.

b) The university is a "training facility" for the highly qualified personnel of specific professions.

c) The university is a "service centre" for solving social problems in the broadest sense of the word.

d) The university is a "starting point for entry into the establishment".[280]

The first of these answers is strongly historicizing, it refers to the origins of the Bologna university and the predestined privileged position of the humanities and the social sciences in the portfolio of university disciplines; something which experimental disciplines and those focusing on professional qualifications would often dispute – though not by everyone and absolutely.[281] The second of these views also has a historicizing subtext and refers to the universities of the 12th–13th centuries, the prestigious sections of which were the professionally focused theological, legal and medical faculties. The last two mentioned also form the backbone of professional education in today's universities. Within these two faculties, however, are a number of disciplines which are mainly theoretical and for which the label "professional" is too narrow. The concept, of course, does not suit interdisciplinary-focused disciplines – not only natural sciences, the humanities and social sciences – but also economics and sport. It is a different style of working, a different style of thinking and a different style of intellectual creativity. Professional education aims at the social operationalization of university study, and is, therefore, mainly "egotistical" in character. A general education, on the other hand, aims at higher goals, at benefiting the whole of society under the label of "searching for the truth", usually at the core of the university sponsio (graduates' ceremonial oath) and the third answer to the question about the usefulness of universities. It denotes the accumulation of knowledge, the training of educated people, the development of new technology independent of economic profit in the narrower or immediate sense of the word, but with a vision for the benefit of society. The different focuses of the disciplines at a university also indicate fundamental differences in their attitude towards the third answer, in particular during a period faced with urgent, complex and global social issues. The fourth answer is

---

280 Wolff, Robert Paul: *The Ideal of the University*. Boston 1969, pp. 3–5.

281 Wagner, J. James: *Multiversity or University? Pursuing competing goods simultaneously*. The Intellectual Community Vol. 9, Nr. 4, 2007, http://www.emory.edu/ACAD_EXCHANGE/2007/febmar/wagneressay.html retrieved 8.7. 2017.

modernist in the way it combines education and power, and is potentially critical of the current social and political order.

Each university is to an extent a heterogenous organism, so it is impossible to unambiguously answer the question about its usefulness; which was why in the 1960s the term multiversity, coined by Clark Kerr in 1963, became popular. The term described *"congeries of communities – the community of the undergraduate and the community of the graduate; the community of the humanist, the community of the social scientist, and the community of the scientist; the communities of the professional schools; the community of all the non-academic personnel; the community of the administrators."* These various communities, with their often conflicting interests, reach out in turn to other communities of the alumni, government officials, city neighbours, business leaders, foundation heads, NGOs, and many others.[282] Kerr saw this term as bridging two traditions embedded in American university culture – the Newman tradition, which he saw as being overly biased towards the humanities and emphasized Bachelor courses – and the Flexner tradition, which applied to those universities grouped around the reforms of Abraham Flexner (John Hopkins University of Baltimore, University of Michigan, etc.), which emphasized scientific research, applied skills and graduate and professional education.[283] The term multiversity was established as a criticism of alleged academic snobbery, which excluded non-university-educated people from influencing public life, and for increasing the chaos and heterogeneity of the *universitas* – this point is the most topical – by opening the university gates to market principles, in particular the highly controversial academic capitalism.[284]

The issue of usefulness in Czech university culture

Every answer to the question concerning a university's usefulness is embedded in the university culture of each country. They differ in the way they prioritize one interpretation over others. Sometimes the differences between university cultures are very small, in particular relating to the unifying tendencies of the Bologna model, where extremes blur and cultures converge. The relationship between university education and the establishment is embedded in the code of French, Russian, British and American university culture, albeit in a handful of elite schools. The concept of professional education is stronger in French, and to a lesser extent Russian, university culture, than in other university cultures. The

282 Wagner, J. James: *Multiversity or University? Pursuing competing goods simultaneously.* The Intellectual Community Vol. 9, Nr. 4, 2007, http://www.emory.edu/ACAD_EXCHANGE/2007/febmar/wagneressay.html retrieved 8.7. 2017.

283 Ibid.

284 Wolff, *The Ideal*, pp. 32–34.

British "Newman" tradition aside, the notion of the university as a "temple of science and education" is strongest with the Humboldtian *universitas* tradition in German-speaking areas, which has also influenced universities in Central Europe. However, there are numerous exceptions which quickly modify or destroy any schematically defined character of university culture, as František Drtina demonstrated in the story about a project for a series of public lectures at Cambridge. Drtina thought the ancient English universities were very elitist because "*the people were completely excluded and only the elite of the nation had access.*" Nevertheless, the Cambridge heads responded positively in 1872 to a call from societies and town leaders to become more involved in people's education, which Drtina quoted: "*We know that in the rural districts a large number of people are demanding the benefits of a higher education. People who are no longer of the age to go to school. They have neither the means nor the time to spend 3–4 years at university. Many of these people are young people belonging to the middle class, employed all day in a shop or office, many are also from the working class. How to care for the education of classes who only have the evening for self-study? In this predicament we turn to the old English universities, the national centres of our education. Why should the universities not come to us, when the people we speak for cannot go to them? Why could they not send us professors, men excelling in their specialist area of knowledge?*"[285]

From the mid-19th century, the Thun reforms (1849) meant that Austrian universities began to converge with the Humboldtian university in Prussia – i.e. more like a research university.[286] The difference was that although the Humboldtian organisational scheme was maintained, in terms of freedom of research there was greater conflict due to the Catholic-conservative nature of the monarchy and its ties to the Holy See (the Concordat of 1855), which under Pope Pius IX was strongly opposed to liberalism and free research at universities. In spite of attempts by subsequent regimes to revise, weaken or abolish Humboldtian ideas about the social benefit of the university in terms of basic research, its transference to teaching, and freedom of inquiry and research, these ideals have remained strongly rooted in the university community. To this day it is a legacy which the humanities tenaciously defends, despite the fact that at the end of the 19th century the Humboldtian university suffered a crisis of legitimacy, and accusations of it being divorced from the real needs of society became increasingly present in debates about the meaning of universities. For nostalgic supporters of the Humboldtian vision, the 20th-century history of Czech tertiary education appears as an era of constant attacks on university ideals, where the main argu-

---

285 Drtina, *Universita*, pp. 10–11.

286 Kernbauer, Alois: An elitist group at elitist universities. Professors, Academics and Universities in Habsburg Monarchy from the Middle of the 19th Centrury to World War I, In: Bieber, Florian – Heppner, Harald (eds.). *Universities and the Elite Formation in Central, Eastern and South Eastern Europe.* Zürich – Vienna 2015, pp. 93–110, esp. p. 100.

ment is the lack of a social contribution in various ideological contexts, always with organizational-economic consequences. Attacks based on arguments on the need to take universities away from the "ivory towers", where their attachment to the Humboldtian ideas had apparently led them, are refuted with the same vehemence as the negations of the very foundation of the university.

Chronologically, the next attempt to redefine the usefulness of the university in Czech and Central European cultural circles was the application of French and then later Soviet models, which meant a narrower reorientation of the university towards professional education. The French cultural influence on Czechoslovak and Polish interwar universities cannot be overstated, whilst in Hungary and Austria the influence was minimal. Several prominent individuals were bearers of the French university traditions – the mathematician Matyáš Lerch and the sociologist Inocenc Arnošt Bláha in Brno, and the neuropathologist Ladislav Haškovec in Prague. The philosopher František Drtina and the Czechoslovak president, Edvard Beneš, were considered by Czech academia to be true experts on French university education.[287] Despite the fact that they were certainly influential as individuals, their work in the academic community did not disrupt the dominant cultural attachment of the majority of academics to Austrian and German higher education. At that time, the leaders of the Czechoslovak sate saw professional education as undoubtedly the most powerful argument for financing universities. Being fully dependent on the state budget meant that universities risked giving decision-making powers to the political class, who saw the steep growth in higher education in the new republic in the years shortly after the revolution as too unstable and economically unsustainable.[288] It is worth recalling that the establishment of the universities in Brno and Bratislava had the character of a revolutionary act – the laws were approved by the Revolutionary National Assembly of the Czechoslovak Republic shortly after the revolution – in January and July 1919 when Hungarian troops were still being fought in Slovakia. At the same time, the Czechoslovak state allowed the German section of the Charles-Ferdinand University to remain open, and in 1920 it was renamed the German University in Prague, at that time the most important state university for members of an ethnic minority in Europe. Financing four universities proved to be no easy undertaking for the Czechoslovak state budget, and in the interwar period the government immediately sought ways to make savings, even employing radical steps.[289] Attempts at interference and cutbacks in the universities in Prague proved to be politically unfeasible as they would have damaged the Czech capital's university – the

---

287 Drtina, František: *Nástin dějin vyššího školství a theorií paedagogických ve Francii o doby revoluce.* Vol. 1, (1789–1814). Prague 1898; also: *Organisace školská předních kulturních států.* Prague 1901; Beneš, Edvard: *Školské poměry ve Francii,* Volná škola 20.8. 1908, pp. 55–57.

288 Jordán, František et al.: *Dějiny university v Brně.* Brno 1969, p. 124 ff.

289 Doležalová, *Ve vleku,* pp. 89–103.

only university catering for the needs of Czechoslovakia's German population in their own language. It also proved to be politically dangerous to make cuts in the budget of Bratislava's university, and although there were numerous minor and less obvious interventions, in view of the relationship with Slovakia, its organizational structure was left more or less untouched. There was also interference in Brno's university in areas which were deemed too distant from the concept of professional education at a university – the natural science faculty and the faculty of arts (1923–1925, 1932–1933). In the case of the natural-science disciplines, the argument concerned the difficulty in equipping the laboratories, which were unable to compete with other schools and private research teams without expensive technology. The argument was more interesting (from our perspective) in the case of the arts faculties, as it pointed to the supposed redundancy of the humanities, which with their general education were apparently unable to respond quickly to the needs of the labour market and produced an unemployed educated proletariat which could be dangerous to the regime because of its political views.

The line of defence from the heads of Masaryk University, the faculties and the mobilized (predominantly Moravian) public is instructive in terms of how people perceived the importance of the university in different ways – its role in the support of a national identity, democracy, as well as provincial patriotism, and its close ideological links to the educated elites of the Moravian towns, where most of the protests were centred. In addition to the committed network of graduates and families of students, there were also declarations of support from municipal representatives, teachers' organizations, cultural organizations, the Sokol movement and members of officers' clubs.

This close link that the university and its arts disciplines had to the national and democratic ideal would later be a reason for Nazi intervention: the universities were seen as being an obstacle to total Germanization. The Nazis acted with greater severity towards the universities in the smaller nations of Central Europe than towards the nations of Western Europe, though conditions in Czech education were not nearly as bad as in Poland.[290] Here the Nazis proceeded with the aim of exterminating the Polish nation, and soon after their victory in 1939 began to move ruthlessly against the Polish intelligentsia as the standard bearers of national identity. The university in Poznań was immediately closed in September 1939, the buildings confiscated by the German authorities and any valuable equipment was transported back to Germany. The Polish intelligentsia were treated mercilessly as part of the objective of Germanizing the area of Greater Poland – a large number of teachers were imprisoned, some were executed and some were sent to the east to the General Government. The only university in operation in Greater Poland – now called Wartheland and transformed into

---

290 Rüegg, *Geschichte*, III., pp. 528–534.

a model province of the Great German Reich – was the Posen Reich University (Reichsuniversität).[291]

It is interesting that the professionally oriented disciplines from the legal and medical faculties avoided the issue of cuts during the interwar period. Medical education had the strongest position in the portfolio of subjects offered by the interwar universities. The medical disciplines were even kept partially open after the Nazis had closed down Czech universities in 1939, which was why they were suspected of collaboration with the Nazis, even though there were only a few reported cases.[292] In the historical memory of the Czech university community, those who resisted the Nazis were seen as mainly scholars from the humanities. Amongst them stood out two symbolic figures who were rectors during the period of the Nazi attacks on Czech universities – the Orientalist Bedřich Hrozný in Prague and the Czech scholar Arne Novák in Brno. The process of the collective remembering and forgetting of events during the occupation was usually recorded by the arts disciplines, with the result that a large number of the victims from the natural sciences were forgotten (e.g. Brno's natural science faculty lost a quarter of its teachers). These people were often involved in the resistance through their knowledge of technological processes, chemicals and explosives.[293]

After the intermezzo of the Nazi occupation, postwar Czechoslovakia, like other countries in the emerging communist bloc, looked to Slavonic systems of higher education for their model, in particular the Soviet university. This influence had only been marginal during the interwar period and was linked to left-leaning academics mainly from the arts faculties and their close intellectual circles – in Brno this applied to Vladimír Helfert and Bedřich Václavek,[294] while in Prague this was related to Zdeněk Nejedlý and intellectuals around the journal *Var* (Ferment) and *Nové Rusko* (New Russia).[295] Within a Central European context, Czechoslovakia was the exception due to its more receptive attitude towards interwar Soviet models, which was attributable to the strong influence of the communist movement in society, the general left-wing orientation of a great number of Czechs and a traditionally sympathetic attitude towards Russia, which still persevered despite the regime's anti-Soviet narrative based around the Czech Legion's struggle against the

---

291 Grot, Zdisław (red.): *Dzieje Uniwersytetu im. Adama Mickiewicza 1919–1969*. Poznań 1972, pp. 304–316.

292 Urbášek – Pulec, *Kapitoly z dějin*, pp. 10–11; Charles University Archive, Čestný soud vysokých škol fonds, i.d. 421–423.

293 Jordán, *Dějiny university*, pp. 228–229, 239.

294 Kubáček, Vojtěch: *Pokrokové tradice Univerzity Jana Evangelisty Purkyně*, Universitas 1/1979, pp. 3–5.

295 Kšicová, Danuše: K některým problémům kulturní politiky SSSR a ČSR v meziválečném období. In: Čerešňák, Bedřich (red.): *Padesát vítězných let: sborník prací z vědecké konference filosofické fakulty Univ. J. E. Purkyně k 50. výročí vzniku KSČ*. Brno 1974, pp. 139–144.

Bolsheviks in Russia. In the postwar Third Czechoslovak Republic (1945–1948), the influence of Soviet models increased and references to Soviet universities became normal in any conceptual debate about the form of Czechoslovak tertiary education, although there were still references to British models, and less so to American ones.[296] For understandable reasons, German-Austrian concepts were beyond the pale.

In 1946, debates between Czechoslovak reformers included ideas about *"industry's long-term mistrust of 'pure science' and universities"*; as well as the thesis concerning *"the close relationship between research and science carried out at universities"*, and it was optimistically stated that at universities there is *"often research of a global standard, as well as a rising, or at least constant, standard."*[297] One of the few clear results from these fevered discussions was a fundamentally Humboldtian conclusion: the university's contribution to society lies in the combination of pure and applied science with teaching; the role of the university is to develop *"normalized education for practical purposes, to cultivate science as an educational tool with international scope."*[298]

This search for inspiration in Czechoslovak tertiary-education reform from the Soviet Union resulted in Soviet models being uncritically and incompetently imported at the end of the 1940s. It was the most significant ever attack on the Humboldtian university tradition and the tradition of freedom of research in Czechoslovakia, when for tactical reasons both supporters of separating research and teaching, as well as its opponents, cited Soviet models.[299] The idea of separating basic and applied research from universities and transferring them to research institutes and the Czechoslovak Academy of Sciences was, in its extreme form, carried out inconsistently and only partially during the height of the reforms from 1951–1952,[300] nevertheless, the division of roles was to remain clear throughout the communist regime's existence. Both basic research and its practical application were the remit of research institutes and academies.[301] Universities were to focus mainly on professional education and partially on the training of science students. From 1952, universities were not supposed to be involved in research activities. For example, a report from the ministry in 1950 was very critical about the state of mathematics: *"...exclusively theoretical teaching at universities, without any connection to practical application; in the technical colleges they amass encyclopaedic knowledge but without any use for the student"*, and the solution was to be provided

---

296 Archive MU, fond H III Sbírka historické dokumentace, sign. 110/7; Archive CU, Fond Akademický senát 1882–1945, box. 31, i.d. 559.

297 NA, MŠK, k. 2085a, i.d. 44 I., Výzkum 1945–1948.

298 Ibid.

299 NA, MŠK, k. 2086, i.d. 44, Výzkum 1953.

300 NA, MŠK, k. 2086, i.d. 44, Výzkum 1953.

301 NA, MŠK, k. 2085a, i.d. 44 I., Výzkum 1950–1952.

by the Mathematical Institute of the Czechoslovak Academy of Sciences as an example of the new research structures built along Soviet lines, which was to remove all of the mistakes from the previous era.[302]

However, by 1953 it was the ministry's view that separating "*comprehensive* (i.e. basic – author's note) *research from universities is economically damaging*" and that it is necessary to find "*a balance between the two, as there is in the USSR.*"[303] In 1954, the rector of Prague's University of Chemistry and Technology produced some material for the minister's committee which criticized the state of research at universities, where he refuted the notion that there had been improvements connected to the management of research institutes, stating that, "*members of departments and faculties who have been employees, or have had experience with research activities at some departmental research institutes, believe that the new directives lead to the same poor state of research in universities as in the departmental institutes: the additional administrative work has a catastrophic effect on research. Instead, university research has to be research-oriented for the needs of industry. It is impossible, however, to foresee periods of completion or the direction and stages of development.*"[304] In 1952, the dean of Brno's science faculty said of research institutes that "*in the discussions the comrades from Brno's research teams stated that they felt it was unhelpful to have so many meetings, different announcements, directives and instructions, which meant they could not carry on with their own work.*"[305]

The separation of roles was indicated mainly by the level of centralism within university management. This could be seen in the guidelines for the admission of university applicants and the resulting system of so-called allocations, i.e. the employment of university graduates according to the needs of the national economic plan in accordance with government directive no. 20/1952 Coll. In Czechoslovakia, "allocations" in medical disciplines had been standard practice during the war and the system was revised again shortly afterwards; from the start of the 1950s it applied to all university graduates. Work places were allocated by directive, the only exception being 1968–1969 when a system resembling competitive management was introduced. When the communist regime tightened its grip, *c.* 1952–1956 and 1970–1974, the system worked quite thoroughly. For most disciplines this was connected to the political vetting of graduates, where it was very difficult to avoid the influence of the allocation committees. However, neither at that time nor later was the decision of the commission absolute and, nepotism and bribery aside, the result of the proceedings was greatly influenced by the applicant's family circumstances (caring for children or parents), the local and professional ties of

---

302 Ibid.

303 Ibid.

304 NA, MŠK, k. 2086, i.d. 44, Výzkum 1954.

305 NA, MŠK, k. 2085a, i.d. 44 I., Výzkum 1950–1952.

the husband and wife, and public activities within the area and region. The system failed due to poor communication between the ministry and the central planning structures on the one hand, and with the universities on the other. It was also impossible to realistically plan for the needs of the labour market over a longer time period, not to mention the ideological restrictions. Following the liberalization of the labour market after 1990 the "allocation" system was transformed into a type of survey whereby the university followed the careers of their graduates, and then used the data to varying degrees of thoroughness during the evaluation of their curricula. "Allocations" are also known to legal institutions in the Western bloc, and even today they are used in the Netherlands and Finland.[306] Their existence is a bond which binds the university to the narrower professional education of its students. "Allocations" as well as surveys about graduate careers legitimize the activities of the university in the eyes of the taxpayers, who are interested in whether or not the money invested in education by the public was not wasted on unemployed graduates.[307]

The majority of the Czechoslovak university community was reserved in its attitude towards the official redirection of universities towards a narrow professional, ideological education. In the eyes of the more experienced members of the academic community, the practical application of communist ideological principles to the level they desired was impossible and was incompatible with the basic rules governing the university. Many of the youngest academics – some students and the youngest teachers who were idealistic members of the Communist Party – believed in the application of ideology to the letter. It was as a result of their youth and inexperience that the image of the communist university-reform experiment from 1948 to 1956 appears as such a chaotic era, full of idealism and a lack of respect for traditions and real life in general.[308]

Older academics in particular spoke *ex post* of a *"dictatorship of the blue shirts* (i.e. the Youth Movement – author's note)," who combined incompetence and a lack of experience with placing ideology above scientific principles.[309] The older generation of academics then suffered from the clear drop in the quality of teaching in comparison with the interwar period. This applied to the new teachers who were loyal to the regime but incompetent from an academic perspective, as well as the drop in standards amongst the newly arriving students. The reforms carried out by the communist regime in sections of the university community – in par-

---

306 https://vsmonitor.wordpress.com/2014/05/13/jak–v–nizozemsku–urcuji–pocty–prijatych–na–vysoke–skoly/ (5.7. 2017)

307 Archive MU, Fond A4 Pedagogická fakulta, k. 1, sign. DXIII; Ibid, Fond A3 Lékařská fakulta, k. 1, sign. DXIII.

308 Novák, Mirko: *Úsměvné vzpomínání.* Prague 1998, pp. 183–184; Urbášek – Pulec, *Kapitoly,* pp. 9–186.

309 Pernes, Jiří: *Škola pro Moravu. 100 let Vysokého učení technického v Brně.* Brno 1999, p. 65.

ticular researchers from the natural science and medical disciplines – offered the possibility of building research teams instead of solitary researchers. In order to fulfil the strategic goals, they had to materially provide for younger scientists and offer them better career perspectives. A more vocationally orientated curriculum for university education was not seen as a problem – not even in the arts faculties, which remained the most important standard bearers of the Humboldtian tradition in the university.

In terms of a professional education, students and their families usually registered the dichotomy between the "ideological" and the "academic" subjects – the first were viewed as padding, the second as necessary for a professional career and a happy life. It was this that the school had to prepare the student for and thus legitimize itself. Naturally, there was an awareness, particularly in the humanities, that it was impossible to clearly separate both groups of subjects, which were often taught by the same teachers.

For the majority of students, their diploma in ideological subjects was the necessary price to pay for the opportunity to gain a professional education, as was stated in a report from Palacký University in 1962: "*The greatest danger* (for the socialist university – author's note) *is certain students' increasing indifference towards what we have built, to what is happening in the world and at home. They care little about the birth pains of our society and all that we have, the blood and toil that it cost. Their parents fought hard for their victory, but students take it for granted and just want to live well.*"[310] A similar situation was also described by the Brno professor of Marxism-Leninism, Silvestr Nováček, in 1983: "*In comparison with 1949, today's students are much younger and less experienced. More than 50% of them come from the families of workers and communists, though you wouldn't recognise this in the majority of them. A significant number seem to me to be politically indifferent, but I do not believe this is their fault – they are only a reflection of the circumstances in which we live... A smaller section of the more conscious students and Communist Party candidates follow my lectures with interest and reward my efforts with agreement and sometimes even with enthusiasm... However, it would please me greatly if they were not so reticent and could express more openly what they were thinking. I think they are afraid their political commitment will compromise them in front of the mass of their passive and indifferent colleagues.*"[311] In 1976 Kurt Starke stated that the relationship between students and teachers in East German universities was complicated and lacked comradeship. According to his research, the social and communication barrier was seldom overcome: "*Contact* (outside of teaching hours – author's note) *is limited to a small section of students, usually those who are more hard-working and socially active, and then the negative individual cases. During the school year there are so many students who never discuss political or ideological*

---

310 AUP, Rektorát UP II., k. 56, i.d. 141, sig. I/9A.

311 *Představujeme vám ... prof. Dr. Silvestra Nováčka, CSc.*, Universitas 3, 1983, pp. 42–45, here p. 44.

issues with the teachers outside of teaching hours, which becomes an even greater number when it comes to their personal problems. It is necessary to work on developing closer social contact between university teachers and students, even on an emotional level."[312]

The lack of understanding the practical side of specific professions was seen as a shortcoming throughout the existence of the communist regime, and in the eyes of the students this failing, alongside the burden of the ideological subjects, were the main problems concerning the legitimacy of university education. On the other hand, the demand for scientific study and the opportunity to participate in basic research were not viewed in this light. In his observation in 1983 "on the state of the student body", the Brno Czech scholar Arnošt Lamprecht noted that for the majority of teachers their work was first and foremost scientific, but the students did not usually share this Humboldtian enthusiasm for science: "*...the situation is basically the same. Even years ago, most people* (students – author's note) *just wanted a diploma so they could teach in a school, while they were not concerned about any deeper academic research. Those who were truly interested even worked outside of any scientific circles, but they constituted a relatively small number.*"[313]

This provides evidence of how the communist management of universities created divisions within the academic community in its relationship towards the Humboldtian tradition of scientifically preparing students. There are also numerous documents revealing uncertainty on the part of the university management during the communist era. This was accentuated by its superficial knowledge of the "Humboldtian" or bourgeoise interwar university, which was, of course, officially supposed to be replaced. They were to imitate models, particularly Soviet ones, but they were also influenced by the everyday reality in local universities, where the main problem was a personnel policy which strove to find a balance between the departmental staff's ideological reliability and their academic competence.

Within this muddled political context the priorities set for the university changed quite rapidly and chaotically over time – at one point the main concern was ideological reliability, atheism and working for the party, at another it was specialization and the ability to carry out scientific work, and then at another it was the ability to work with industry in developing the socialist economy.[314] All of these changes in emphasis were hidden under the concept of comprehensive evaluation, which in practice was an extremely variable tool.[315]

---

312 Starke, Kurt: K vývoji osobnosti socialistických studentů v NDR. In: *O komunistické výchově na vysokých školách v BLR a NDR.* Prague 1977, pp. 37–79, here p. 64.

313 *Představujeme vám .. prof. Dr. Arnošta Lamprechta,* Universitas 1, 1983, pp. 48–51, here p. 50; a similar assessement from PU Olomouc cf. AUP, box 441, i.d. 1488, sig. D/II/5.

314 David-Fox, Michael – Péteri, György: On the Origin and Demise of the Communist Academic Regime. In: (eds.): *Academia in Upheaval. Origin, Transfers, and Transfromations of the Commuist Academia Regime in Russia and East Central Europe.* London 2000, pp. 3–38, here p. 11.

315 *Hodnocení výchovy na vysokých školách.* Prague 1977, pp. 54–56.

A resolution from a meeting of the faculty council of the faculty of arts at Palacký University in Olomouc (FA PU) in 1951 criticized the lack of a link between research and education at the faculty, basically the absence of the Humboldtian ideal, albeit with a Marxist nod towards collectivism: "*In general the academic work of the individual members of departments does not correspond with the material from the lectures, they thus remain thematically and methodologically individual matters, matters of private interest. ..University work is not a purely private issue as the teacher is subject to criticism and has a responsibility towards the collective. The revision of academic attitudes in the development of Marxist science within a sociable collective becomes a personal matter for each individual.*"[316] Shortly after a visit by a leading Soviet academic, interest in applied research led to a campaign by the university community of Olomouc University to demonstrate its contribution to socialist management in this area: "*Scientific departments used to have the wrong approach: they would try to discover something new, write an article about it, but then show little interest in what significance this discovery had for practical life. That was for another category of scientists whose role it was to put these new ideas into practice. It smacked rather of science for science's sake.*"[317] In other words: disregarding the role of the university in basic research and scientific training, while on the other hand defining itself as a centre of specialized expertise and initiatives for the manufacturing sector. Another report arrived at the ministry from Charles University's Faculty of Arts in 1958 which saw the greatest success in the "*harmonized alignment of scientific work in the departments with educational requirements,*" while basic research was given "*centre stage*" in the first sentence of the report.[318]

Documentation relating to personnel policy at Palacký University's Faculty of Arts again testifies to the complicated combination of the awareness of the mission and ideas of the university in the daily life of the departments. To a large extent personnel policies were framed within "the situation", therefore, the requirements set were quite vague and, in many respects, conditional. The ability of an academic to carry out independent scientific research remained one of the most important requirements for a university career, even though it is impossible to overlook the various forms of clientelism and political influences. In particular for young academics, a lack of scientific research was a reason for losing their job, despite the fact that they might be politically committed, loyal to the regime, open towards the Soviet Union, etc. The formal route was to start the interview process once their contract had expired. If there was a more suitable candidate from the interviews, then the scientifically inadept applicant would fail, despite being

---

316 AUP, Rektorát UP I., k. 41, i.d. 83, sign. III/25.

317 AUP, Rektorát UP II., k. 56, i.d. 141, sign. I/9A.

318 Národní archiv, MŠK, k. 2089 (1958), document Zhodnocení práce na Filozoficko–historické fakultě UK.

strong ideologically. For the less politically committed staff, there was always the threat of a special interview for the post, where any scientific work was of secondary importance and not usually a powerful enough argument to save a university career. The third important factor in personnel policies was the worker's general behaviour, which took into account both positive features in political activity as well as activity in the research team – such as attitudes towards the opinions of the authorities, independent judgment, the level of self-confidence, work rate and communication skills.[319]

As a result of the relatively frequent ideological U-turns and course corrections by the communist parties of the Soviet Union and Czechoslovakia (1953, 1956, 1967–1969, 1985), it was difficult for any politically committed discipline to maintain its scientific integrity within the academic community on the one hand, and its political credibility in relation to the party authorities on the other. The result was basically a position whereby the importance of a discipline, its power within a university and its "penetration" into other disciplines was assured by its basic compatibility with the regime, but also by the political clout of its leading specialists. And this was determined by people's ability in high academic and party functions to accept the aforementioned political-ideological U-turns, often at the cost of intellectual contortions leading to psychological problems, alcoholism etc.[320]

The creativity in finding ways to circumvent ideological demands was also reflected in the university's contribution to the national economy. Here social-science students could only make a minor contribution at best – for example, by carrying out sociological or psychological surveys – and so they were forced to defend their social contribution by using ideological arguments about their part in creating the "new socialist man".[321] A last resort was industrial companies' formal patronage of faculties – for example, the shoe manufacturing Gustav Kliment Works in Třebíč and their patronage of the Medical Faculty of Brno University[322], or volunteer brigades of students working in industry and agriculture. There was no shortage of anecdotes about this collaboration, and there was no need to be under any illusion about its effectiveness: for example, in 1957 a group of "*forty comrades from Charles University Faculty of Arts*" volunteered for construction work. The comrades apparently "*caused many problems*" on site, but the ideological objective had been achieved.[323] One particularly absurd idea came from the Youth Organisation of Olomouc's Faculty of Arts in 1959–1960, calling for a separate

319 AUP, FF UP, k. 59, i.d. 71, sig. C/I/3.

320 Petráň, *Filozofové*, esp. pp. 168–196, 231–278.

321 Archiv UK, Fond Kolegium rektora, k. 38, zápis z jednání dne 9.4. 1990.

322 AMU, H III, i.d. 110/7.

323 AUK Celozávodní výbor KSČ, k. 1, zápis ze dne 28.3. 1957.

factory of the PREFA national construction company to be established on the faculty grounds.[324]

However, these issues should not disguise the fact the communist regime also enjoyed some successes in its reform of tertiary education. In the mid-1960s, Czechoslovakia was still able to compete in quantitative terms with West Germany, Austria and France; in global terms an impressive 12.5% of the year's population were university students while higher education's share of GDP was 3.5%. In qualitative terms, however, Czechoslovakia was not so successful; research gradually became less international, levels dropped, as did graduates' knowledge of foreign languages. The overall undemocratic atmosphere in society, coupled with the recurring purges in personnel and rigid centralism constricted and exhausted universities. However, the real deathblows to Czechoslovak tertiary education were to come in the 1970s and 1980s when the depleted universities were instructed to intensify their links with industry, which at the time was stagnating due to mistakes made by the heads of state and a lack of modernization and effectivization in manufacturing. The reforms to higher education in Western Europe, which were carried out to make mass education more effective and were linked to the changing economy, exposed Czechoslovak schools to a merciless and considerably gloomy backlog of underdevelopment.[325]

The fall of the communist regimes forced Central European universities to look for inspiration from the global *universitas* network, the centre of which was clearly the USA in the 1990s. It is remarkable that no-one attempted to imitate models from the Central European university tradition – in this regard, communism represented a complete rupture from the past. There was, however, a minority strand within academia and university management for whom the Humboldtian ideal remained an important value. The experience with pressure from the communist regime and isolation from developments in the West allowed the Humboldtian ideal of the university to survive in a form which the Czech academic community recognised from the interwar period and had been preserved in the collective memory. Some academics connected the reconstruction of the scattered glory of Czech universities with the need to closely follow on from the interwar traditions of university culture, forgetting the huge gap in time which separated the university in 1990 from its idealized example. Naturally, it was more nostalgia than an established programme that was apparent in the humanities, where academics focused on the ideal of the university and where the historicization of their attitudes to the theme was the discipline's approach to reality. Alongside a combination of historicizing ideas, the academic community was confronted by – as it was in other post-communist countries – phenomena which shocked

---

324 Urbášek – Pulec, *Kapitoly*, p. 251.
325 Fiala, Jiří a kol: *Univerzita v Olomouci 1573–2009.* Olomouc 2010, pp. 117–118.

it: the problematic standards of private academies and some newly established public universities, the sale of diplomas, and the fusion of political, economic and academic clientele.[326] These factors, combined with the chaotic state of the educational system, prevented any focus on conceptual and strategic issues for the long-term development of the university.

Few people in Czech academia at the start of the 1990s were aware of what was really happening in Western European public universities, and only a few people appreciated the level of Americanization in Western European and German higher education. It was seldom acknowledged that the large Western European universities had moved to the periphery of the global university network as a result of the enormous dynamism of the top private American universities and Oxbridge. There was little reflection on the loss of the prestige of their research in favour of specialist research centres or professionally orientated academies in Germany and Austria. The countries of the former Eastern Bloc saw the situation in Western European university education through rose-tinted spectacles, which was in contrast to the critical discourse in the Western world at that time.[327]

One special chapter is the relationship forged between some Czech academics and French universities, something which developed within the global university network in a quite specific and, for Central Europe, unique manner. The relationship was based on the distinctive political position of France within the Western bloc and the historical openness of some French universities towards their Czech partners during the communist period. The influence of the Francophile community on the post-November management of Czech universities reached its height shortly after the revolution in 1989, for example, in the figure of the rector of Brno's Masaryk University, Milan Jelínek. He was an exception, however, and was followed by those looking towards Anglophone countries for models. The symbolic victory of the Anglophiles can be seen in the establishment of English as one of the three official languages in Czech universities (alongside Czech and Slovak). Since the 1990s, English as the lingua franca of postmodernism has cemented its position in Czech university culture. Despite voices from the humanities calling for the maintenance of greater linguistic plurality in order to keep contact with cultural wealth of the world, the dominance of English would appear to be unstoppable, sometimes even at the expense of Czech.[328]

---

326 Udrescu, Claudia Maria: University and Politics between East and West. Faciing Challenges in post–communist Romania. The Case of University of Bucharest, In: Bieber, Florian – Heppner, Harald (eds.). *Universities and the Elite Formation in Central, Eastern and South Eastern Europe*. Zürich – Wien 2015, pp. 215–225, esp. p. 224.

327 Reading, Bill: *The University in Ruins*. Cambridge 1997².

328 Liessmann, *Teorie nevzdělanosti*, p. 91.

Challenges from Western European debates

The debate surrounding the social contribution of universities underwent dramatic developments in the West from the 1960s to the 1990s, something which went virtually unnoticed by the majority of Czech academics. There were five aspects in particular which influenced the direction of the Western European debate:

a) The fall in the prestige of Western universities in comparison with the elite American schools, with only a few of the ancient European schools being able to compete, while the others were greatly harmed by the flow of their most talented scientists across the ocean, the economic problems of a war-torn continent, and the discredit caused by academia's collaboration with the regimes defeated in the Second World War, most obviously in the case of the top German universities.

b) The Americanization of European universities, most markedly in the defeated countries of the Axis powers, but generally across all of Europe, holding up American universities as a suitable model and direction for the development of their country's own higher education system; naturally the image of American higher education being reduced to approximately ten elite private schools and several top public universities (University of Florida, University of California).

c) The democratization of universities in the 1960s, which definitively took away the influence of traditional teachers' committees in favour of more open academic institutions, led to students having more influence in universities, which significantly altered the debate about the objectives of university activity. This was reflected in the integration of a number of new disciplines into the academic community, resulting in a movement towards a left-liberal political ideology in most of the important universities.

d) The development of mass higher education in Western European universities, often multiplying the number of students and educators, auxiliary and technical personnel in enormous facilities with 50,000 or even more than 100,000 students; in the countries of the OECD, up to 80% of the year's population attend higher-education institutions.

e) The knowledge that public budgets are not capable of supporting the policy of "a university education for everyone" and are not large enough to develop high-quality tertiary education, but at the same time, the political leadership of the state is not willing to reduce the number of students or increase tax for education. As a result, this forces universities either to make internal savings or implement the academic capitalism known from private universities. This would require a significant part of the finance for the running of the university to come from the school's own entrepreneurial efforts, particularly through applied research.

Without being aware of it, the attempts by post-communist universities to return to the family of "European universities", the westernization of their own teaching and research, and the establishment or development of their contacts with the West, have brought them into a debate about deep structural problems which have been discussed in Western European universities since at least the 1960s. It has proven to be a very sensitive issue. For example, Hans Peter Herrmann used the example of the university in Freiburg im Breisgau to talk about an 80-year crisis (1933–2010) and attempts at reform which in one way or another moved the university further away from the Humboldtian ideal.[329] Since opening up to mass higher education in 1977, the West German university has dramatically changed. The number of students rose by 73% between 1977 and 1990, 48% of whom were in full-time study, and 106% were outside full-time study, but the number of graduates only rose by 20%. The rise in academic and non-academic personnel was only by 7%, the space for studying rose by 11%, university expenditure increased in absolute figures by 12%, but the share of university spending dropped from 0.78% to 0.65%.[330] This data was not analysed in the Czech Republic and only a few people realized that the Western European university – which many people wanted to copy – was going through a serious structural crisis and was at a crossroads in the search for answers to the question about its own social usefulness.

West German discourse on academic policy in the 1980s did not harbour many doubts about mass higher education being the correct response to the challenges of the era. It was only *ex post* and with a distance of approximately twenty years that the argument began to develop that the 1970s-1980s had witnessed the gradual end of the Humboldtian tradition and an undermining of the foundation of the university's identity.[331] In the 1980s the memories of the oldest generation of academics of the Humboldtian universities appeared as curiosities. They subconsciously interpreted it as a "golden age", while acting in an evident quandary when aware of the contrast with the current form of study. Johannes Weissinger, a professor of mathematics at Karlsruhe University, recalled his student days at Jena, and compared the position in 1930 with the current situation in universities: "*The professor's lecture* (in 1930 – author's note) *was attended by several assistants and senior lecturers, and if the professor had a coffee break over the two hours of teaching, the*

---

329 Herrmann, *Krisen*, pp. 9–24.

330 Müller–Böling, Detlef: *Entfesselung der Wettbewerb. Von der Universität zum differenzierten Hochschulsystem*, pp. 353–365, here pp. 353–354.

331 vom Bruch, Rüdiger: Langsamer Abschied von Humboldt? Etappen deutscher Universitätsgeschichte 1810–1945. In: Mitchell G. Ash (Hg.): *Mythos Humboldt. Vergangenheit und Zukunft deutscher Universitäten*. Vienna, Cologne, Weimar 1999, pp. 29–57; vom Bruch, Rüdiger: Universitätsreform als Antwort auf die Krise. Wilhelm von Humboldt und die Folgen. In: Sieg, Ulrich – Korsch, Dietrich (Hg.): *Die Idee der Universität heute*. München 2005, pp. 43–55.

assistants would remain in the classroom and debate broader scientific issues with the students. Today this scene would be held up as an example of the professor's elitism, as a waste of people and time. I am now so overloaded that it would be impossible to teach so freely, and neither would the students dare to get involved in a conversation with the assistants, they would probably not even listen. Students are more timid in the rude, impolite atmosphere of today, the senior lecturers thus maintain their elitist thinking and do not want to engage with the students. And students used to have a more general interest in their discipline and did not concentrate on one aspect as is the case today." Weissinger repeatedly apologized to readers for his *"elitist memories"*, but nevertheless, he stood up for a positive Humboldtian tradition, which he saw as becoming extinct due to mass higher education. The professor took a very positive view of the tradition of a new colleague's opening lecture on a broader academic topic for the other professors, bringing them personally closer into the debate and *"their subsequent collaboration was thus far more less formal than today."*[332]

The university culture within post-communist countries in the 1990s did not allow for complaints about the university being in political and economic crisis, which was a common feature in Germany and Western Europe. The academic community's vision was to aim for the same standards as Western universities. This position – perhaps slightly naïve – was hardly surprising given the dramatically backward conditions and the general greyness of post-communist universities.

"Bologna"

The real start to the debate about the objectives of university academics within the wider academic community was a very important political step – the Czech Republic's signing of the Bologna declaration on 19 July 1999. The original group of 30 countries, rising gradually to 49 (and the European Commission), agreed to increase the quality and accessibility of tertiary education. It was basically in response to the problems and challenges that postwar European higher education faced as outlined above.[333]

The objectives of the Bologna Process can be summarized in four points:
1) The convergence of higher education across Europe.
2) The increased internationalization and mobility of study.
3) The differentiation of the missions of the individual universities within the system.

---

332 Weissinger, Johannes: Die Universität gestern, heute und morgen. Erinnerungen und (unsystematische) Gedanken, In: Kahle, Heinz Gerhard (Hg.): *Die Hochschule in der Herausforderungen der 70en Jahre*. Karlsruhe 1980, pp. 11–26, here pp. 12, 15.

333 http://www.ehea.info/pid34248/history.html (6.7. 2017).

4) Developing links between university courses and the needs of the labour market.

There was a pluralistic character to the implementation of the Bologna system into the higher-education systems of the different countries – there was no single interpretation, nor will there be in the near future, of all the recommendations from the Bologna declaration for individual countries. The smaller European countries in particular have little choice and are under pressure to respond to the situation in the larger European countries and attempt to align their university education with the "main current". Ján Figeľ, the then Euro Commissioner for education, described the position of Slovak university management: *"Being part of the Bologna process does not mean that the other countries will acknowledge everything, it means it will be easier for them to acknowledge things."*[334] Different aspects of the system are stressed differently, while the tempo for applying the principles also differs dramatically. Some examples: although a credit system for the Bachelor's and Master's degree was introduced, there were large differences. Nineteen countries opted for the system of a three-year Bachelor course and two years for a Master's, seven countries chose a 4+1 system and 23 offer a hybrid system. As for student mobility, smaller countries such as the Netherlands and Austria boasted the most mobile students, with 20% of students having studied abroad. On the other hand, larger countries such as Britain and Poland did not even exceed 5%.[335] A total of 76% of travelling students went to four countries within the Bologna system (Great Britain, France, Russia and Germany)[336], with the British system being the far most attractive. Smaller countries fared less well from these exchanges and there are particularly high deficits in Central, Eastern and South Eastern Europe. Some smaller countries have responded to the national weakness of a "small language" by making their education system more open (Austria, Finland, Norway), and the ratio between outgoing and incoming students is quite balanced overall; some countries are slower and less thorough at opening up their education system, and when taking into account the factor of a "small language", the result is a dramatic disparity in the number of outgoing students – a phenomenon often viewed negatively by the public as the sign of a brain drain, exacerbating demographic problems due to the predatorial policies of the richer Western countries (Slovakia, Lithuania, Serbia, Croatia).[337]

---

334 Čikešová, Mária: *Aplikácia Bolonského procesu na Filozofickej fakulte Univerzity Komenského.* In: Slobodník, Martin –Glossová, Marta: 95 rokov Filozofickej fakulty UK. Pohľad do dejín inštitúcie a jej akademickej obce. Bratislava 2017, pp. 503–524, here p. 504.

335 Teichler, Ulrich: Bologna – Kontinuität und Wandel der Hochschulentwicklung, In: Kellermann, Paul – Guggenberger, Helmut – Weber, Karl (Hg.): *Universität nach Bologna? Hochschulkonzeptionen zwischen Kritik und Utopie.* Vienna 2016, pp. 74–95, here pp. 74, 78–79.

336 Čikešová, *Aplikácia principov*, p. 518.

337 Ibid.

Interpreting the statistics from the Bologna Process is a tricky affair. The academic community is interested most in student mobility, which is relatively well quantified among the Bologna objectives. In the period 1999–2007, student mobility within Europe rose from 3% to 3.3% of the student year population,[338] which is not a particularly radical change. Questions are then asked about how effective these significant resources are in changing the university course system. A barrier to mobility – particularly for people going from East to West – is the cost of accommodation, a lack of course programmes in world languages, and the difficulty of incorporating a foreign study stay into a course plan, particularly for a Bachelor's course. In addition, much of the mobility is directed towards countries which are similar in language – students from Slovakia, based on their linguistic affiliation, study in Czech or Hungarian universities; Austrian students travel to Germany; Bavarian and Southern Tiroleans to Austria; Walloons to France, etc. Greater motivation to study abroad is often lower course fees and cheaper student accommodation rather than the Bologna principles.

In other areas the benefits of the Bologna Process are practically impossible to measure. Its supporters claim that the opportunity for the student to influence the speed and type of course is more suited to the mentality of today's youth, who are strongly focused on their individual interests and hobbies, with an almost exaggerated attachment to self-realization and the idea that courses should be "fun". In the "pre-Bolognian" European system of higher education, the system of a 4–6 year course prevailed, at the start of which the student usually chose a narrowly defined discipline – the extremes in specialization were particularly evident in the social sciences and the arts. Reform was based on the fact that with such a high percentage of university students in the population year, it was no longer tenable to target universities solely for producing graduates either in science or educational work for the lower school levels, and that in the first years it was necessary to make the courses more open in terms of the subjects to enable a narrower academic focus in the higher years. This Bologna system had, to a certain degree, already been implemented in the medical, legal and theological disciplines, which were more obviously vocationally orientated, unlike the majority of the more generally focused university subjects. The two-cycle course tried to limit the lack of success in courses and the loss of public money invested in the student, which did happen for some disciplines, though not for others, and it is debatable whether this aspect of the Bologna system had any major influence.

It is clear that the Bologna system was the death knell for the pointlessly specialized disciplines of the social sciences and the arts. But did this also bring about a demise in scientific thinking as part of the study? It is impossible to expect Bachelor's students in the majority of subjects to be able to delve deeply into the

---

338 Teichler, *Bologna*, p. 74.

discipline's scientific discourse – the courses are too short, they have to make up for the weaknesses in secondary-school education, while the majority of students do not set great store by an academic training. But this was a reality which university educators faced long before Bologna![339] The problem had accumulated over decades; its roots were in the vague answers to the question of what scientific education actually was, or rather scientific thinking, and what specific competencies for resolving problems does the graduate acquire in comparison with other types of study and individual personal development. It would appear that academics argue strongly in its defence in a way which the public does not listen to because they do not see the need for scientific education in this form and level.[340]

Humanities teachers at Masaryk University have subconsciously admitted for many years that they have been providing academic training to students with the awareness that in a (large) year group, only a few individuals are interested in an academic career, while the others are headed to a career in education or elsewhere.[341] For a long time this failure of the university to meet the public demand was deflected using references to academic freedom in teaching and research. A gulf thus started to emerge between the public (taxpayers) and academics, which manifested itself in waves of anti-intellectualism and anti-academism, made all the more powerful with the new communication methods in alternative media and social networks where everything is permitted. Placing "scientific thought" above social need, and work for the "wisdom of the majority", creates an explosive mixture of anti-university aversion amongst sections of the public.[342]

Was "Bologna" the final nail in the coffin for the Humboldtian ideal of the university's useful contribution to society? Yes and no.[343] From the perspective of respect towards the university traditions of different countries and regions, the Bologna reform was based mainly on the British tradition of Bachelor's study; it more or less leaves untouched the tradition of the narrow vocational education of the French and Russian university culture, and interferes to the greatest extent in the German or Humboldtian tradition. If we ignore the extreme views that have been heard in the long and contentious debates, then the Bologna Process can be characterized as an effort to adapt the Humboldtian tradition to the challenges

---

339 Arnold, Rolf: *Bildung nach Bologna! Die Anregungen der europäischen Hochschulreform*. Wiesbaden 2015, p. 14.

340 Ibid, p. 15 ff.

341 *Představujeme vám .. prof. Dr. Arnošta Lamprechta*, Universitas 1, 1983, pp. 48–51, here p. 50; a similar assessment from PU Olomouc viz AUP, box 441, i.d. 1488, sig. D/II/5.

342 Teichler, *Bologna*, p. 92.

343 Cf. Seibt, Gustav: *Ende einer Lebensform. Von Humboldt zu Bologna: Der atemberaubende Untergang der deutschen Universität*, In: Süddeutsche Zeitung 21.06.2007; Langewiesche, Dieter: *Ende einer Lebensform. Welche Folgen hat der Umbau der europäischen Hochschullandschaft?* In: Süddeutsche Zeitung 29./30.12.2007; Bollenbeck Georg – Wende Waltraud (Hg.): *Der Bologna–Prozeß und die Veränderung der Hochschullandschaft*. Heidelberg 2007.

of globalization, digitalization and the curricular changes (the content of education) – thereby maintaining the positives contained within the Humboldtian tradition. One of the positives from the process is the systematic attempt to shift rigid tertiary education to a direction where it reflects public demand, despite the fact that from the outset the package of Bologna reforms contained many problematic elements and ill-considered consequences.

There are many critics of the Bologna Process. In many academic communities it is difficult in the lower levels of the university hierarchy to find anyone with anything positive to say about "Bologna". These include academics and political traditionalists and conservatives, who often quite understandably refer to the Sorbonne declaration of the ministers of education from France, Italy, Germany and Great Britain from 1998, which proposed a united framework for European education with the objective of mutually recognizing academic courses. The subsequent implementation process, which was increasingly associated with the structures of the European Union, was seen as bureaucratic and overly complicated in the manner in which it arrived at its objective, and fundamentally harmful and dangerous due to its unintended repercussions.[344] Its critics also include supporters of various forms of identity movements who are against external interference in the national interest of education. In addition, there are university trade unionists, concerned by the academic capitalism inspired by the Bologna Process in the USA and Great Britain, and also members of the reform movements in Western countries which tried to transform academia "pre-Bologna".[345] Rather than its actual substance, many critics base their dislike of the process more on its clumsy presentation, bureaucratism and reforms stimulated by large sums of money from development funds. They look on with suspicion at the conflict between the superficial adoration of Humboldtian traditions in gala speeches by "pro-Bologna" university dignitaries and politicians, and the sequence of major as well as minor managerial and bureaucratic steps which are in fact removing that Humboldtian tradition, or at the very least altering its foundations.[346]

The mid-1990s was an auspicious time for "Bologna" to arrive in the Czech Republic as it helped politicians and university managers overcome their quandary concerning the future direction of university education. It offered them an opportunity to respond credibly to two of the main problems contemporary universities face: the lack of a link between teaching and the needs of the labour

---

344 Liessmann, *Teorie nevzdělanosti*, p. 73; Arnold, *Bildung*, p. 19.

345 Stucke, Andreas: Mythos USA – Die Bedetung des Arguments „Amerika" im Hoschulpolitischen Diskurs der Bundesrepublik. In: Stölting, Erhard – Schimank, Uwe (Hg.): *Die Krise der Universität.* Wiesbaden 2001, pp. 118–138, here p. 125.

346 Schwarz, Karl: *Die Bologna–Reform erzwingt die Frage nach einer neuen Universitätskonzeption.* In: Kellermann, Paul – Guggenberger, Helmut – Weber, Karl (Hg.): *Universität nach Bologna? Hochschulkonzeptionen zwischen Kritik und Utopie.* Vienna 2016, pp. 217–225, here p. 217.

market, and the high level of course failure in many university disciplines.[347] It was precisely in the usefulness of its work for students and its contribution to society that the university began to lose its credibility and social prestige, and it was this situation which led to the German, Dutch and British attempts at reform in the 1980s, which would later form the basis of "Bologna". In the post-communist countries of Europe the Bologna process was a welcome sequel to the first waves of reform in the 1990s which attempted to expunge the legacy of communist rule over universities. Here "Bologna" was part of a wide-ranging political programme of European integration and a decidedly idealistic attempt to "catch up" with the West.[348] Nevertheless, the position of university graduates in the fast-changing labour markets of the post-communist countries was significantly different from Western countries and more favourable due to the higher demand in the labour market for university graduates with a knowledge of languages and the basics in information science. An important element of the public debate surrounding tertiary education in the Czech Republic has been the fact that universities and university teachers have manged to maintain a relatively prestigious position within society.[349]

In its initial stages the implementation of the Bologna directives in universities with a Humboldtian culture was considered by many to be a shocking change, particularly due to the doors being opened to mass higher education and the threat to the scientific character of disciplines from the influx of students with only a general and superficial interest in the subject. These were people with no ambition to participate in the highly academic and specialized debates of what supporters of the Bologna vision and many students would term the "ivory tower", a place where a large number of academics perhaps unwittingly found themselves.

According to its critics, Bologna has reduced the academic level in Bachelor's courses. Graduates from Bachelor's courses have difficulties finding employment in the labour market and many of them become proverbial employees at call centres or make deliveries to drinks machines in fast-food restaurants. Those students who continue on to a Master's have to write a thesis at the end of their Bachelor's course, often of dubious academic quality due to the level of knowledge and skills acquired. Notwithstanding, usually two years after writing their Bachelor's thesis, they can expect to write a Master's thesis.

The Master's course found itself at the centre of demands for "excellence". This pressure was implicit within the Bologna rules as an argument for the defence of every school on the university map. The constant and increasing pressure

---

347 Hüther, Otto – Krücken, Georg: *Hochschulen. Fragestellungen, Ergebnisse und Perspektiven der sozialwissenschaftlichen Hochschulforschung.* Wiesbaden 2016, pp. 35–61.

348 Cf. Roth, Oto: *Integrace vysokého školství v EU a česká vysokoškolská politika.* Prague 1997.

349 Prudký – Pabian – Šima, *České vysoké školství,* p. 68.

on excellence, whether in terms of exceptional research quality or the quality of the vocational education, threatens to sharply differentiate university disciplines. Those disciplines which search for a "golden middle way" are seen as uninteresting, grey and worthless in the competitive university struggle. Value lies in excellence: therefore, some universities focus on teaching and throw overboard the relevant research, others do the exact opposite. As a result, however, the relationship between research and teaching is destroyed and the university's identity along with it. In its place might be an academy of sciences research centre, the Max Planck Institute, or an academy focused narrowly on professions.[350]

Nevertheless, the Bologna Process is just the first, albeit symbolically the most important stage, in fundamental curricular reform which aims to prepare universities for the challenges of the 21st century. In the Czech Republic, a country with an extremely unstable ministry of education and chaotic development in educational policy, the visionary aspect of curricular reform fell away in the mid-1990s, and after many twists and turns, the reformist vision returned with the education act of 2016, particularly in relation to changes to subject accreditation.[351]

If the university as an institution is to survive the changes in the public's demands, it will have to find a way of adapting its culture to six sets of challenges. Each of these will mean – optimistically speaking – important innovations in the historically rooted university culture. From a more pessimistic view, these are changes which are so fundamental that many of the ideals formulated by Wilhelm Humboldt and John Newman will cease to exist. Therefore, what are these challenges that universities face on a global level?

– *Reacting to the demands of society*

The university has to react to the demands of society – it cannot shut itself off in a realm of "pure science" in the style of the early 19th century and expect to receive in this apotheosis the support of the administrators of public budgets who have to answer to taxpayers and voters. The idea that universities are given a considerable sum from the public budget each year to spend as the administration of the university sees fit is erroneous from the outset and incompatible with the way in which democratic societies operate. Historical reminiscing on this point is unhelpful and misinterprets the reality – the modern university has either been entirely economically dependent on the state and carried out its wishes (the French and Russian model), or there has been a combination of state and private financing (the British and German model) with autonomy in some competencies. In the Czech and Central European tradition there has been a huge dependency

350 Matuschek, Stefan: *Zerreißprobe. Zur gegenwartigen Hochschulreform.* In: Jamme, Christoph – Schröder, Asta von (Hg.): *Einsamkeit und Freiheit. Zum Bildungsauftrag der Universität im 21. Jahrhundert.* Munich 2011, pp. 125–138, esp. pp. 128–135.

351 Walterová, Eliška: *Kurikulum – proměny a trendy v mezinárodní perspektivě.* Brno 1994; http://www.msmt.cz/ministerstvo/novinar/poslanci-schvalili-novelu-vysokoskolskeho-zakona (6.7. 2017)

on state financing in the modern era, and the arguments made to taxpayers either referred to vocational education or the national character of a university's activities – during the communist era there were references to building a national variant of a socialist society. Today this concept of state financing is unsustainable. Taxpayers may hear about the role of universities in vocational education, but the other aspects of a university's work – more or less political and ideological – are considered by the public to be untrustworthy, problematic, replaceable or unnecessary. This section of the public endorses the idea of introducing tuition fees on a sliding scale, noticeably in course programmes with unclear links to the labour market. This section of the public does not listen to arguments about the abstract cultural mission of universities, and suspects academics of quietly misusing public funding and influencing the youth in certain ideological directions. This might include the national dimension of a university's activities, its regional or provincial importance, concepts of multiculturalism and Europeanness, or of a democratic forum for free discussion and thus an incubator of democracy.

The role of the Humboldtian university as an unbiased participant in public (national) decision-making was generally accepted up until the 1870s. These were wonderful times for Humboldtian professors, and even today a substantial number of academics look back on them with nostalgia. José Ortega y Gasset cited two famous quotations idolizing Humboldtian-Newman education: the statement by Arthur Wellesley, the Duke of Wellington, that "*The Battle of Waterloo was won on the playing fields of Eton,*" and Otto von Bismarck's remark to the French emperor, Napoleon III, that: "*the victory of 1870 was a victory for German teachers and professors.*"[352] There was also a somewhat more sober voice from across the ocean: "*The German professor was a legendary figure in educational circles in the USA at the time. He was regarded as infinitely wise. As a servant of the throne he could educate young people to serve the Crown, and as a representative of high German culture he could demand befitting, seemly and formal treatment from those around him. The government would ask him for advice... Amongst the German public and academic circles, pride in the position of the university was connected to pride in the growing importance of the German Reich amongst other nations. The position of the German professor was leagues away from the position of the professors of little renown as was typical in the USA.*"[353]

As a result of democratization, political pluralization and the radicalization of the public from the 1830s, this concept has been eroded and the university's authority has become a relative concept. For some, the university continues to be an authority and impartial institution, standing apart from daily political skirmishes, while for others it is an institution which has been discredited by pompous political activism, concealing its separation from the general concerns of ordinary

---

352 Ortega y Gasset, José: *Mission of the University*. London 1946, p. 37.
353 Cited Paulus, *Vorbild USA?*, p. 61.

people. The role of the university as the provider of impartial, complex analyses to solve social problems is an extremely difficult challenge, but failing to accept it would lead the university to losing its legitimacy as an authority in society. Its demise goes hand in hand with the demise of rational experts' credibility in public life, and in the best case scenario the university will survive as just one of many participants in a multipolar debate.

– *Global contextualism*

Some of a university's tasks are global in nature, while others are more local – what is needed is for them to be interconnected. It is necessary to remember that some university subjects respond more to global challenges, while others respond to local or regional challenges, and that it is through concerted interdisciplinary teamwork that the demands formulated by the public and political leaders can be met. Whether a discipline has mainly global or local ties has to be reflected in its curriculum, its financial model, as well as the demands on educators. Globally focused disciplines are not qualitatively superior to locally or regionally focused subjects, and vice versa. Overrating global perspectives leads to an ideological assessment of reality; in an extreme form this can lead to the position that the challenges of globalization are the only ones today that every "modern and rational" person has to face. The acceptance that disciplines are different has to be the foundation for decision-making at university. Often small signs of simplistic thinking can be phenomena of the utmost importance for university culture, such as the failure to take into consideration the different traditions and ties of disciplines – one typical example is the complete superiority or dominance of English compared to other languages in everyday academia, which is particularly harmful for the humanities, characterised as they are by their linguistic variety. Or there is pressure to publish in high-impact academic journals which are predominantly Anglophone in their cultural references. The concept of *global contextualization* has emerged from current academic debates. The idea means considering global theories in all of their political, historical, religious and geographical aspects, raising unsettling questions and looking for appropriate responses. The search for context has been the principle objective of the humanities and social sciences since the Enlightenment – the Humboldtian tradition in particular was predestined to help the public perceive contexts. Unfortunately, the specialist areas of the disciplines have lost their ability to broadly contextualize, while there are usually very few opportunities for universities to provide the public today with comprehensive interpretations which link the global and local.

– *Redefining academic freedom*

The main reason why the university community seldom responds to the global challenges of interdisciplinary-oriented academic expertise within the framework of global contextualization is a poor understanding of academic freedom. In the Euro-American university tradition, the true holders of the absolute right to freely research are the professors – the chair holders. Due to economic dependence, that freedom is inaccessible to lower-level academics at the start of their career or PhD students. Changes to this tradition have been brought about by the assessment processes of the European Research Council (ERC), but also by national research councils, which in the first case systematically, and in the second as the result of organisational chaos, facilitate a situation whereby a professor's projects and work are assessed in some cases exclusively by lower-grade academics, sometimes even by people without any basic academic titles. The influence of academic capitalism also brings a hierarchization of professorships and professors according to scientometric and economic perspectives. The principles of change management in universities encourage the university management and its bureaucratic apparatus to weaken the ties between the professor and his/her institute or department, and instead transfers the competencies for evaluating the work of a professor from the departmental head to the dean. But in spite of all of the modernist pressure, the Humboldtian-Newman tradition is quite clear: at university, only the professor can investigate whatever he/she chooses.

This arrangement proved to be highly productive in terms of research, and it is not a thesis which is only advocated by nostalgic and stubborn Humboldtian conservatives. The weak point of the thesis – within the Humboldtian tradition of *Freiheit, Lehre, Forschung* – was and remains the transfer of research activity to teaching. Many professors simply teach what corresponds to their research activities. Therefore, they often focus on very detailed, specialized areas of research, or research with an applied character which is incredibly difficult for students. The link here between the topic and the subject curriculum is often very loose or completely inadequate. And this trend weakens the relationship between the social responsibility of the academic, the discipline and the narrow specialization. From the perspective of students and taxpayers, this is an evident abuse of academic freedom and an avoidance of social responsibility. By being overly detailed and specialized, the academic community cuts the branch of social legitimacy from underneath itself. With the expansion of such bad practices it is not surprising that the public and political leaders demand restrictions to academic freedom, tighter control of universities and economic cutbacks, which in turn provokes a response from the academic community, which attempts to barricade itself in, referring to the historical principles of university autonomy at any cost – even at the cost of excessively ideological arguments.

- *Fundamental reforms to the curriculum*

Responding to mass higher education through fundamental changes to the curriculum, whereby each discipline, according to its own specific characteristics, has to come to terms with the fact that only a relatively small number of students display any academic ambitions. From an academic perspective, some of them even show only a very superficial interest in the subject, its methodologies and research inquiry. A significant number of students are not sufficiently motivated for specialized course study and require a more eclectic education, which through good management of the university's courses could be transformed into a demand for interdisciplinary education with practical potential – something which the labour market greatly requires. And most importantly – the curriculum has to reflect the fact that in the digital age the university has lost its centuries-old undisputed position as the sole accumulator of knowledge, with this role being taken over to a large extent by the internet. The role of the teacher is also undergoing fundamental change. Under the influence of mass higher education, the Humboldtian ideal of the teacher-scientist has been divided into three groups of university teachers. The first contains those who take on a large share of the teaching and as a result – in many cases also due to their competencies and priorities – are not part of larger research projects, they do not generate any finance for the university for research from external sources, they do not form research groups around them, and their publishing activities are below average. The advantage of these educators is their ability to handle the teaching material and to interest and motivate students who are not properly prepared for university study, who are poorly motivated and out of their depth. The second group of educators are those who are nearest to the Humboldtian ideal: people who teach but who are also scientifically active. However, their research results are usually average or slightly above average, but not excellent in a wider international context. These educators have a difficult role. They have to be adept teachers who have an influence on students in their later years of study, as well as scientists who are capable of presenting students with a comprehensive range of scientific inquiry. They select some of them to be trained for research work and others for a more vocationally orientated education according to the subject's requirements, and – particularly in the arts and social sciences – they show them the way towards a broader interdisciplinary grasp of reality. It is with this group, forming around 80% of the academic community, that it will be the most difficult to implement the challenges facing the university. The third group consists of academics who are visible on the international scene in their specific disciplines, *principal investigators* and *visible researchers*, whose goal within the framework of university research is to generate and lead research teams across generations of researchers, link up to prestigious research projects and grant competitions, bring in external funding for research and "look after the brand" of the discipline and the university in relation to politicians, the public and the commercial sector.[354] In the digital age, university teachers can no longer rely on their role as an unwavering authority and a superior guardian of knowledge and facts. They will have to come to terms with the existence of alternative sources of knowledge and respond to a new educational role

---

354 Dörre – Neis, *Das Dilemma*. Berlin 2000, p. 95.

where they manage the debate on various interpretations of reality by emphasizing different contexts.[355]

– *Bridging the gap between vocational and general education*

In the future the differences between the demands of vocationally orientated education and interdisciplinary/general education will increase. Presently, the tendency for disciplines to develop their own path towards vocational education has been muted by Czech higher-education legislation which required an unacceptably high share of practical teaching for accreditation in vocationally focused courses. As a result, many *de facto* vocational disciplines at the university preferred not to define themselves as such and found themselves straddled between the general focus of the discipline *de jure* and the professionally focused content of the teaching *de facto*. It is likely that the medical and legal disciplines will try to improve the narrow definition of a vocational course rather than develop research, in particular research of an interdisciplinary nature; such a narrow definition of a discipline will obviously be incompatible with the university's complex role in society. It can be expected that some of the disciplines which are not willing or able to respond to the challenges of interdisciplinary research will move outside of the university – one example has been the rapidly expanding network of universities specializing in law in Germany since the 1970s, and the specialist medical universities (Medizinische Universität) in Austria that have been established since 2004. The binding role of the university community will be increasingly passed on to the arts and social sciences, the courses of which are now the closest to the structure of the three-stage education: i.e. the general Bachelor's course aimed at developing critical thought, the more professionally orientated Master's course, and the academic preparation of the PhD course. However, as a result of political turbulence and radicalization, the legitimacy of the arts and social sciences amongst the general public has been shaken. Additionally, over the long term these disciplines have suffered from the incompatibility of the results of their work with the dictates of economizing scientometrics as established by the political leaders of the country. Some of them have fallen into line with the state's rules and have looked for financial sources mainly in educational activities, including the acceptance of mass higher education and lower requirements from students, while others strive to preserve the research character of their discipline and the selective nature of the course, and subsequently suffer economic restrictions due to their "virtuous poverty". The conditions for the humanities acting as a university bond do not seem particularly favourable. Maintaining both the unity of the university and its legitimacy as a socially useful institution is obviously going to be the toughest problem in the coming decades.

---

355 Brzeziński, Jerzy Marian: Od uniwersytetu Humboldta do e-uniwersytetu, In: Drozdowicz, Zbigniew (red.): *Uniwersytety. Tradycje – dzień dziesiejszy – przyszłość*. Poznań 2009, pp. 109–122.

- *Meeting the challenges of academic capitalism*

From today's perspective this is perhaps the most fundamental challenge of all. For example, in 2016 the Austrian legal expert Manfred Nowak approached the issue of the social contribution of the university very reductively and defined the university as *"a community of highly specialized academics designed to look for and create new knowledge and maintain and expand their scientific disciplines by recruiting students whose activity is based on the traditional demand for independence and self-determination."*[356] He saw the greatest tension resulting from the incorporation of the university's independence as a basic element in a university's identity and *"the increasing calls to be more orientated towards the customers, for the university structures to adapt to their demands, including management and control mechanisms."*[357] According to Nowak, with the loss of its own self-determination in terms of its objectives, the university as an idea has come to an end, as society will no longer need it, turning instead to specialist academies.[358] Concerns are raised by theoreticians of science regarding the narrowing of scientific knowledge as a result of economism and the pursuit of international visibility, which disregards basic research with its unclear link to a tangible result at a predetermined time.[359] The successes in this pursuit are interpreted as a foregone conclusion because the approach of the handful of top universities towards their financial sources, including their attractiveness to elite researchers, is already very different today from the other universities. As a result of academic capitalism this difference will increase and prevent any real changes within the hierarchical status of universities. He thus refutes the thesis that it is possible for them to raise their profile due to the quality of the research work and teaching, at least in certain parts of the world.[360]

Klaus Dörre and Mathias Neis even had the courage to predict the development of the relationship between the university and academic capitalism, which is obviously very rapid and largely unpredictable. Universities will become increasingly entangled in a global system of competition and mercilessly judged according to criteria set by the top American universities; the Americanization of university culture will gain in intensity in spite of the fact that the principles of academic capitalism are presently being questioned in the USA as a foundation for the holistic development of the university network. They predict a movement of power in universities into the hands of the *visible scientists* or groups partly made up of professors – the top researchers, as well as people in various opaque

356 Nowak, Manfred: *Universitäten zwischen Freiheit und Verantwortung. Entwicklung und Perspektiven einer Rechtsbeziehung.* Wien 2016, p. 5.

357 Ibid, pp. 5–6.

358 Ibid, pp. 7, 12–24.

359 Münch, Richard: *Akademischer Kapitalismus. Über die politische Ökonomie der Hochschulreform.* Berlin 2011, 155–180.

360 Ibid, pp. 218–235.

though undoubtedly exclusive and close relationships with the commercial sector, the state bureaucracy, the political class and the media. The importance of these elite teams will continue to grow. One typical example is the role of the Central European Institute of Technology (CEITEC) in Brno, a successful research centre established by a consortium of universities and other research institutes. The internal culture of the CEITEC is clearly managerial and international, the official internal language is English. The existence of the CEITEC brings elements into the institutional culture of Masaryk University and other universities which often conflict with the culture of faculties and traditions. An interesting and understandable aspect is the gradual movement of the CEITEC culture towards the culture of the science and medical disciplines, where there is a crossover in terms of research projects and personnel, while the humanities perceive the CIETIC as a foreign body in the university corpus. The ruthlessly efficient character of the management is sometimes literally viewed with horror, giving rise to further reflection on the theory of a multi-speed university. Sometimes it is even seen as a foretaste of management practices for research at universities, where the objectives of a university's work are set by managers and regional political representatives and their definitions of policy development.[361]

However, Jacek Sójka has rejected such a catastrophic scenario. By referring to the Polish experience, he pointed out that some elements of academic capitalism have always been part of universities, while he also used the example of Cambridge to demonstrate that academic culture is compatible with university capitalism. He also highlighted the fact that a large number of disciplines will respond more to the demands from the public sector rather than enter into close contact with commercial firms, and thus capitalism will be able to be regulated and managed, with pressure also applied from the European Union.[362] Finally, in his famous work from 1988, *Homo academicus,* Pierre Bourdieu pre-empted the main debate on academic capitalism when he spoke about four varieties of capital on the university grounds: scientific (reputation, innovators); social (personal ties, connecting science with furthering a career); economic (links to external financial sources, influence on financial channels within the university), and political (the right to strategic decision-making).[363] From this perspective, the academic-capitalism invasion is (slightly) deflected by the ancient university culture and the powers at universities towards economism, which evidently signals another stage in the long historical develop of university culture, though not its extinction.

---

361 Dörre, Klaus – Neis, Matthias: *Das Dilemma der unternehmerischen Universität. Hochschulen zwischen Wissenproduktion und Machtzwang.* Berlin 2010, pp. 18–23.

362 Sójka, Jacek: Zarządzenie strategiczne a idea Uniwersytetu. In: Drozdowicz, Zbigniew (red.): *Uniwersytety. Tradycje – dzień dziesiejszy – przyszłość.* Poznań 2009, pp. 169–188, esp. pp. 181–185.

363 Bourdieu, Pierre: *Homo academicus.* Frankfurt am Main 1988, p. 151 ff.

Conclusion

The current narrative about the usefulness of the university is basically the result of institutions, disciplines and individuals searching for their place within a system of differentiated higher education, the power of which we have seen around us for almost two decades. The system has emerged without clear political goals, without defined objectives which could be traced back to long-term trends in financing higher education and research, or from the response of universities and their external partners to these long-term issues. A chain of the actors' actions and reactions emerges, along with a sequence of strategic and less strategic moves and countermoves. It is difficult to distinguish its beginning and ascertain who was exactly reacting to what. The disorientation of the academic community is the logical outcome from this confusion, and academics become attentive and grateful listeners to mythical narratives. This makes it easier for them to adopt a position in this chaotic situation, face to face with the complex and difficult issue of determining the university's position in today's society. And in pragmatic terms, it makes it easier for them in the struggle for posts and control of decision-making and influencing financial channels. At present this narrative has maintained an eschatological character and, therefore, has the distinct contours of a myth which combines the social usefulness of the university with extremely important values: social progress, democracy, freedom, truth...

There are three basic forms of myth. The literature terms the first of these as traditionalist or conservative, and its objective is to defend the classic form of the university as best it can, and in Central Europe this is linked to the Humboldtian ideal of the university. This myth disguises the fact that the Humboldtian university is a product of the Early Modern Age from the 18th and 19th centuries, related to the level of a discipline's specialization, the development of the national state and the parameters of market development. It removes one segment of the university ideal from its context – academic freedom in deciding the direction of research and education. The mythical narrative states that all contemporary trends limiting this freedom are dangerous for the very foundation of the university. The bell tolls for the university either due to the mass increase in students, pressure on the effectiveness of its financing, or for a number of other reasons seen as part of a dangerous modernizing experiment.

The second type of mythical narrative is also historicizing, but it searches for a compromise with the challenges of the period: the challenge of considering the early modern ideal of the university anew. This mythical narrative has a more dynamic form – it reflects on the Humboldtian-Newman vision, but focuses more on attempts at reforming it and on the successes and failures of the 20th century. Experiments range from attempting to surpass the Humboldtian ideal, to not necessarily viewing it bipolarly it as dangerous, but simply as an attempt which was successful in some aspects and less so in others. It is inhibited in its approach to the two most famous Central European attempts at reforming the Humboldtian university – the Nazi and communist experiments – and in this regard it is an incomplete discourse and, therefore, untrustworthy. However, one of its advantages is its openness to counter-arguments and the subsequent attempt to reflect on the changes in public demands and admit that the university is required to respond to them, without losing its own identity by so doing.

The third mythical narrative is labelled modernist due to its links to the differentiated system of higher education – a decades-old innovation in the long history of higher education. Conservatives view it as the anti-myth to the Humboldtian ideal, but more precisely it is an extensive revision of the university ideal from 1810 with a view to the needs of the 21st century. This narrative explains the reality which has existed in the Czech Republic over the past twenty years – that in the future, universities will have to count on a much greater level of differentiation than the academic community of traditional universities has been used to. The traditional "bricks and mortar" universities will continue to be incorporated within the global university network. Alongside them will be universities with highly differentiated levels of disciplines, or schools with incomplete discipline structures with ties to the region and regional employers. And finally, narrow, vocationally focused, specialist (private) universities with a limited choice of subjects and little research, but with an unusually high reputation within a narrow professional community. The mythical narration does not interpret this in a bipolar way as the defeat of the Humboldtian university. The pluralist demands of society are capable of inundating all of these aforementioned parts of the university landscape, and each in a specific way without it being possible to say that one way was superior or inferior. It accepts the fact that external partners will have a greater say in the running of the university, but weighs up the pros and cons which are associated with it.

THE MYTH OF AUTONOMOUS UNIVERSITY GOVERNANCE

The belief in the need to preserve and further develop the autonomous governance of a university, allegedly one of the fundamental preconditions for the successful implementation of a university's mission, is one of the central pillars of academic culture. The historically grounded myth of the indispensability of university autonomy in its decision-making is seen as part of the academic community's defence against external pressure; as a support to the university administration's claim for some kind of special or explicitly privileged treatment by the state bureaucracy and political representatives. Naturally, this myth has its own use within the university. Here the motives of its narrators become less clear and there are at least four narrative sources within the cultural circles of Central European universities – the level of central power divided between the academic functionaries led by the rector, followed by the level of non-academic managerial staff, the faculty level, while the fourth level is represented by the individual departments, seminaries and institutes. Each of these sections of the university community narrates its myth according to its own needs and interests, and selects supporting arguments from the historical aspects of the university's autonomy when deciding its interests. One will narrate a story with great urgency and mobilize the public behind it, elsewhere there is a long-held silence – though this does not in the least signify giving up on a goal.

University governance in the pre-modern era

For more than eight hundred long years in the history of the European university, since the start of the 11th century, there have been two basic models of organization – the Bolognian and the Parisian. The first was the model of a community of masters and students on an equal basis, due to the fact that the students were the most important source of finance. And they also had decision-making powers. The Bolognian model mainly consisted of adult men from aristocratic families, who were used to deciding public matters through the bureaucratic elite; and so, understandably, they claimed this right at the university as well. In the Parisian case, the main source of university finance came from the church and so the teaching was not reliant on student finance, which led to power being in the hands of the masters. Both models had followers, though the model of the Paris university was by far the most popular, and was also a model for Central European universities founded as "*universitas magistrorum, doctorum et scholarium*".[364] Here the financing of higher education was taken over by the monarch, thus the influence of students waned over time, in some cases to an insignificant level.

However, it would be a mistake to view the two models as dichotomous. If we disregard the differences in the division of power, the university community operated in similar ways. The medieval university was basically a guild, where matters were decided by an assembly of full members of the academic community – most often all of the professors (*concilium generale*) in the Parisian model. For "Parisian model" universities, the limited direction downwards was variable and sometimes the council could also include doctors and holders of lower academic titles. The assembly would elect a rector, usually every half a year, either directly or through electors. The rector had the right to manage the university's assets, resolve disputes within the academic community and defend the university's privileges externally. The rector had at his disposal the advisory body of the collegiate of deans and procurators, though even here the development in universities was somewhat different as sometimes a body might emerge from the advisory group which would take over some of the competencies of the rector. Often the division of competencies and powers was not fully determined by codified norms, instead a large role was played by university traditions, where a clear signal of the division of power was the university insignia and the form of university rituals.

Medieval universities did not have powerful administrative forces, and in an overall European context these were only small institutions. Most often, the number of actively registered students was around 100–200 people, and the administration was effective in dealing with such numbers. However, there were also several large universities with thousands of students. By the Late Middle Ages, the last remnants of the "Bolognian" model – universities formed by a free association of scholars – had completely vanished, and universities were founded by higher authorities, and given property, privileges and guarantees for their existence by

---

364 Boháček, Miroslav: *Založení a nejstarší organisace pražské university*. Acta Universitatis Pragensis 1964, issue 1, pp. 5–31, here p. 16.

the supreme political authorities of the period – i.e. the popes and emperors. One typical privilege was the guarantee of autonomy, which strengthened the drawing of resources from underwritten property, while some historians believe that universities managed to manoeuvre between the political influence of the secular ruler, the church and the town communes, and thus exempted themselves from some of their duties. This is difficult to verify because the situation was different for each university and was highly variable over time. For example, the foundation of the university in Prague is linked to one papal and two royal decrees; in addition to the emperor and king, Charles IV, one prominent supporter of the new university was Arnošt of Pardubice (1297–1364), who was the king's advisor and confidante. The university maintained friendly relations with the Roman Church as one of the guarantors of its existence and autonomy until 1417, when it issued its approval for receiving Utraquists, and was thus separated from the influence of Rome. The church's influence returned to full strength on university soil with the transfer of the Jesuit school in 1622, and remained there until the reforms of enlightened absolutism.[365] It was not until between 1784 and 1841 that the percentage of theology students at the university dramatically fell from 50% to 8%.[366]

In its relationship with students, the university was very mindful of maintaining its reputation for autonomy, as this freedom in decision-making was demanded by students, and any shortcomings would have affected the reputation of the school within the university network. Therefore, any intervention by secular, or less frequently, religious powers, was usually conducted with discretion by the university, as normally the university had nothing to gain from open conflict. The complicated and very often individual search for and discovery of a relationship between university autonomy and dependence began to form lines of conflict in the medieval history of universities, which are still topics of public debate and sources of mythical narratives.

Economic governance

External powers usually made use of economic issues to make their way through the doors of the university. When they were founded, medieval and many early modern age universities were provided with important property – in the case of Charles University this was the Carolinian foundation. The university's holdings usually consisted of property, village holdings, privileges, duties and various salaries, while several universities kept valuable art collections or moveable property.

365 Svatoš, Michal (red.): *Dějiny Univerzity Karlovy I. (1347/1348–1622)*, Prague 1995, pp. 33–35, 78–84; Beránek, Karel (red.): *Dějiny Univerzity Karlovy II. (1622–1802)*, Prague 1995, pp. 27–29.

366 Havránek, Jan (red.): *Dějiny Univerzity Karlovy III. (1802–1918)*, Prague 1997, p. 19.

The problem was usually administering these possessions. There were frequent changes in office personnel, who had limited competency to manage often considerable but in general quite disparate assets, while the university's small-scale bureaucratic apparatus did not provide the necessary support. Universities were unable to respond to fluctuations in the market and were unable to effectively administer their property, but traditionalism prevented property being transferred to a more suitable lease. One obstacle was the overall atmosphere in the university's teaching bodies, which often tended to approach trusteeship without any strategic thinking, without any long-term perspectives, often basically predatory – which was why the professors' committees prevented the leasing of university property due to concerns over increasing the transparency of the financial flows. The proceeds from the foundations would be squandered and the professors sometimes made successful attempts at selling off the university's core property. One typical feature concerned prospective personal promotion within the university hierarchy; for example, in Prague, many professors expected employment at the larger, wealthier and more prestigious university in Vienna, and thus behaved very short-sightedly and inconsiderately when it came to issues of property in their own departments.

The result of the problems in the university's economic management system was a general *"administrative failing"*.[367] With the exception of some of the large, rich universities (Cambridge, Paris, Vienna and Padua), the daily management of early modern age European universities was characterized by arrears in payments to teachers, employees and suppliers, while teachers sought to earn money outside of the university, e.g. from private tuition, various types of fraud when issuing and transferring university charges (matriculation, exams, graduation), demanding hospitality and gifts from students, etc. The governance of Prague's university, as with many others, was adversely affected by the military conflicts of the 16th and 17th centuries. The financial problems slowly accumulated from the first half of the 16th century, and from 1638, teachers did not receive any salaries or their full benefits in kind for several years. A report from 1660 estimated the arrears at an enormous sum. This decline in the university's economic fortunes can be seen symbolically in the state of the buildings, including the most important and prestigious ones – in 1714, the home of Prague university – the Carolinum – was closed due to the dilapidated state of the structure.[368]

Typical of the period was a concept for far-reaching university reform written by Peter Theodor Birelli.[369] He saw the decline in university finances as the tip of

367 Cf. Rüegg, *Geschichte,* II., pp. 162–165; Ibid, III., pp. 104–107.

368 Klabouch, Jiří: *K dějinám hospodářství pražské univerzity v 17. a 18. století.* Acta Universitatis Carolinae 1963, year 4, issue 2, pp. 87–114, here pp. 90–97.

369 Beránek, *Dějiny Univerzity Karlovy II.*, p. 41.

the iceberg in an in-depth critique of the conditions at the university, and called for intervention into the failed university governance. Teachers apparently taught nearly 60 hours per year, and the majority of their best lectures were given privately (i.e. paid), with the result that the lectures open to the public were empty. According to tradition there was no teaching on Wednesdays, Fridays, Saturdays and Saints' days, or during the university holidays, graduation, matriculation and faculty assemblies. According to Birelli, this meant that in practice a teacher did not work for three-quarters of the year. Characteristically, this critique of conditions at the Prague university came from someone with experience from Western universities – Birelli was from today's Luxembourg – and it was typical of his analysis that he focused on the so-called secular faculties – mainly law and medicine.[370] Due to the influence of the Jesuits and the supervision by the episcopate, there was stricter discipline in theological faculties and also a greater degree of autonomous exclusiveness.[371] Overall, however, university autonomy in Prague in the early 18th century made for a rather grim picture.

Introducing statist practices into university governance and their boundaries

The state normally intervened in times of university crisis – in dealing with vices and glaring injustices, renovating university buildings, moving universities to more appropriate places, etc.[372] In particular, the removal of the influence of the Jesuits in education (1773) brought about a sharp rise in state intervention in the Catholic countries of Europe, and even universities which had been founded by the Roman church gradually found that in the 19th century ecclesiastical funding became a marginal source, even for theological faculties.[373]

In Austria, the enlightened absolutism of Maria Theresa and Joseph II represented a watershed for many reasons, including the *Studienhofkommission* (1760) with its numerous subsequent statist measures in Habsburg-controlled lands,[374] where universities were completely administered by the state from 1783–1784.[375] The same level of dependence on the state budget was typical for other Austrian

---

370 Kučera, Karel: *Raně osvícenský pokus o reformu pražské university*. Acta Universitatis Carolinae 1963, year 4, issue 2, pp. 61–86, esp. pp. 64–65.

371 Klabouch, *K dějinám hospodářství*, pp. 90–97.

372 Rüegg, *Geschichte*, II., pp. 162–163.

373 Rüegg, *Geschichte*, III., p. 106.

374 Stanzel, Josef: *Die Schulaufsicht im Reformwerk des Johann Ignaz von Felbiger (1724–1788). Schule, Kirche und Staat in Recht und Praxis des aufgeklärten Absolutismus*. Paderborn 1976, pp. 237 ff., 379.

375 Beránek, Karel (red.): *Dějiny Univerzity Karlovy II. (1622–1802)*, Prague 1995, p. 51.

universities.[376] Rich universities with effective governance in German lands were spared state intervention, and many of them were only partially affected by the state's grant policies and the concomitant supervision. Newly established universities, however, were usually completely dependent on state budgets, or state property was only entrusted into their administration. In particular for universities from the Middle Ages and the Early Modern Age, the share of the finance from the original foundation was still significant in the first half of the 20th century; for example, in Marburg in Germany, teachers in the 1960s were still receiving benefits-in-kind in the form of wood from the forests owned by the university.[377] But the intervention by the strongly statist regimes meant that this was a curious exception in 20th century Central Europe. Walter Rüegg estimated that in Europe in 1938 the percentage of public finance in university budgets ranged from 25% to 100%, while Czechoslovak universities at the time were completely reliant on the state budget.[378]

However, accompanying this loss of economic autonomy and the transfer of power away from the university came the flourishing of Central European and German universities, which were now largely financed by provincial budgets. At the same time, however, there was also a change in how their mission was understood. The upswing was due to the fact that the public model of university financing provided certainty and a future which could not be found in the previous regime of "administrative failing". The change in the understanding of their mission was on the flipside of the same coin: it was reasonable to expect that public authorities would want the right of control in exchange for finance, and that this would lead to a greater level of bureaucratization of universities. In addition, politicians in the modern era were accountable to their electorate. With increasing democratization and the politicization of the public in the 19th and 20th centuries, universities were no longer allowed to become independent bodies or nonpartisan institutions, nor were they even allowed to be bureaucratic organizations outside of public debate. The power of the civil servant coupled with taxpayers' demands led to university governance, management and efficiency becoming open topics for discussion.[379]

Walter Rüegg considered secularization, bureaucratization and specialization as being the most significant symbols in the development of European universities from 1800 to 1945. Universities became the subject of state-education poli-

---

376 Lemayer, Karl von: *Die Verwaltung der österreichischen Hochschulen von 1867–1877*. Vienna 1878, p. 41; Dybiec, Julian: *Finansowanie nauki o oświaty w Galicji 1860–1918*. Kraków 1979, p. 22.

377 vom Brocke, Berhard: Universitäts– und Wissenschaftsfinanzierung im 19./20. Jahrhundert. In: Schwinges, Rainer Christoph (Hg.): *Finanzierung von Universität und Wissenschaft in Vergangenheit und Gegenwart*. Basel 2005, pp. 343–462, here p. 344

378 Rüegg, *Geschichte*, III., p. 106.

379 Taylor, *Crisis*, pp. 54–55.

cies, which in the case of nation states meant the so-called national interest. In multinational monarchies, the equivalent relationship was blurred – in Austria both the ruling dynasty and the Roman Catholic Church saw the university as "state property", as did a large section of the public and, albeit more gradually, representatives of the state bureaucracy. In place of the medieval models from Bologna and Paris came new models. The French "Napoleonic" model had a high degree of bureaucratization, statization and faculty specialization, it was strongly orientated towards vocational education and a rigidly defined curriculum, typically with a subordinate role for the arts faculties (*Faculté des Lettres et des Sciences Humaines*), which usually only provided part of the bureaucratic exams and organised lectures for the public. In many ways, the Prussian model or Humboldtian university was in direct contrast to this. This held aloft a university model which focused on realizing a vision of universally focused study and the mutually enrichening harmony of research and teaching, with arts faculties playing an important consolidating role. With its idealistic universalism "directed towards the truth", the Humboldtian university somewhat disguised the reality that it was also a state-supervised institution, and that a significant number of the disciplines had never strayed from their close focus on vocational education, where there was far more emphasis placed on satisfying the (state's) demands for specialists, rather than a universally and philosophically grounded relationship between research and tuition.

Therefore, with the Prussian model we encounter a mixture of idealism, (particularly in the arts faculties), and the professionally orientated pragmatic specialization of the medical and law faculties. From the start of the "Humboldtian" era, then, this loyalty towards the interests of the state proved to be one of the conflict lines in universities. While the legal and medical disciplines were not particularly troubled by state supervision and its attendant bureaucracy, as the state demand for experts quite suited them, the humanities saw state supervision more to their detriment and struggled to defend their own usefulness in the eyes of the state bureaucracy, where the only defence mechanism open to them was the idea of the harmony between state and national interests – something which the Humboldtian humanist scientists usually strongly supported. From a legal perspective, the university during this golden era was a *mixtum compositum*, where there was more corporative autonomy in curriculum issues, the conferral of titles and honours, and the organization of the school, while there was state management in the material side of running the school.[380]

In Central Europe the trend towards the state supervision of universities led to a sharp rise in the number of universities. The extensive developments were obvi-

---

380 Beran, Karel: Proč je univerzita veřejnoprávní korporací? *In: Historie, současný stav a perspektivy univerzit. Úsvit nebo soumrak akademické samosprávy.* Uspořádal Josef Staša. Prague 2008, pp. 110–120, here p. 118; expanded on in Wolff, Hans J.: *Die Rechtsgestalt der Universität.* Cologne 1956.

ous, but the quality and prestige of the schools remained relatively low compared to the rest of Europe, with the exception, of course, of the University of Vienna.[381] During the Early Modern Age, the countries of Central Europe under Habsburg rule still had relatively few universities, particularly when compared with Western Europe. The main universities in this network were the universities in Prague (founded 1348), Krakow (1364), Vienna (1365), Graz (1586), Lviv (1661) and Innsbruck (1668). In addition, there were several schools of insecure standing, where – typically for the situation in Central Europe – the influence of the state and the church became intricately interwoven; for example, the Order of the Benedictines in Salzburg and the Jesuits in Olomouc. One typical organizational characteristic was the clear predominance of the theological faculties within the academic communities. The Austrian state did not assume complete control over these schools. It did not entirely reduce the church's influence and either transformed them into theological-philosophical academic lyceums (Olomouc 1782, Salzburg 1810) or different types of universities (Ljubljana 1783–1791). The teaching statute for Olomouc changed two more times: in 1827 the school was recognised by the state as a university again, but then abolished in 1860, leaving only an independently functioning theological faculty. In the 19th century the Austrian state continued with its rapid expansion of universities, enjoying more success with technical colleges (eight schools in total) than universities (1875 Černovice, 1882 Prague university divided into Czech and German sections), where the interests of the dynasty and the state clashed more often with the interests of the individual nations. The emergence of small nation states in Central and Eastern Europe after the First World War signalled the start of a competition between 1919 and 1922 to see which nation could fulfil its ambition to build more universities: Brno (1919), Bratislava (1919), Poznaň (1919), Ljubljana (1919), Pécs (1921), Szeged (1921).

The Austrian state did not command the strength of the Prussian or French states; the Habsburg bureaucracy did not proceed – with the exception of the Josephine era – as uncompromisingly and ruthlessly as its Hohenzollern or Napoleonic counterparts. The Habsburg state took into account the interests of the Roman Catholic Church for much longer than in Western Europe. However, it was the reforms of Leo Thun in 1849 and the higher education law of 1873 which created space for university corporative autonomy, which Czechoslovakia also introduced with a law in 1918.[382] Autonomy remained *lex lata* until the issuing of the university law in 1950, when universities became state institutions for all intents

---

381 Teichler, Ulrich: *Hochschulsysteme und quantitativstrukturelle Hochschulpolitik. Differenzierung, Bologna–Prozess, Exzellenzinitiative und die Folgen.* Münster–New York 2014, p. 149, translation of the original Japanese text by Hiroshi Yamazaki.

382 Lentze, Hans: *Die Universitätsreform des Ministers Graf Leo Thun-Hohenstein.* Wien 1962; Engelbrecht, *Geschichte*, pp. 234, 240–241; the effects on the Czech lands Havránek, *Dějiny Univerzity Karlovy* III., pp. 99–103.

and purposes. In reality, though, university autonomy had been a fiction as a result of the Nazi occupation and the communist coup in 1948.[383]

From the 1880s, the Austrian authorities had become increasingly hamstrung in their activities due to internal political problems, in particular the rivalry of the Central European nations. Their ambition was not to unpick the Austrian monarchy, but to use it to their own ends – specifically to dominate any territory with a majority of speakers of one language, or where there were historical claims to that land. Therefore, it was not primarily a struggle of nations *against the state*, but a *struggle for the state*. Territory, universities – in fact, practically everything was seen as national property, and in the struggle to seize it, people who belonged to a national community, but who were formally in the service of a transnational Habsburg state, had to subordinate themselves to this goal. The identity and social status of Austrian officialdom was changing.[384] An Austrian official could now be a Czech or a German, and this corresponded to the change in the relationship between the state and the university, at least on the practical level of decision-making. The state sphere was being rent asunder by national interests.

Although the Central Europe of the Habsburgs followed Western European or Prussian university models, it copied them inconsistently with particular regard to its own specific cultural characteristics, and as a result was less statist and bureaucratic. Therefore, the universities in the Habsburg empire were a peripheral part of the Prussian model of higher education. With their considerable eclecticism in adopting the Prussian models, rather than resembling Germany or the West, they were much more similar to the haphazardly modernizing universities of Southern Europe – famed historically, but which had become ossified in the 19th century and were on the periphery of the university network. Additionally, the unstable regimes of the successor states to the Habsburg empire continued with these eclectic, conceptually vague policies. The enthusiasm at the start of the postwar era for building universities as the flagships of the nation's education policies soon began to wane when faced with financial restrictions. In Germany, Poland and Hungary this was compounded by dramatic inflation and the increasing pressure from national conflicts and chronic internal-political instability. Therefore, the interwar Central European university presented the picture of an institution whose teaching corps happily harked back to the ancient traditions of European universities and their governance, clinging to symbolic expressions in science and teaching, while ignoring the fundamental changes in politics and society. Most importantly, they happily forgot the fact that universities were completely dependent on the decisions of the state when it came to the most crucial organizational

---

383 Beran, *Proč je univerzita*, pp. 110–120, here p. 118; Morkes, František: *Zákony o vysokých školách z let 1948–1989*, Pedagogika 49/1999, pp. 115–127, pp. 116–118.

384 Klečacký, Martin: *Iluze nezávislosti. Sociální status c. k. soudce v konfliktu loajalit mezi národem a státem na přelomu 19. a 20. století*. Český časopis historický. Year 112, no. 3 (2014), pp. 432–462.

and management issues. This was a contradictory type of dependence. Although the state had taken over all responsibility for universities, and the political leadership had signed up to the idea of universities as the nation's flagships, at the same time they refused to allow enough money from the budget to go towards the development of tertiary education.[385] Compared to Austria there was a sharp rise in the money spent on education from the Czechoslovak state budget, though most of the expenditure was on lower school levels, while the state's approach towards universities was inconsistent. One reason was the prioritization of technical education at four of the fifteen Czechoslovak universities, another was that state expenditure on research was minimal.[386] The state had a vision for universities where research and teaching would be in harmony, but in reality this applied only to teaching. In addition, the state was doubtful that universities were being efficiently managed and opened a debate concerning the reduction or even closure of some schools. It demanded greater efficiency from the investment of public funds through tighter bureaucratization, but which was difficult to implement in a disorderly political climate. For example, the idea that the Czechoslovak state would be able to gain absolute control over Prague's German university came up against the realities of politics: any heavy-handed treatment of the university by the state could escalate the problems surrounding Czech-German cohabitation, with numerous ramifications for foreign policy. The situation was similar to the relationship with the Slovak university in Bratislava, and to a lesser degree with the university in Brno, which twice enjoyed waves of support from the provincial patriotism of Moravians.[387] The corporative governance of universities was also a target of criticism from people within its own ranks – the influential lawyer František Weyr, a teacher at Brno's Masaryk University and one of the architects of the Czechoslovak constitution of 1920 – systematically called for it to be limited. According to Weyr, the surviving administration was the reason for the unfortunate isolation of universities from public life, and Weyr was forthright in his criticisms of the failure of teachers' bodies in relation to regulating research and teaching, and of the administrative incompetence of the academic corps.[388] Therefore, during the interwar period in Central Europe there was a confrontation between the surviving ideal of the autonomous governance of universities and inconsistent and basically contradictory bureaucratization. The entire Humboldtian university culture found itself in a similar position, in particular the once-famous German university.

---

385 Rüegg, *Geschichte*, III., pp. 104–107.

386 Doležalová, Antonie: Fiskální politika. In: Kubů, Eduard – Pátek, Jaroslav (red.): *Mýtus a realita hospodářské vyspělosti Československa mezi světovými válkami*. Prague 2000, pp. 24–40, here 34.

387 Fasora, Lukáš – Hanuš, Jiří: *Masarykova univerzita. Příběh vzdělání a vědy ve střední Evropě*. Brno 2009, pp. 60–86.

388 Urbášek, *Vysokoškolský vzdělávací systém*, p. 12.

The birth of academic capitalism

Between 1871 and 1914, German universities were the global benchmark – in the eyes of observers they came closest to the ideal of academic education. Many historians consider the "spread" of German universities and German science abroad as the most significant *soft power* of Wilhelmine Germany.[389] At that time, American universities, in particular the elite private schools, used German universities as their model.[390] During the first half of the 19th century, the USA was particularly influenced by the teaching methods at German universities, in particular from the humanities and philology. It was only a few decades later that they started to become interested in the methods of organizing research activities. What was important here, however, was that when looking for a model for a research university this did not apply to the German Humboldtian university in general, but almost exclusively to German technical and applied-science research – i.e. where investment produced fast and clear results.

On the other hand, neither research into the humanities or basic research in science and medicine was of any particular interest to the Americans. It was in the research disciplines adopted by the Americans that the managerial or capitalist way of perceiving universities was most thoroughly implemented. These disciplines had provided German science with its greatest successes at the world exhibitions in the USA (1876 in Philadelphia, 1893 in Chicago and 1904 in St Louis). And it was thanks to imitating and developing these European models, coupled with its excellent laboratories, that even before the First World War the USA had become the global frontrunner at the expense of Germany and Great Britain.[391] This opened the way for the development of "academic capitalism" as a result of the shift in influence within the global network of universities towards the USA. From the somewhat ridiculed periphery of the university system, America gradually became the model for the 20th century, and imitating it in other parts of the world became a mantra – even if a university was shaken by crises, paralysed by uncertainty and unable to find a way out from their problems – this would be a panacea for their troubles. Nevertheless, any outward adoption of the American model in Central Europe in the interwar period was done quietly and with some embarrassment. After 1945, it was done openly in Germany, and after 1989 it became a magic formula for a modern style of university management. The "American" style of university management legitimizes university dignitaries in their

389 Stern, Fritz: Deutschland um 1900 – und eine zweite Chance. In: Hardtwig, Wolfgang – Brandt, Harm–Hinrich (Hg.): *Deutschlands Weg in die Moderne*. Munich 1992, pp. 32–44, here p. 32.

390 Paulus, *Vorbild USA?*, pp. 44–65.

391 Röhrs, Hermann: *Einfluss der klasisschen deutschen Universitätsidee auf die Higher Education in Amerika*. Weinheim 1995, p. 93 ff.; Paulus, *Vorbild*, p. 46 ff.

functions and silences critics – such and such measures in the "American" style are necessary – just look at how high the famous American universities are in the rankings and where ours are! Stricter controls are needed in the name of improving efficiency! We might recall that the university accreditation system originally came from America. From 1819, the principle of freeing schools from state supervision was recognised, but it brought with it a great widening in the spectrum of curricula and varying levels of teaching quality, and as a result the accreditation system emerged "from below", with the support of the public, as a supervisory body overseeing the quality of education. Characteristically, however, there were large differences between the disciplines and an emphasis on vocationally focused curricula – the earliest from 1874 for the medical disciplines, law from 1890 and forestry from 1900.[392]

The use of the USA as a model was not confined to Germany in the period immediately after 1945 – contemporary Central European debates on university reform also reveal strong links to American models, particularly the elite private universities. Hundreds of others – often schools with very controversial reputations – are left out of the picture. Meanwhile, the picture of their management and financing is viewed reductively, omitting the fact that there are massive financial resources from the private sector behind the high quality of the top American schools, resources which for the foreseeable future will not be available to European universities, which are mainly financed by public sources. According to Sylvia Paletschek, in Germany the state financing of universities reached its peak in the 1990s,[393] and the situation has not changed since. Some figures might help to illustrate this shift from elite to mass education. When the Humboldtian (or "elite" in today's language) model was at its height, universities normally had between 2,000 and 5,000 students; in 1914 Berlin University was considered to be exceptionally large with 10,000 students. During this period a total of approximately 60,000 students studied at 21 German universities. In Austria, only the University of Vienna with its 9,000 students (1914) could compete with Berlin.[394] After 1960, the idea of mass universities began to take root in all European countries.[395] Today, the important public universities in Central Europe regularly have between 30,000 and 60,000 students. In 2017, Charles University had a total of 50,000 students, while Masaryk University had 35,000. In comparison, the prestigious private research universities such as Yale had some 16,000 students in 2017,

---

392 *Hodnocení kvality*, p. 30.

393 Paletschek, *Die permanente Erfindung*, p. 525.

394 Engelbrecht, *Geschichte*, p. 236.

395 Moraw, Peter: *Gesammelte Beiträge zur deutschen und europäischen Universitätsgeschichte. Strukturen – Personen – Entwicklung*. Leiden – Boston 2008, p. 365 ff.

Harvard 21,000 and Oxford 23,000.[396] From 1200 to 1900 the number of university students in Europe represented 1% of their population year, while in the countries of the OECD today, 30% to 80% of the population year are students.[397] Over recent years the pan-European trend in public tertiary education has been towards stagnation or even a reduction in state financial support, which does not correspond to the high number of students, while under the banner of academic capitalism the regulations have become increasingly strict for how the funds are used, with the attendant bureaucratic pressure.[398]

The confidence of Czech academic governance, undermined by the loss of control over university management, was dealt another blow by the concept of academic capitalism. The fact that universities are completely economically dependent on public financing has not yet dealt a killer blow because the state still provides resources. Although not much, it is enough to ensure the basic running of the university, while more importantly – the state does not demand a great deal in return. Although universities are involved in annual disputes with ministers over additions to the budgets, the state shows relatively little interest in how effectively these resources are used. With the change in the political climate and growing pressure from the public for a managerial method of running the state, three exceptionally important themes have cropped up in the negotiations between Czech universities and the state authorities, symbolizing the allegedly uneconomic use of public funds: the large number of students prematurely abandoning their studies; the high percentage of graduates with poor prospects on the labour market; and research activity aimed at accumulating knowledge without any practical application.

Academic capitalism is an answer to these incongruities. It stresses the need to increase the efficiency of university methods, but does not take into account the specific characteristics of university governance and management, and basically administers universities using the same tools as any other commercial enterprise, or the same way as private universities have been managed over the years.

The changes in academic identity were indicated by the contrasting answers in a questionnaire which was based on a humorous idea by Stefan Collini[399]:

---

396 https://www.yale.edu/about–yale/yale–facts; https://www.ox.ac.uk/about/facts–and–figures/student–numbers?wssl=1; http://www.harvard.edu/media–relations/media–resources/quick–facts (29. 6. 2017).

397 Schofer, Evan – Meyer John W.: *The Worldwide Expansion of Higher Education in the Twentieth Century*. American sociological Review 70, 2005, pp. 898–920.

398 vom Brocke, *Wege*, pp. 208–210.

399 Collini, Stefan: *What are universities for?* London 2012, pp. 132–133.

Your profession?	I work in human resources and research	I am a university teacher.
Your institution's specialization ?	We produce highly qualified workers and highly useful and accessible scientific knowledge	I teach students and write books.
Your position in the institution?	I have a middle-management position, directly accountable to the managing executive	I am part of a large community of scholars; I fulfil certain administrative tasks and can influence the running of the school through elections, as the members of the board are elected from amongst my colleagues
Condition of the firm?	In recent years we have achieved a solid year-on-year growth of around 5%, we managed to increase our work efficiency by 3%	I feel that the amount and quality of teaching has worsened over the past twenty years, as we don't have enough time to complete our tasks to the same level as before
Global position?	Outstanding. Our brand has established itself on the global market and there is a high evaluation of our firm on the ratings ladders	Hm... we are a Czech university...we're trying to improve our international standing, so far we've been successful mainly with Slovaks.
Company motto?	Global quality for a good price	We don't have a motto.

In praise of academic capitalism

Advocates of the theory of academic capitalism argue that it is strongly modernist, progressive, centralist, superior from a material viewpoint and very technocratic. Their view is strongly focused on the present and predictions for the future, while the historical aspects of the tradition of university administration and culture of decision-making are trivialized, or even completely ignored. In the Czech Republic this discourse began to appear in the mid-1990s, when it was part of the official programme for catching up with the advanced nations – i.e. a search to find a way to modernize local universities by simply adapting to the universities of the West, which were interpreted generally and slightly naively as cultural models.[400] Today,

400 Hendrichová, Jana – Čerych, Ladislav et al.: *Terciární vzdělávání ve vyspělých zemích: vývoj a současnost.* Prague 1997, p. 90.

in comparison with countries from Western Europe and the USA, the Czech debate on the theory of academic capitalism is less intensive, occasionally based on sociological research, but strongly technocratic due to the absence of research into any cultural-historical context.[401] It is precisely the technocratism and economism, characterized by an ignorant or even contemptuously negative attitude of the historical context of running a university, which is grist to the mill for critics of academic capitalism, and the primary cause for academia dividing into two camps – the supporters and opponents of the new system of decision-making, where both employ mythical narratives to legitimize their positions.

The basic ideological application of the theory of academic capitalism consists of general scepticism towards the ability of history to speak to the present, the conviction that the various historicizing mythical defence narratives within the academic community merely serve to block a progressive programme while preserving redundant and hopelessly backward university principles and traditions. Their anti-historical scepticism is often justified and their arguments in this regard are convincing to many people. In addition, the theory of change management, which is also applied to universities, is able to skilfully prepare its proponents for any critical responses, providing them with a whole series of tools from various fields of science aimed at overcoming any initial shock and confusion which the proposals might cause amongst the public; from rational, albeit sceptical acceptance, to emotional acceptance, and finally to integrating the community into the vision.[402] Critics of academic capitalism do not have such sophisticated tools and alternative visions of progress, and clearly never will. It is little wonder that the managers of universities who are loyal to this vision of academic capitalism are surrounded by professionals from change management – it is thanks to them that this vision can be implemented, even if at the initial stages of the process fewer than 10% of the academic community are convinced it is the right path, while within the disciplines it is difficult to find any supporters. The administrative character of decision-making is formally maintained, the tradition of the university does not suffer any harm. But on the road towards decision-making, two camps meet and come into conflict: in the first fragmented and disunited camp is a victory for basically unclear, rather emotionally based doubts about developments based on the complex overlapping and clash of departmental, faculty and university identities and interests; influential academics from this camp have doubts which are usually supported by a wealth of experience. And alongside them, or rather opposite them, are the precisely focused psychological, sociological and managerial competencies of a phalange of workers from the rectorate and other

---

401 Závada, Jiří et al.: „Benchmarking" v hodnocení kvality vysokých škol. Aula 14/2006, special edition, pp. 83–96; Vinš, Václav et al.: Vnitřní hodnocení na vysokých školách. Analýza výročních zpráv a dlouhodobých záměrů vysokých škol, ibid, pp. 61–82; Prudký – Pabian – Šima, České vysoké školství, p. 79.

402 Wehrlin, Ulrich: Hochschul Change–Management. Göttingen 2014², pp. 46–54.

central departments, freed from doubts thanks to their unambiguously defined university identity, as well as the directness and rapacity of youth.

Let us look more closely at the three central arguments from the "optimists' camp":

a) *Academic capitalism is an inevitable consequence of globalization and technological developments and the way in which science and research are linked to these processes*

Economic globalization is seen as an unstoppable process, bringing the conceptualization of science into a transnational framework.[403] Additionally, according to this theory, faced with globalization, the university will have to fundamentally redefine its relationship with the social and political environment.[404]

Mark Taylor, a professor of religion at Columbia University, predicted that by 2020 the study of this discipline would be very heavily influenced by the global choice of universities and digitalization. Students, who have been used to spending much of their time online with their "circles of friends" from across the world since childhood, will see it as completely natural to study online, to have e-learning, and to combine the skills and information gained at university with those from the virtual world. It will be entirely natural to put this theoretical knowledge into practice on a global scale, and students will be able to decide for themselves the length, type and financial cost of study. Symptomatically, Taylor mentions the astonishment and uncertainty that students' parents will face as a result of this type of study, particularly those from small-town mid-west America. However, they will have little choice when faced with the unavoidable changes brought about by new technologies.[405]

This represents a widely used, convincing, but at the same time, very contentious set of arguments. Those who use them have the advantage of the indisputable developments in new digital technologies and their gradual impact on practically all areas of life in the advanced world. It is difficult to find any opposition to the need for universities to utilize the new technological trends, and it is precisely at this point that the credibility of all critics of academic capitalism is lost. At the university in Brno there have also been on-going debates about the need to gradually digitalize all systems since 1979 – at first it was the agenda of the admissions system, then personnel, then later the allocation of student accommodation; since

---

403 Slaughter, Sheila – Leslie, Larry: *Academic Capitalism. Politics, Policies, and the Entrepreneurial University*. Baltimore 1997, pp. 31.

404 Kauppinen, Ilkka: *Towards transnational academic capitalism*. Higher Education, Vol. 64, No. 4 (October 2012), pp. 543–556, here p. 545.

405 Taylor, *Crisis*, pp. 218–221.

1995 the development of digital technology has been one of the decisive factors in the further development of the university.[406]

The theory of globalization as a driving force has another two weak points, stemming from the concept of globalization as a process which brings advantages to one and all; the older, simplified win-win interpretation of globalization has been shown to be untenable in the light of the financial crisis of 2008 and increasing inequality, and requires new, more in-depth analyses.[407] In the Czech, Central and East European academic environment, the greatest concerns are about the "brain drain" and the so-called scientific imperialism of Western European and American universities and research institutes.[408] Even in the Anglophone centre of the global university network there have been strong voices stressing the university more as a national and regional, rather than global institute, especially in relation to its teaching mission.[409] It fulfils the function of an important regional employer, an organiser of significant national and regional events, it is a constructor and important actor in the creation of the city's public space, it is a taxpayer and a member of numerous consortia of regional institutions.[410]

And the same applies to two additions to the theory of globalization as a driving force. Firstly, that the Western European left-wing idea about the imminent demise of nation states, the role of which would be transferred to transnational organizations, and the approaching triumph of "global thinking",[411]has been shown to be a chimera in the context of political developments in Europe and the USA since roughly 2005 (the referendum on a European constitution in France, identity and isolationist movements in many countries). This applies to the countries of the Visegrád Four (the Czech Republic, Poland, Hungary, Slovakia) more than anywhere else in Europe. And then there is academic capitalism and the role of the humanities and social sciences. Their research results are seldom commercially viable, any global comparisons are difficult to measure due to their ter-

406 Archive MU, A6 Science Faculty, box 4 (Automated systems).

407 Milanovic, Branko: *Global Income Inequality by the Numbers*. Global Policy Volume 4. Issue 2 . May 2013, pp. 198–208.

408 Hryniewicz, Janusz – Jałowiecki, Bohdan – Mync, Agnieszka: *Ucieczka mózgów ze szkolnictwa wyższego i nauki. The Brain Drain in Poland. Regional and Local Studies*. Warsaw 1992; https://financialobserver. eu/cse-and-cis/serbia/serbia-experiencing-health-sector-brain-drain/ (2.1. 2018).

409 Gibbons, Michael: A Commonwealth perspective on the globalisation of higher education, In: Scott, Peter (ed.): *The Globalisation of Higher Education*. Philadelphia (PA) 1998, pp. 70–87.

410 Spoun, Sascha – Seyfarth, Felix C.: Die Vetreibung aus dem Elfenbeinturm: Sebstverständnis, Attraktivität und Wettbewerb deutscher Universität nach Bologna. In: Jamme, Christoph – Schröder, Asta von (Hg.): *Einsamkeit und Freiheit. Zum Bildungsauftrag der Universität im 21. Jahrhundert*. Munich 2011, pp. 193–220, here p. 201.

411 Kauppinen, Ilkka: *Towards transnational academic capitalism*. Higher Education, Vol. 64, No. 4 (October 2012), pp. 543–556.

ritorial limitations, while they also respond to new technological innovations with reservation and strong cultural scepticism.[412]

b) *University governance is marked by outdated and historically discredited forms of organization which restrict free competition in education and research.*

This is corporativism and governance expressed using professional or statist principles, previously known as guilds. The unsustainability of this form is demonstrated through the reliance on state regulation, and its supporters are those members of the academic community whose quality of teaching and research is not competitive in an international or global context.[413] The enclosed nature of academic bodies and their antipathy towards integrating outsiders is a blind alley for scientific progress, preventing many universities from becoming part of the international network of university education. So-called academic inbreeding (building a career only in the school where the academic studied)[414] characterizes the tendency for creating a group of researchers around a professor made up exclusively of his own pupils, whose academic career is pursued exclusively at their alma mater and no attempt is made to acquire long-term work experience abroad or in other more local universities. In the Czech Republic and Central Europe this is exacerbated by the language barrier, limiting the integration of foreigners into the work collective. A very effective way for regulating attempts at bringing in outside staff into Central European universities is the salary conditions, which discourage academics from Western Europe and the USA. The supporters of academic capitalism tend to belittle these two problems, and usually point to the natural or technical sciences, where due to the predominance of an Anglophonic culture, internationalization is easier and it is possible to receive (temporarily) a higher income thanks to European structural funds.

In the eyes of the optimists, the strength of academic capitalism is in dealing with that aspect of academic governance which is blatantly dysfunctional – the heads of individual institutions. If the professor/head of an institution avoids provoking the senior academic bodies with catastrophic cases of mismanagement, and if the person is not completely unproductive in the field of research, then their position is assured. They can build a clientelist network with their subordinates, who repeatedly elect them to their function in return for guaranteed security, i.e. overlooking or playing down obvious long-term failings in their research or managerial and teaching work. Within this power network, the institution usually perceives the outside world – the faculty and university leadership of

412 *Hodnocení kvality*, p. 30.

413 Rhoades, Gary – Slaughter, Sheila: *Academic Capitalism, Managed Professionals, and Supply–Side Higher Education*, Social Text, No. 51, Academic Labor (Summer, 1997), pp. 9–38, here p. 34.

414 Pabian – Prudký – Šima, *České vysoké školství*, p. 73.

other institutions – as latent enemies disturbing the status quo. If a university's decision-making process is based on models from the public or non-governmental sectors, then this closed-off world will remain undisturbed. Any intervention by the dean into the often poor conditions of the institution is incompatible with the institutional culture, and as a result, intervention is highly improbable; one exception is the clear bankruptcy of a department due to a lack of students or research outputs. A statutory body's decision to close down a team due to unconvincing research results is standard in the Czech Republic in some of the central university departments or at specialist research university centres, but not at faculties with their autonomous decision-making and often long traditions of existence.[415] With its instruments of evaluation and economism, academic capitalism might change the institutional culture to the extent that any steps taken by the dean or rector away from isolationism will not be viewed negatively by the academic community, but as the normal reaction of a crisis manager.

> c) *Academic capitalism introduces new ideas and fresh air into the conservative climate of the university, where the old dichotomies and conflict lines lie petrified, little understood by anyone outside of academia*

Public universities take the positives from the management practices of commercial institutions, including private universities, while discarding the negative habits from the non-private, regulated sector, especially some of the relics of customary law.[416] The driving force for change will be the change in students' mentality – from being a consumer of education, they will become a customer who plays a far more important role in determining the form of the educational process. A similarly optimistic view of academic capitalism is held by the stakeholders, i.e. all of the external actors in a university's educational and research work. For a university to be accommodating in its approach towards its "customers", it is necessary to standardize the products on offer, which is provided by quality control mechanisms (Total Quality Management – TQM).[417]

This will lead to dialectically surmounting the conflict between the interests of the individual faculties and disciplines, where into one melting point will be combined the interest groups of the academic community, whose strategy will be to bet on market mechanisms, including those which rely on regulation. University autonomy thus gains new meaning through its responsibility for the school within the market relationships in education and research; the old clientelist system of professors and lecturers loses its raison d'être, there will be an end to certain

---

415 https://www.ceitec.cz/evaluace/t1133 (20.12. 2017)

416 Vondrák, Ivo: *Proč zavádět systém managementu jakosti na univerzitní pracoviště*. AULA, year 13, 03 / 2005, pp. 26–31, here p. 26.

417 Rhoades – Slaughter, *Academic Capitalism*, p. 14.

academics and disciplines leeching off public budgets, the work of the university will gain new meaning – for academics themselves, but particularly for all of the external actors connected to university work and also for the taxpayer.[418]

The arguments of academic capitalism's supporters are not usually as ideologically restricted and technocratic as their opponents suggest. They recognize that the application of academic capitalism and TQM in public universities with long traditions and deeply embedded institutional cultures cannot be an imperative – it has to progress step by step, taking into consideration the specific missions of each section of a university.[419] In the discourse, academic capitalism is usually seen as being affiliated to a specific circle in academic culture, whilst the Humboldtian university is usually regarded as the most traditionalist in a global comparison. Here, more than anywhere else, it is necessary to respect the fact that the components of a university have different goals and ways of achieving them. It is not an "industry" in the narrow sense of the word as it revolves around working with people, and so each university has to carefully examine the TQM path with regard to its appropriateness and effectiveness. It is necessary to always take into account the motivated participation of the academic public in the entire transformational process of the university, and minimize any approaches which might be considered authoritarian, centralist or overly hasty. Close contact has to be maintained with the managerial and expert (i.e. professorial) bodies to prevent alienating the two groups, which is a *conditio sine qua non* for the university's successful overall transformation. In their enthusiasm for change, the leadership of each university has to progress very sensitively, as universities are institutions which are very vulnerable to political, technological, economic and social changes. In particular, the academic community's cohesion is paramount, and it is necessary to use democratic forms in decision-making to continually renew the consensus regarding any changes and the ways in which they are brought about.[420] The specific paths towards the selective and successful application of academic capitalism have been documented in numerous university case studies, for example, at the Vienna Wirtschaftsuniversität.[421]

---

418 Ibid, p. 16.

419 Sporn, Barabara: *Managing University Culture: An Analysis of the Relationship between Institutional Culture and Management Approaches.* Higher Education, Vol. 32, No. 1 (Jul., 1996), pp. 41–61; Rhoades, Gary: *Capitalism, Academic Style, and Shared Governance.* Academe, Vol. 91, No. 3 (May – Jun., 2005), pp. 38–42.

420 Ibid, pp. 42–43.

421 Ibid, pp. 48–51; Yokohama, Keiko: *Entrepreneurialism in Japanese and UK Universities: Governance, Management, Leadership, and Funding.* Higher Education, Vol. 52, No. 3 (Oct., 2006), pp. 523–555; Tuunainen, Juha: *Hybrid Practices? Contributions to the Debate on the Mutation of Science and University.* Higher Education, Vol. 50, No. 2 (Sep., 2005), pp. 275–298.

Criticisms of academic capitalism

Who are the critics of academic capitalism? They tend to be people who are connected by their shared negative impression of the changes in universities in recent years, rather than people who have a similar type of academic career or social background. In their eyes, the university today has suffered from a type of social dethronement, which *pars pro toto* also applies to the position of teachers. It is painful for them to accept the loss of public trust in universities, as a result of which they have to permanently struggle for media attention and persuade politicians and grant agencies of the relevancy of their research. There is also the uncertainty of generational experience, as most of the academics who have influence in today's universities were students at a time when the situation was dramatically different. And there is also real trauma resulting from the cases of academics' drastic ethical failings[422] – in a Czech context, the turning point was a scandal at the Law Faculty of the West Bohemian University in 2009 surrounding plagiarism and the sale of titles to people from the business sector, public administration and politics.[423] There is a similar view of academic titles from certain Slovak universities, as well as of the unduly high financial payments which academic functionaries have been awarding themselves.[424] Academics from traditional universities are particularly sensitive to the presence of numerous new universities and private higher-education institutions, which have made the university landscape more incomprehensible and untrustworthy for the general public.

Critics of academic capitalism have developed a distinctive mythical discourse. It is based on an awareness of the university in crisis, and an almost desperate hope of finding a way out – at the same time, though, there is scepticism towards the methods of addressing the problems offered by the apologists of academic capitalism. This pessimistic discourse is characterized by a disrespect for managerial practices and digitalizing technocratism, which are rejected as absurd and fundamentally flawed due to their separation from any historical context. As part of this discourse, the university has a right to deferential treatment and a place outside of TQM solely because it is *per se* a university – an institution which has signed up to the truth, with pure science as the way of achieving it, an institution with a strong ethical mission, unlike any TQM or change-management.

---

422 Seyfarth – Spoun, *Die Vertreibung*, p. 197.

423 https://zpravy.idnes.cz/kvuli-plzenskym-pravum-se-poprve-sejde-komise-titul-zatim-ode-bran-nebyl-14s-/domaci.aspx?c=A100626_171702_studium_jan (21.12. 2017)

424 https://archiv.ihned.cz/c1-64640160-slovenska-vysoka-skola-danubius-uz-nesmi-rozdavat-doktorske-tituly-doktorat-z-ni-ma-i-hejtman-hasek (21.12. 2017); https://www.lidovky.cz/super-plat-dekanky-na-dotaz-na-neumerne-vysoke-odmeny-jsem-odpoved-nedostal-rika-byvaly-rek-tor-iga-/zpravy-domov.aspx?c=A180323_115043_ln_domov_mpr (23.3. 2018).

This obvious distance, bordering on contempt, from the principles of managerism, from economic rules and their political connotations, is what binds these critics together, but which at the same time is their greatest weakness. The absence of economic and political aspects to their thinking prevents the creation of a plausible alternative theory to academic capitalism, which is very strong precisely in these points. Therefore, the arguments of its critics are inconsistent and are unable to respond to a number of serious questions. It is the apologetic idealization of a Humboldtian golden era, the epoch of the elite university which disappeared without trace when it stopped fulfilling its social function. In this idealization of university history, the mythic narrative of the "pessimists" is often strongly manipulative and reductive concerning the important historical context of how the Humboldtian model operated, similar to the arguments of the supporters of academic capitalism. The difference, however, is in the language – the pessimistic myth is accompanied by as rich a language as the intellectuals can muster to reflect the fact that this discourse has a distinctly intellectual character and is connected mainly to the humanities. It differs from the optimistic mythical narrative, which likes to use numbers and graphs; the frequent Englishisms of the optimists contrasts with the ostentatious use of Latin and the Romance languages in the pessimistic narrative – but neither one is a condition of trustworthiness – the manipulative aims of both groups of narrators are quite obvious here.

Despite the fact that the critical narrative is incoherent and often not particularly trustworthy, it still has value. Although it does not provide an alternative to academic capitalism, it does offer food for critical thought and for doubting the wisdom of the paths that universities have blindly embarked on in recent years. There is variable quality in these disquieting ideas. Some of them point to the failings of academic capitalism ad hoc, while others doubt the entire system and the ethical aspects of its operation and objectives.

Examples of ad hoc criticism include cases of the failure of internationalization programmes, which touch more upon areas of science which are demanding in terms of language competency and territorial and cultural links. The cases of foreign "flying professors" – symbols of the modern struggle with academic inbreeding, who take advantage of short-term high salaries but do not become part of the environment or the collective, and after a while change their workplace in search of a better career and even higher salary (often to the annoyance of the other team members) – are definitely arguments to be welcomed. One Austrian critic of academic capitalism, Konrad Liessmann, is also critical of the overuse of English in academia, where it has indeed become the lingua franca. In itself this phenomenon is usually seen positively, but Liessmann views the situation through the prism of the humanities, which draw upon their legitimacy from a linguistic and cultural plurality that is being damaged by the insensitive dominance of English.[425] Liessman offered a compelling, albeit absurd case, when he presented the career path of Immanuel Kant as being completely at odds with today's contemporary academic evaluations. As is well known, Kant never left his home town of Königsberg, but in spite of this he was awarded a definitive professorship, which TQM would define today as typical of academic inbreeding. Immediately after this appointment he more or less stopped publishing and only wrote two newspaper articles over ten years. According to Liessmann, today he would *"have to answer for his lack of effort and ineffective research work. At the very least he would have been placed into an innovative and interdisciplinary minded research project."* At that time, of course, he was a dean and had several other functions, but it was also then that he came up with his Critique of Pure Reason. And when it was finally published, the scientific community – along with the peer-review incantations of today's scientometrics and TQM – ignored it and even ridiculed it as a work which was *"unintelligible, too complex, not aimed at the user, therefore useless."*[426]

But it is precisely with Liessmann's theory of miseducation, so popular in the circles of sceptical judges of the present state of higher education, that it is easy to see some ad hoc critical arguments develop into a deeper critique. Liessmann unmasks the allegedly beneficial motives of TQM as an untrustworthy veil covering the real motives – among them is the unacknowledged unwillingness of a large part of society, represented by the head of state, to financially support the university as a provider of abstract knowledge, the practical use of which is hard to define, rather than support the university as a buttress for the cultivation of society and the development of critical thought, which leads to the abstract values of freedom and democracy. Those who uncritically stand by the principles of TQM and academic capitalism do not like to admit that the basic source of its legitimacy is by making savings in resources aimed at higher education. The development of economic management in American universities was the direct result of a reduction in public spending as a consequence of the economic turmoil in 1973, and savings made by Ronald Reagan's administration in the 1980s.[427] Savings, savings...according to Liessmann, this is the true objective behind the interference in institutions, fields of study, other educational and research workplaces, or the movement of finance to places which in the future can expect higher places in the rankings.[428] All other arguments are merely smokescreens.

A favourite target of critics is the ratings mania of the university heads, rushing around worrying about movement in the Shanghai rankings; and every critic is

---

425 Liessmann, *Teorie nevzdělanosti*, p. 91.

426 Liessmann, *Teorie nevzdělanosti*, pp. 62–63.

427 Bok, Derek: *Universities in the Marketplace. The Commercialization of Higher Education*. Princeton 2003, pp. 8–13.

428 Liessmann, *Teorie nevzdělanosti*, p. 60.

capable of collecting a great deal of evidence on the absurdity of such behaviour and the low evidential value of similar measurements.[429] Here the arguments have their global as well as national dimension, and familiarize readers with the problem of evidence in the life of an academic. For example, in the Czech university landscape any drop in the quality of teaching or research at Charles University could never reach such a level that it would endanger the position of the school in the elite national rankings or even the existence of the school as such. This is also true for its visibility on the international stage, where the attractiveness of Prague as a tourist destination, its cultural variety and transport accessibility, will always be important for the exchange of academics and "internationalization". It is unimaginable in the Czech Republic, Germany, Austria or Poland that they would close down universities which had founding charters dating back to the Middle Ages and whose notable previous research successes include a Noble Prize – albeit from the more distant past. Even if they have not been able to capitalize on that success in the subsequent fifty years, it is still produced as a tool of visibility for the local and international public. Neither is it important that some Nobel Prize winners were only loosely associated with a particular university, perhaps even controversially – one example is the sharing of the Noble Prize for polarography (1959), awarded to Jaroslav Heyrovský, between the Czech Republic Academy of Sciences and Charles University – or the assumption of awards from the German section of Charles University by the Czech part. The political rules of visibility are written into university culture to the extent that universities a priori belong to a group of elite, and in many respects, untouchable schools, which would be considered too new in Western Europe, having barely celebrated the centenary of their foundation.

Another strand of the argument points to the pitfalls of applied research being financed at universities by private sources. Here there is no clear evidential value concerning any of the problematic forms of cooperation in relation to the entire enormous sector, but the argument resonates effectively due to people's deep mistrust of capitalism in the Czech Republic and Central Europe. We can only speculate on how the public would react to symbols linking the commercial sector and universities – in the USA, after the initial shock, the public has grown accustomed to such things as the introduction of the *K-Mart Professor of Marketing* or the *Yahoo Professor of Computer Science*.[430] In his book *Bought Research*, Christian Kreiß presents dozens of cases of ethically dubious research projects procured by the well-known sharks of global capitalism (so-called contract research), in par-

---

429 Münch, Richard: *Akademischer Kapitalismus. Zur politischen Ökonomie der Hochschulreform.* Berlin 2011, pp. 53–67.

430 Bok, *Universities*, p. 2.

ticular by the tobacco, food, chemical and pharmaceutical industries.[431] Sections of the Czech public are especially interested in the connection between research and the powerful oligarchical institutions with clear political ambitions (Agrofert, PPF). However, manipulation of research on their part has not been proven either in court or by the ruling of a university ethical commission or similar body, without which it would be impossible to imagine the effective legislative regulation which Kreiß proposes in his book.[432] In Czech academia there is a precedent from Masaryk University in Brno, where attempts by the university management and the Law Faculty to cooperate more closely with the Energy and Industry Holding of Daniel Křetínský, a graduate of the university, came up against objections from the faculty's Academic Senate. Regarding the establishment of a joint research centre (the Institute of Energy Studies), the senate argued that there was a lack of regulation to prevent the work of the faculty being subordinated to the interests of a private subject, particularly in the situation where research results negatively affected his interests.[433] On one side of the debate on similar cooperation is the argument about the need to bring academia closer to the commercial sector, on the other is the concern that this will lead to a decline in the credibility of public institutions and their research, which has already been viewed anxiously by many experts, particularly in sociological and political research. This topic receives relatively little attention in the mainstream media (owned in the Czech Republic by the captains of industry) or in the academic press, though it is a frequently discussed subject on social media, and the subject of unfounded or partially founded rumours and myth.[434]

The most sophisticated of these arguments concerns the normalization of science through mechanically applied scientometrics in the service of academic capitalism. The hunt for the impact factor and various forms of *peer-review journal articles* places the monopolization of strategic decision-making for the future direction of research into the hands of a few institutions and their governing academic coterie. A frequent subject is the proven or, more often, perceived profiles of various "citation mafia" made up mainly of Anglophonic academics from the leading global universities. Room for independent research, sometimes truly creative and original in its approaches, has dramatically shrunk over recent years with this normalizing system. This understandably applies more to sciences with a global reach, where scientometrics has become much more embedded, than in

---

431 Kreiß, Christian: *Gekaufte Forschung. Wissenschaft im Dienst der Konzerne*. Berlin – Munich – Vienna 2015, esp. pp. 21–81.

432 Ibid, pp. 175–183.

433 https://brno.idnes.cz/daniel-kretinsky-pravnicka-fakulta-masarykovy-univerzity-poh-/brno-zpravy.aspx?c=A180207_381505_brno-zpravy_dh (8.2. 2018)

434 http://www.ceskatelevize.cz/ct24/nazory/1368357-byznys-a-pruzkum-verejneho-mineni; https://technet.idnes.cz/volebni-pruzkumy-0zx-/veda.aspx?c=A131016_152300_veda_pka (20. 12. 2017).

the humanities. And the fact that criticism of this "scientific imperialism" often has anti-American political connotations is of secondary importance here.

In his unique work on the state of Austrian higher education, Christian Badelt considers the impact of academic capitalism on labour-law relationships in universities and on the employment culture in general. He claims that the introduction of TQM and commercialization has shifted competencies to a higher level, i.e. from individual academics to the department heads, and from there to the deans and rectors. In his view, the identity of a subject or faculty becomes lost within an identity bound to the university. An academic has to become used to an entirely new way of handling resources – the school will be able to get rid of unused space or people much more flexibly than before. The academic community will have to become accustomed to the very noticeable reaction of their superiors to any mistakes in their teaching or research work, including the termination of employment, closing down a research team, etc. And the new atmosphere is also apparent in the relationships between universities and research teams. Brno academics will start to view their counterparts at Charles University much more as competitors than the colleagues with whom they have sat together on academic committees or collaborated on projects. According to Badelt, the entrepreneurial university is both a challenge and – in the light of these briefly outlined problems – *contradictio in adjecto*.[435]

Conclusion

Public pressure and a decline in prestige have forced Czech and Central European universities to become part of public debates, often highly political and ideological, and make themselves accountable for the way in which they invest public money. The academic community has thus found itself in an onerous position as this change in the public perception of universities threatens the illusion of their loftiness, created by even the smallest, newest and most obscure universities, who use the name to suggest membership of the ancient tradition of the *universitas* and a superior global network of knowledge.

The clash of these two mythical narratives lies at the heart of the struggle for the very identity of the university itself, and it is particularly interesting because it is occurring in universities almost every day – i.e. in relation to clarifying opinions concerning the immensely important and also controversial issues of decision-making competencies, forms of control and evaluation, and the possibilities and limitations of the university's response to undertakings devised by external actors

---

435 Badelt, Christian: *Die unternehmerische Universität: Herausforderung oder Widerspruch in sich?* Vienna 2004, pp. 30–40.

or stakeholders. From the viewpoint of the critics of academic capitalism, it is a matter of the proverbial cogwheel, which turns quickly here, slowly there, but in each case, tooth by tooth, inevitably brings the university closer to its new unloved role. Every interaction with the commercial sector is viewed as a Faustian pact by some sections of the university community.[436] With the economization of its operation, the university loses the rest of its identity as a multipurpose, non-political and independent expert, and becomes just one more hungry mouth to be fed by the taxpayers. And there are more links in this causal chain: if a university is no longer an independent arbiter and expert – or at the very least is not accepted in this role by a significant part of the public – then it can hardly be surprised when opposition forces stand up against it, calling for a reduction in its budget, always of course with arguments about higher work efficiency, the social relevance of its work, avoiding waste, etc. The narrators of the academic-capitalist myth tell their story with this as their defence, while the more sophisticated of them use it as an apology – by introducing TQM they are only trying to protect the university from the more drastic aspects of economism, the supporters of which would *never* take university tradition into account.[437] The only alternative, after all, is the privatization of university education, as they have done in the USA. With the growing importance of private sources of finance, the top public schools (University of Michigan, University of Virginia) have become de facto private or semi-private – without taxpayers even seeming to notice.[438] A similar trend in Czech and Central European education, whether directed or not, is very unlikely. What is more likely is that the state will increase its supervision to the extent that the university will be managed like a company, and the state will no longer fund the "non-productive" parts to the same extent as before. In 2017 with the formation of Andrej Babiš's government – the man behind the vision of "to run the state like a company" – the academic environment might come closer to this concept than we at present suspect.[439]

The theme of a noble and distinguished independence – the ivory towers – has been part of the university's mission since the Middle Ages. It was only in the 19th century that this idiom was used as a symbol of the arrogance of universities which had turned away from social reality and the world. In the 12th century, however, this idea was embedded in the mission of the first universities, that it was preparation for *healing the world*. It was about sparing a young person who was

---

436 Bok, *Universities*, p. 200.

437 Nantl, Jiří: *Mechanismus tvorby vůle orgánů univerzity. (Podmínky jejich legitimity a efektivity)*, In: Historie, současný stav a perspektivy univerzity, pp. 54–60, p. 57.

438 https://www.chronicle.com/blogs/innovations/the–privatization–of–state–universities–it–makes–sense/31744 (20.12. 2017).

439 https://www.parlamentnilisty.cz/politika/politici–volicum/Babis–ANO–Ridit–stat–jako–firmu–A–proc–ne–499512 (20.12. 2017).

the hope for a better tomorrow and the world, allowing him time to mature so he can carry out his task.[440] And despite many years of continued criticism, this idea is still a strong part of the identity of university communities, which like to stylize themselves as islands of positive values in a society convulsed by controversy and unease due to pessimistic visions of the future. The old issue of the mutual compatibility of the world of finance and the world of noble goals receives a new form here, this time the issue of the (level of) compatibility between capitalism and democracy.

For critics, a key role is held by the academic senates, which are seen as a symbol of the main defence of university governance. As the voice of the academic community it is expected that the senate will come up with ways to thwart the machinations of academic capitalism. The strong position of the academic senates and the privileged position of students within them was viewed in Czechoslovakia at the start of the 1990s as fulfilling one of the key demands of the revolution in 1989, the driving force of which was the students. Some universities and faculties, in particular Charles University, used the legal means at their disposal to grant students the maximum representation in the academic senates, which approaches 50% of the mandates.[441] Thus in practice the students have a significant say in the running of the faculty; the level of the constructive policy of the senate, though, is highly dependent on individual senators. A handful of people with great (political) ambitions, with complicated personal relationships with their colleagues and no small level of exhibitionism can seriously disrupt the relationship between the heads of the faculty and the senate. The authority and legitimacy of Czech university senates has been inadequate for a long time now, the electoral participation in the students' chamber is often in single percentage figures, while in the chamber of the academic employees there is the usual problem of finding trustworthy candidates. The meetings at the university administration committees are filled with arguments and formalities.[442]

The problems with the legitimacy of the senates are too great to be able to fulfil their mythical role as defenders of academia. They stem from democratic limits, in particular the failure to respect the rule of *one person – one vote*, particularly in the case of student representation. A more serious problem is that the members of the senate are rarely the more senior academics, people who have experience and have some scientific or pedagogical renown; they normally feel overburdened with work and show no interest in a senator's post.[443] As a result, during the election of a dean or rector, the professors and senior lecturers nerv-

---

440 Rüegg, *Geschichte*, IV., pp. 32–33.

441 https://web.natur.cuni.cz/student/studentska–komora–akademickeho–senatu–prf (31.3. 2018)

442 Rodriguez–Moura, Enrique: *Freiheit und Macht an der Universität*. Berlin 2016, pp. 59–71.

443 Vanderziel, Jeffrey: *Senát hájí zájmy univerzity*. MUNI, December 2017, p. 12.

ously watch the election determined by the votes of students and lecturers.[444] And finally there is also the divergence in interests of the university senate and the faculty senates, which is reflected in the differences in the interests of departments and disciplines, and the complex mergers and struggles within the identity of each academic in terms of the department, faculty and university.[445]

In the struggle with their opponents, critics of academic capitalism and change management usually lose their position step by step. This is even the case in those clashes where they have more powerful arguments, and the modernism, centralism and progressivism of the exponents of academic capitalism and TQM are shown to be primarily ideological tools for the overall economization of decision-making in universities and society as a whole, with very unpredictable and potentially very risky consequences for people and society. Critics of academic capitalism lose out in their arguments because they are unable to combine a vision of academic governance and the value of social responsibility, and thus present a complex and trustworthy alternative for the decision-making mechanisms in university against TQM, which can respond with a simple truth: by representing taxpayers, the state has the right to oversee the public investment into higher education.[446]

A section of academia uses the myth of the right to a special style of management and the grave danger posed by academic capitalism as a defence mechanism against the uncertainty of following through the implications of their own dependence on state funding to their logical conclusion. By using some historical examples – usually somewhat misinterpreted – they talk about the university as a black box where public money pours into, but it is impossible to find out what society actually derives from the university.[447] This section of academia is basically satisfied with the present system of financing Czech higher education. Although the resources provided are modest, the supply is somewhat unstable and is accompanied by degrading procedures, as a result of the absence of thorough supervisory mechanisms, when the advantages and disadvantages are weighed up, the situation is actually quite acceptable. The myth is a product of the uncertainty of one's role: the university, or more precisely, those departments which are completely reliant on state financing, find themselves in the precarious situation of consumers of public resources, which relativizes the value of public control over their activities, and at the same time, portray themselves as the guardian and beacon of democratic principles, but one of which – the flow of public money supervised by representatives of the taxpayer – has been in existence for a long time.

---

444 http://ceskapozice.lidovky.cz/akademicka–samosprava–musi–byt–stavovska–nikoli–demokraticka–p6q–/tema.aspx?c=A160623_165535_pozice–tema_lube (6. 1. 2018)

445 Nantl, *Mechanismus*, p. 57.

446 Watrin, Christian: *Studenten, Professoren und Steuerzahler. Die Gruppenuniversität in ökonomischer Sicht*. München 1979, pp. 29–34.

447 *Hodnocení kvality*, pp. 7–8.

THE MYTH OF TERRITORY

In 1691 the Jena scholar Caspar Sagittarius was searching for the answer to the question of what the university meant for the town and what the town meant for the university. He initially focused on calculating the economic benefits, highlighting the volume of work which scholars provided for Jena's shoemakers and washhouses, but gradually he turned his attention towards the more complicated and ambiguous social and cultural ties between the two institutions. He was also interested in the development of the "marriage trade" in the university town because *"a burgher's daughter who could hardly be fond of a local shoemaker or tailor could look favourably upon some of the master's students, another might favour a doctor, a superintendent, or even a counsellor and chancellor..."*[448]

Amongst the university myths, the myth of the school's territorial identity finds itself in a contradictory position. It is a myth that is shared and narrated by the academic community as one of the central features of its identity: either the school emerged as a provincial university (Landesuniversität), or it had been fought for over many years and was an expression of the country's provincial and national emancipation. This is one of the reasons why in a commemorative work for the 100th anniversary of the Brno Technical University it is histrionically called the *"School for Moravia,"*[449] and why Brno's Masaryk University has always identified itself as *"a Czech-language university in Moravia"* as an expression of the strength and success of the Czech emancipation movement in this territory.[450] This myth is spread with particular strength and intensity by the humanities, whose disciplines

---

448 Quoted from Leiß, Jürgen: *Justin–Liebig Universität, Fachhoschule und Stadt.* Giessen 1975, p. 90.

449 Pernes, Jiří: *Škola pro Moravu. 100 let Vysokého učení technického v Brně.* Brno 1999.

450 Halas – Jordán, *Dokumenty II.*, pp. 13–23.

are strongly connected to the culture of the province and region, and who feel called, if not duty-bound, to protect their interests.

But other no less important parts of the academic community do not even register the myth, and when they do, they doubt it provides any long-term context in the creation of the school's identity. The example of Torun's Nicholas Copernicus University shows that if we take a few steps away from the humanities towards the social sciences and some related sciences (e.g. geography), the awareness of the territorial link begins to weaken and the myth loses its function as a formative part of the identity of the discipline and the wider academic community. The Torun example is interesting because unlike in Moravia, Silesia or Greater Poland we are dealing with a relatively weak regional identity and provincial patriotism. Difficulties arise when merely trying to find a consensus amongst the disciplines on how to define the region. Although the disciplines agree on finding universal links worthy of the name "universitas", they also agree on their link "to the region" – for historians this is the historical territory of Pomerania (Pomorze Nadwiślańskie), though the majority of disciplines see it as "northern Poland" (e.g. archaeology, botany), while for physicists and chemists the region was the whole of Poland in the sense of their contribution to national science and the national economy.[451]

Since the 1970s the debate on the relationship between universities, towns and regions has been very lively and is a forum which attracts specialists from across disciplines. One of the main areas of debate is the attempt to quantify the benefits that universities bring to the labour market, the consumption of goods and services, innovation, etc. These efforts are undermined by the inability of those involved to agree on research methodology. The debate has also long been in the grip of the notion that the establishment of a university in a specific region necessarily helps it to catch up in economic terms. The policies of the regional and local political elites in the Czech Republic, Slovakia and Poland led to a boom in small public universities as well as universities with ties to specific regions which were often relatively small.[452] It is worth remembering that after 1989 the number of universities in Central European countries grew significantly: there are now 77 universities operating in the Czech Republic, 434 in Poland, 70 in Hungary and 38 in Slovakia.[453] Many regions were unhappy with the idea of only having

---

451 Kalemba, Sławomir (red.): *Miejsce Uniwersytetu Mikołaja Kopernika w nauce polskiej i jego rola w regionie*. Toruń 1989, pp. 5–7.

452 https://aktualne.centrum.sk/status-univerzit-ohrozil-najma-vysoky-pocet-studentov/slovensko/spolocnost/ (5.5. 2018); Raczyńska, Magdalena: *Od elitarności do masowości. Stan szkolnictwa wyższego w Polsce po transfomacji ustrojowej z 1989 r.*, Policharia: Kultura, religia, edukacja 1/2013, pp. 217–244; *Diagnoza stanu szkolnictwa wyższego w Polsce*. Warszawa 2009; Bendyk, Edwin – Maron, Olaf: *Ranking naukowy uczelni akademickich*, https://www.polityka.pl/tygodnikpolityka/nauka/1621163,1,ranking-naukowy-uczelni-akademickich.read (5.5. 2018).

453 http://www.msmt.cz/vzdelavani/vysoke-skolstvi/prehled-vysokych-skol-v-cr-3; Adámek, Vladimír: *Financování veřejných vysokých škol*. Brno 2012; http://www.vysokeskoly.sk/katalog; *Szkoły wyższe*

a specialized college and from the outset wanted a university with all the various disciplines. The network of higher-education institutions also significantly expanded as improved educational accessibility was seen as a precondition for regional development – something which was met with by the approval of voters and taxpayers. There had been little reflection on Germany and Austria's experiences, where specific conditions had to be met before the university could contribute towards regional development. If these were not met, the existence of universities could even have a harmful impact on the region. It has been shown that in underdeveloped or slightly underdeveloped regions, the university is mainly responsible for the outflow of active and educated people from the region, thus deepening its structural problems, while the establishment of a university with a properly established curriculum in a region with slight economic growth will operate more successfully.[454] The sustainability of curricula linked to the needs of the region is one of the most serious long-term issues for the strategic development of higher education. The excessive and chaotic establishment of the university network in the above-mentioned countries in the 1990s created a line of conflict between central management bodies and regional political elites, who saw each attempt to limit or restructure the regional university as an encroachment on their own position, and would call on the help of voters under the banner of defending regional identity. However, it is a much more difficult process to close down a badly structured or superfluous university than it is to establish one, which is why in the Czech Republic, for example, regional demands for higher education tend to be met by opening special sections of universities which already operate than by founding new ones.[455]

An important aspect has been missing in the debate on universities' regional ties, which few authors raise: universities have to share cultural links with the region and attach themselves to the regional (provincial) communication network of experience exchange. Only then will they be successful, and as a result this success in the region will help them connect to the global science network, thereby strengthening their identity and the confidence of the academic subculture. The relationship between the university, town and region is much more than one of calculating profit. In the debates it is also necessary to focus more attention on the towns which have not been successful in the "competition" for a university, or which voluntarily decided against having one, often for good reasons. This is why there are various jokes doing the rounds in German regional universities that each

---

i ich finanse w 2014 r., pp. 26, 29–30, 164, Poland : quarterly statistics 2016. Główny Urząd Statystyczny; http://www.nefmi.gov.hu/felsooktatas/felsooktatasi-intezmenyek

454 https://slovacky.denik.cz/zpravy_region/zlinska–univerzita–roste–20071.html (5.5. 2018).

455 https://www.aktuality.sk/clanok/518391/kiska–by–zrusil–tretinu–univerzit–ktore–by–to–moh-li–byt/ (5.5. 2018); https://restartregionu.cz/univerzita–karlova–zahaji–vyuku–ve–varech–pomoci-muze–program–restart/ (5.5. 2018).

city politician would like a university, but few would also want the academics and students to go with it...[456] This is no wonder as the presence of a university is very costly, while the impact on the lifestyle, culture and identity of the population is also considerable.

The Czech experience has shown that "fusion" with the region is more of an issue for the smaller and relatively new universities, which are able to respond better and more sensitively to regional conditions than the large metropolitan schools, and are more distant from the main political and ideological struggles which prevent meaningful cooperation. Regions with stronger identities – here the Silesian "tradition of difference" is appropriate – are better able to bring the university into their network of cooperation. Ostrava University is an example of a regional connection that works well. It was established in 1991 in a region which was referred to as the humanities' "black hole" of Czechoslovakia – an area hit hard by rapid industrialization and by the equally rapid deindustrialization of the 1990s, with its attendant problems in social and cultural structural trans-formation. Although the prestigious Báňska Mining University had operated in Ostrava since 1945, the populous region did not receive any schools to promote its cultural development. In this respect, the university has played a very impor-tant role by contributing significantly towards the transformation of the region and its economy, supporting cultural life, developing tourism, as well as working with memory institutions. The university's character reflects the demands of the region, represented by a varied portfolio of partners including business groups, museum representatives and the leadership of the Roman Catholic diocese. Par-ticular attention should be given to the work of Ostrava's arts and social science disciplines, which have tried to retain the specific characteristics of Silesia and use this platform to develop cooperation with their Polish, Slovakian and German partners. The examples of Ostrava, Brno and Pardubice demonstrate that the presence of students can change a previously unattractive industrial town into a vibrant centre of services, culture and leisure,[457] albeit that this is very difficult to quantify economically, while the residents themselves – in particular businesses in the catering and cultural sectors – are well aware of this fact during the academic holidays.

If the scientific, technical and medical disciplines represent an open window to globalization for the university, and the humanities more a link to the region, it is necessary to ask how a university's cooperation with memory institutions might operate on a local and regional level. Such cooperation might lead to the coveted end of tension between globalism and regionalism, as some memory institutions

---

456 Briese, Volker: Universität und Umland am Beispiel einzelner Hochschulen: Universität Paderborn, In: Kellermann, Paul (Hg.): *Universität und Umland. Beziehungen zwischen Hochschule und Region.* Klagenfurt 1982, pp. 107–122, here p. 122.

457 http://fajnova.cz/historicke-centrum-mesta-ozivi-ostravska-univerzita-jeji-studenti/ (10. 5. 2018)

are already well connected to a wide European network and are thus an equal partner of the university and an important source of inspiration. Here the role of the Ministry of Culture is particularly important, which grants some regional institutions and not others under its control human-resources and financial support in a form that allows them to join similar supra-regional networks. The Ministry of the Interior has a similar role, administering the network of archives. The co-operation between Brno's university and the local and regional memory institutions (the Moravian Museum, the Moravian Library, the Moravian Archive, the Moravian Gallery, etc.) has positive long-term effects because the university can find partners which are often older than itself, well-established in their field and have the ability to cope with tasks on a regional and wider level. The possibilities are limitless for such a group of research institutes. On the other hand, the groups around the universities in Ostrava, Pardubice and Plzeň are more heterogeneous and have different objectives, which the local museums, galleries and archives tend to pursue on their own with support from central institutions.

Since the Early Modern Age, when the universal identity and network of universities weakened, while links to their sovereigns, province and residential town strengthened, the mutual benefits for the university and town or province became an important public issue and part of a widespread debate on both sides over prestige, identity and the costs which both would have to bear. The pros and cons of their economic relationship were still quite clear, which is well illustrated in the relationship between the town of Gießen and its university, which was established in 1607. During this period the relatively small and insignificant town gained in prestige from its university and, due to the confessional (Lutheran) character of the university, became an attractive centre of learning for the more extensive area of north Germany and Scandinavia. Property owners reacted quickly to the influx of foreigners and students by increasing rents, while local craftsmen, innkeepers and merchants all benefited; many burghers could now provide their sons with a relatively cheap university education. However, there was disquiet in the town due to the need for more extensive investment – the modernization of the sewerage system, enlarging the town's cathedral, even the town hall had to provide the university with space for teaching and accommodation for the masters. There was also unrest in the town community due to the fact that some of the local townspeople had been unable to take advantage of the newly created market for goods and services, and as a result of higher prices had found themselves worse off; the local poor were particularly badly hit, which led to increased social tension within the town. The Gießen townsfolk also responded badly to the blunt enforcement of privileges on the part of the university and its individual masters.[458] Today Gießen is held up as a model example of a town coexisting with its university – its sym-

---

458 Leiß, Jürgen: *Justin–Liebig Universität, Fachhoschule und Stadt*. Giessen 1975, p. 13.

bols are an attractive campus near the centre of the town and the popular-science Liebig Museum (1920) and Mathematikum (2002).[459]

The territorial character of institutional identity is a situational phenomenon.[460] Charles Taylor points out that we are constantly defining our identity as part of a dialogue, sometimes even a struggle, with what our significant "others" want to see in us.[461] Therefore, running a successful university means sensitively nurturing and cultivating a process of mutual learning between scientists and the regional recipients of their output. Here the position of the university is extremely delicate: as bearers of high truth ("lord guardians of the seal"), its scholars tend to put theory above practice, and if there is any inconsistency, many of them believe the fault lies in the practical application. University scholars pay a price for their social isolation, which is seen negatively by most people as arrogant privilege; they pay a price for looking at the world too narrowly through their own discipline; they pay a price for their inability to cultivate a transversal communication network between disciplines in order to tackle social problems. Another aspect of the university's regional role is as a services market for the region, as well as a kind of missionary outpost and window, opening out from the region to the rest of the world.[462]

University territorial identity in the countries of Central and Eastern Europe

In the countries of Central and South Eastern Europe the role of universities on a regional level is more complicated than in Western or Northern Europe. This is because there is a greater need for universities to unite the identity and culture of nations, regions and towns – an identity which may have been fractured over the course of time. The demands of the global elites and the structures they support lead these schools to participate in establishing standards of social behaviour which are similar across the European Union. This ignores the fact that there is a mixture of identities at play: the imperialist French identity embodied in its "Napoleonic" circle of universities, the anti-imperialist identity of the German universities in response to Nazi guilt, and the identities of the small nations from Central and South Eastern Europe with their history of oppression and struggles

---

459 https://www.giessen.de/index.phtml?La=1&mNavID=640.4&object=tx%7C684.4427.1&sub=0 (25. 5. 2018).

460 Roubal, Ondřej: *Když se řekne identita – regionální identita III. část.* SOCIOweb 15–16, Prague 2003, pp. 1–5; Sökefeld, Martin, et al.: *Debating Self, Identity, and Culture in Anthropology.* Current Anthropology. 1999, vol. 40, no. 4, pp. 417–447.

461 Taylor, Charles: *Multikulturalismus: Zkoumání politiky uznání.* Prague 2001. p. 49.

462 Laske, Stefan: *Auf der Suche nach der regionalen Identität der Universität.* St. Pölten 1988, pp. 4–11.

to maintain at least the basic elements of national existence – which universities are an important symbol of.[463] In this light, the emphasis on a policy which brings European nations ever closer appears as the product of the dominant ideology and values of left-liberalism amongst the leadership of the main Western European powers and the European Union over the past decades, who behave with mistrust or even hostility towards conservative values, particularly the values of religion, the nation and the traditional family. However, in Central and South Eastern Europe these have not lost their importance and may appear in university traditions or even in curricula.

It is also necessary to remember the complicated regional identities, which are often obscure to outsiders, and the attendant competitive struggles, rivalries and various "sisterly fights" between universities for a place in the sun, transforming themselves under the circumstances into coalitions of various interest groups. For Czech academia the line of conflict is seen as between the "proper" universities with a tradition of at least fifty years, and the group of newer schools. At other times though, the line of "proper" universities is weakened as Charles University occasionally likes to distance itself from the others. In every country the standards of teaching at the oldest university are seen as the benchmark for the whole country and all of its regions – in this way the Belgian universities are inspired by Leuven University and the Polish by the universities in Krakow and Warsaw. At the same time, the numerous new universities hope to create an identity as a new force to be reckoned with, which is trying to catch up with and overtake the original model. And if the competition between the small regional universities and the old metropolitan schools is seen as counterproductive and fails to help the identity or activities of the school, then a more suitable opponent is at least found in some of the smaller, newer and less famous schools in the area.

Establishing a credible and coherent academic community while strengthening the links with the university's regional identity is unthinkable without placing the historical experience and historical awareness of the people of the town and region into the "story" of the university. Only in this way will the university "suffer with the city" or accept all of the good with the bad, which in the pre-modern era was considered a basic civic virtue. But the question then arises of how to overcome the contradiction between the struggles the university went through to develop its identity in the past with today's calls for reconciliation and cooperation, often under the ambiguous terms of "European values" or "Europeanism"? Here history encounters the present, and the encounter is not always positive on both sides. Are historical aspects still productive in establishing the identity of the

---

463 Barban, Andris: The Magna Charta and the Role of Universities in the Development of the Danube Region, In: Rozman, Ivan – Lorber, Lučka (eds.): *The Role of Universities and the Competitiveness of the Danube Region/Vloga univerz in konkurenčnost podonavske regije*. Maribor 2006, pp. 55–68, here p. 61.

university when there are so many concomitant risk factors, oppression, hatred and revenge which make the future so uncertain? And why in fact talk about a university's regional identity when the vast majority of students (and their parents) do not choose a university because of regional patriotism, but simply because of transportation, the curriculum on offer, the prestige of a diploma, the cost and availability of accommodation, safety and so on?

The coexistence of territorial identities

When does the myth of the regional bond within the academic community acquire such significance that it becomes not only a spur for academia but also for the non-academic community? All of the different facets of the university's struggles with identity can be observed in Moravia, where it has been demonstrated that the university can be part of Brno, Moravia or the nation, depending on the context.

From the Late Middle Ages the territory of the Habsburg monarchy had relatively few universities in comparison with Western and Southern Europe. There were only three medieval university foundations operating on its extensive territory – in Prague, Krakow and Vienna. In the Early Modern Age, the medieval network of universities was not particularly extensive – some of the important new schools were to be found in the cities of Olomouc (1573), Vilnius (1579), Graz (1585), Trnava and later Pest (1635), Lviv (1661) and Innsbruck (1669). One typical feature of these newly founded universities was the cooperation between the state and the Jesuit Order, which was very influential in the running of the universities until its dissolution in 1773. With the new wave of foundations in the Habsburg monarchy in the mid-19th century, several technical universities were established (including in Brno in 1849), though at the same time the emperor abolished the university in Olomouc (1860) due to ongoing disputes with the Catholic Church. During this period Moravia, an important, well-populated and economically dynamic province of the Habsburg empire, became a royal province without a university – all it had was one technical university based in Brno and an isolated theological faculty as the remains of what had been Olomouc's university.[464] In this vacuum it was obvious that the theme of a Moravian university would become a contentious political topic in the liberal political situation of the Habsburg empire after 1861. A university-style school was generally viewed as

---

464 d'Elvert, Christian: *Geschichte der Studien-, Schul- und Erziehungsanstalten in Mähren und Oesterr. Schlesien insbesonder der Olmützer Universität*. Schriften der historisch–statistischen Section der k.k. mährisch–schlesischen Gesellschaft zur Beförderung des Ackerbaues, der Natur– und Landeskunde. Bd. X., Brünn 1857, p. XVIII ff.; Nešpor, Václav: *Dějiny university olomoucké*. Olomouc 1947, pp. 30–32, 40–43, 59–65;

a great boon for the economy of Moravia, as the existing situation whereby Moravian students travelled to the universities in Vienna, Prague, or more seldomly to Krakow, significantly lowcred access to education in the province and restricted its economic growth. However, leaving the economic aspect of the matter to one side, the struggle for a Moravian university became a fight over identity. On the one hand was the "Moravian" theme, which had been highlighted by the Moravian estates since the mid-18th century, when the difficulty of the estates, the state and the Jesuit Order sharing in the governance of Olomouc's university had become increasingly clear. The attempt by the estates to extricate university education from ecclesiastical influence and redirect the school's work towards the benefit of the province – in the secular and economic sense of training medical, legal and economic specialists – was evident when the university was briefly relocated to Brno (1778–1782) as the political and economic centre of the province. However, this was not only a dispute between political representatives in Moravia and the universal power of the Roman Catholic Church, it was also a dispute between the secular and religious powers in Moravian society – another line of conflict which would accompany the Brno university into the 20th century. Meanwhile another battle over identity loomed on the horizon which was connected to the university – the conflict between the Czech and German emancipation movements over which language any future university courses would be taught in.

The encroaching "Czechization" of teaching at the university in Prague, which led to its division in 1882, and the Polonization of Krakow University, which gathered pace from the 1860s, provided the Czech national movement in Moravia with examples to follow. It was clear that without a comprehensive education network in the Czech language from primary-school level to university, the emancipation of the Czech nation in Moravia would always be just a chimera. The Slavonic population of Moravia would continue to be exposed to German cultural influences, while the patriotically conscious Moravian Czechs would always remain an appendage to the much stronger national movement in Bohemia. A large number of Czech intellectuals and national politicians in Bohemia viewed the actions of the Czech educated elites in Moravia in the 1880s–1890s with misgivings as they did not want to divide their forces, preferring instead to concentrate on properly equipping the only Czech university in Prague. As a result, the public case for a Moravian university had to be made by intellectuals from Moravia living in Prague,[465] especially university students and some university teachers such

---

465 Havránek, Jan: *Moravané na pražské univerzitě v 19. a 20. století*, In: Malíř, Jiří – Vlček, Radomír (red.): Morava a české národní vědomí od středověku po dnešek., Brno 2001, pp. 111–121; Pešek, Jiří: *Prag und Wien 1884 – ein Vergleich zwischen den Universitäten und deren Rolle für die Studenten aus den Böhmischen Ländern*, In: Corbea-Hoisie, Andrei – Le Rider, Jacques (eds.): Metropole und Provinzen in Altösterreich (1880–1918). Wien – Köln – Weimar 1996, pp. 94–109.

as Tomáš Masaryk, who was originally from Moravian Slovakia.[466] Among the influential political circles in Prague it was felt it would be more desirable to mollify their countrymen in Moravia with minor political concessions extracted from the Vienna government, and focus their efforts on more important themes (for Prague), such as constitutional and linguistic matters and economic demands. At the same time, some of the Czech national leaders in Prague were worried that any direct refusal to support a Moravian university would lose them support among Moravian political representatives, pushing them towards a separatist route to achieve their goal.[467]

Moravian Czechs had another alternative – to cooperate with Moravian Germans based on provincial patriotism, which might have led to the establishment of a bilingual university. Although there were not many positive experiences from the small number of such universities in Europe,[468]hypothetically it was a possible route to their objective, and a route which could be relatively quick, as the Vienna government had signalled that the key to establishing a university was an agreement between the Czech and German politicians in the province. If a bilingual university had been established in the 1880s, it would undoubtedly have been a great triumph for the Moravian Czechs, as they had previously lacked the political strength to achieve such an objective. However, such a political decision would have meant the Czechs would still have been clients of the Vienna government and hostage to the agreement with their German partners in Moravia. Of the approximately 70% of the population who spoke a Slavonic language (not only Czech, but also different dialects), the majority came from the urban and rural populations, for whom a university education had always been an expensive and unnecessary luxury. For many from the lower classes the issue of national identification was not a defining one, and they had stronger ties to their religion, their patrician's family or the region than to their language and nationality. As the Czech national movement became more democratic and took on more of the characteristics of a mass movement (the Camps Movement from 1868–1871), people from the province who had previously been indifferent were becoming increasingly attached to the idea of Czech identity, and this began to take on more of a national than provincial character.

Naturally, the attitude towards the university also changed amongst Moravian Germans. What had begun primarily as an economic interest also gradually changed to an aspiration to improve the cultural status of their own ethnicity in Moravia. One common feature of the petitions from the 1860s for a new univer-

---

466 Masaryk, Tomáš: *Jak zvelebovati naši literaturu naukovou.* In: Athenaeum II, 1885, pp. 272–288, esp. p. 275.

467 Jordán, *Dějiny university*, pp. 43–45.

468 Cf. Turczynski, *Czernowitz*, pp. 25–36; Bostan, Grigore: *Der Beitrag der Universität Czernowitz zur Entwicklung der rumänischen Kultur und der ukrainisch–rumänischen Beziehungen.* Bern – Wien 1998;

sity in Brno to replace the defunct university in Olomouc was the self-evident link between the university and the German language. Czech was seen by the Germans as an inferior language with an uncertain future, and it was assumed that the Moravian people who spoke various Slavonic dialects rather than standard Czech would accept this fact as benefiting themselves and the whole country. It was incomprehensible to German intellectuals that the entire Moravian population might not want to become part of the globally famous network of German science and culture through a German-language university. Engineers in the economic sector had been trained in Brno since 1849 using both Czech and German, but even here German began to dominate, and by 1873 it was the only language used in teaching. Therefore, under these circumstances, establishing an expensive university for a small, underdeveloped, predominantly agricultural nation with an uncertain future appeared to make no sense, even to the more moderate German leaders. However, by the 1880s German politicians were becoming increasingly concerned that due to the success of the national-emancipation movement, Czech Moravians could no longer be counted on as mere consumers of high German culture. The Germans were gradually discovering that subordination to "Germanness" in Moravia was coming to an end and it would be necessary to face the fact that Moravian Czechs, following the example of their countrymen in Bohemia, would wish to create a fully-fledged alternative to German culture. German politicians were faced with the question of whether to be more accommodating with a timely, symbolic concession such as a university, or whether to maintain a tough, inflexible position and insist upon the superiority of German culture over Czech.

There was cause for concern here, but also reasons to be optimistic. The Moravian Czechs at that time were not nearly as economically powerful as the Germans.[469] The large Moravian towns were firmly under the control of the Germans (Brno, Olomouc, Jihlava, Moravská Ostrava etc.), where the use of Czech in public had long been considered to be the sign of an outsider. In addition, the Czech camp was still heavily influenced by the Catholic Church, which was loyal to the emperor and conciliatory in its attitude towards the escalating Czech-German conflict. However, the smiles on the lips of the optimists soon froze when confronted by the demographic predominance of Slavonic inhabitants over Germans amongst the youth. It was evident that the culturally advanced and wealthy German community was dying out in the language islands, and not even the assimilation of the non-German population would prevent this. The Moravian Slavonic population was now much more inclined towards recognising its Czech linguistic and cultural ties than being assimilated into German culture. The network of Czech primary and secondary schools in Moravia began to improve from the 1860s, then rapidly so in the 1880s when the Old Czech representatives acquired more influence over

---

469 Janák, Jan: *Hospodářský rozmach Moravy 1740–1918*. Brno 1999, pp. 49–59.

the decisions made by the Austrian government; it was particularly important to improve the state of the Czech gymnasiums whose graduates, naturally, wanted to move into higher education. Overall, the Moravian Czechs were making significant progress – more so in culture than in the economy – nonetheless, they could no longer be overlooked.

Although the German politicians in Moravia did not overlook the progress of their rivals, the German liberals were becoming increasingly worried about their own leadership standing within the German camp. They were coming under more intense pressure from radical nationalist forces, who were supported by the less well-off bourgeoisie. As a consequence, of the two possible ways to respond to the progress being made by the Czechs, they decided to choose the confrontational one, opting to boycott any emancipatory steps the Czechs took in the field of culture.

The university issue thus became of symbolic value – a special prize for the victors of the nationalist contest, the golden apple of its day. The result was that the German side refused any kind of bilingual university, insisting on a German-language university as the answer to the Czechs' allegedly excessive demands. There was also uncertainty among Moravian Germans as to whether it was politically productive to adopt such a prominent position in the university issue. For many young Germans in Moravia a higher education was fairly easily accessible even without a university in Brno – towns in the south such as Mikulov or Znojmo liked to present themselves as distant parts of the Viennese agglomeration, while for Germans in north or north-west Moravia, the educational institutes in Prague, which had many places for German students, were accessible by rail. It transpired that the Brno city politicians were the most vociferous supporters of a German university, and despite being powerful, they were somewhat isolated on this point. Although other German interest groups were prepared to block the idea of a Czech university in Moravia, at the same time they were resigned to the fact that there would not be a German-language university and could thus concentrate on more important issues. There were also compromise solutions from the more politically creative politicians in Brno city hall, namely the establishment of two universities – a German one in Brno and a Czech one in another town with Czech municipal leadership. Here national identity became intertwined with provincial as well as local identities. Possible locations for a Czech university included Kroměříž and Prostějov, while one shrewd solution was Královo Pole. A Czech university could benefit from its proximity to the provincial capital of Brno due to the fact that both municipalities were adjacent to one another and practically unified, but at the same time the university would in fact be outside of Brno and would thus not provoke the more radical elements amongst the Brno Germans.

From 1895–1897 both political camps were confronted by the mass character of the Czech-German struggle, where bourgeois political forces were upstaged in

public life by the mass political parties with their large though poor and less liter-
ate membership.[470] This mass engagement reached its peak when socialist forces
also joined in demonstrations in 1905. Politics left the negotiating table for the
streets, resulting in the death of a young Czech joiner, František Pavlík, who was
killed by the police during a demonstration in support of a Czech university in
Brno.[471] There was now no escaping the spiral of oppression and violence, the
moderate forces lost their influence and the university question became one of
"who will defeat whom".[472]

The breakup of the Habsburg empire and the foundation of Czechoslovakia
in 1918 meant that the university issue could be reopened in a different context.
The decision by the Revolutionary National Council in January 1919 to establish
a university in Moravia was not motivated by provincial patriotism. Instead the
motivation was clearly the symbolic and practical culmination of the national
triumph as confirmed on the territory of Moravia.[473] From the perspective of
the Prague political elites, it had not been linked strongly enough to the Czech
national movement. It was a kind of missionary area, and in the eyes of some critically minded contemporaries, it was a colony of triumphal Czech nationalism and
imperialism.[474] After the Habsburgs and Germans, the third to lose out was the
Roman Catholic Church, which until the last moment had postponed and blocked
the establishment of a university, fearing it would become a hotbed of secularism
emerging from revolutionary fervour. It was punished for this in several ways including the absence of a theological faculty in the new university.[475]

However, the strong words from this time of triumph were not accompanied
by deeds, and it soon became clear that the Brno university was the Cinderella to
Charles University, and that its equipment was woefully inadequate. This fact was
again grist to the mill of Moravian provincial patriots, who were frustrated with
and sharply critical of Prague and the overly centralized Czechoslovak state. In
1923–1924 and again in 1932–1933, the Prague government first drew up proposals to close down one faculty, then later two faculties at the Brno university in
an effort to reduce the burden of social and education expenditure on the state

---

470 Malíř, Jiří: Systém politických stran v českých zemích do roku 1918. In: Malíř, Jiří – Marek, Pavel:
Politické strany. Vývoj politických stran a hnutí v českých zemích a v Československu 1861–2004. I., Brno 2005,
pp. 17–57.

471 *Die tschechischen Ausschreitungen und Gewalttätigkeiten,* Neues deutsches Blatt 7.10. 1905, year 1, no.
31, p. 4; Křen, Jan: *Konfliktní společenství. Češi a Němci 1780–1918.* Prague 2013, pp. 191–196; Pernes,
Jiří: *Nejen rudé prapory aneb Pravda o revolučním roce 1905 v českých zemích.* Brno 2005, pp. 115–120.

472 Zur Forderung der czechischen Universität in Mähren, Deutsches Nordmährerblatt 12. 3. 1904,
year 6, no. 11, pp. 1–3.

473 http://www.psp.cz/eknih/1918ns/ps/stenprot/022schuz/s022007.htm ff. (10.5. 2018).

474 *Krise zvěrolékařské fakulty v Brně,* Lidové noviny 21.4. 1921, year 29, no. 197, p. 1.

475 Cyrillo–Methodějská universita na Moravě, Hlas, 24.5. 1894, year 46, no. 116, p. 1; http://www.
psp.cz/eknih/1918ns/ps/stenprot/022schuz/s022007.htm ff. (10.5. 2018).

budget. This was met by a wave of solidarity by Moravians, criticizing the centralism of the Czechoslovak administration and the harsh attitude of Prague's central organs towards Moravia.[476] There were protests by the Czech public in Moravia and Silesia, with even the long-running rivalry between Brno and Olomouc being set aside.[477] No significant support was forthcoming from the educated Czech elites in Bohemia, while the Slovak intelligentsia were also lukewarm in their support, so it was left to the Moravians to defend their university themselves. Its spokespeople claimed the university was Moravia's contribution to the expanding power of the Czech nation and the Czechoslovak state; Moravian patriotism was presented as benefiting the national idea.[478] German political circles did not become involved in the matter, and it is possible that they observed proceedings with a certain schadenfreude.

The aversion of a great number of Germans towards the Brno university manifested itself in the support given by Brno Germans to Nazi officials after Brno was occupied in March 1939.[479] The cutbacks to the university and its eventual closure in 1939 were met with the approval of the majority of Germans in Brno, as a resurgent German nationalism viewed the university as a symbol of German subjugation in the past. There was no element of Moravian or local patriotism in this discourse as the university had long been viewed as part of the national conflict. The Germans had never managed to coexist with the university – only a handful of German-speaking students studied there, usually from mixed-national or Jewish backgrounds. Therefore, the closure of the school in 1939 and its reopening in 1945 was the story of Czech national suppression and triumph. Meanwhile, accounts were settled with the German adversaries in 1945 when the German population of Brno was resettled in Austria and Germany.[480]

With the end of Czech-German rivalry, the university in Brno took on a distinctly Czech character under the influence of its war generation of academics, though its international links were still valued. In comparison with the interwar period, when international ties were undermined by a chronic lack in finance and were mainly with France and Britain, the international dimension was now assuming too much significance. The period 1945–1948 saw a dramatic increase in the importance of the links to Slavonic countries, especially the Soviet Union. There was still respect for the liberating Anglo-Saxon powers, but France had lost much

---

476 Halas, František X. – Jordán, František: *Dokumenty k dějinám Masarykovy univerzity v Brně II.*, Brno 1995, pp. 78–96.

477 Národní archiv, Fond Ministerstvo školství a národní osvěty, k. 1115, sign. 5I2A, čj. 138493/23.

478 Halas – Jordán, *Dokumenty II.*, pp. 78–96.

479 Jordán, *Dějiny university*, pp. 213.

480 Dvořák, Tomáš: Brno a německé obyvatelstvo v květnu roku 1945. Pokus o anatomii historické (ne)paměti. In: Arburg, Adrian von – Dvořák, Tomáš – Kovařík, David: *Německy mluvící obyvatelstvo v Československu po roce 1945.* Brno 2010, pp. 89–113.

of its standing following the trauma of the Munich Agreement. The "Moravian" aspect had virtually no role to play in these links, which were about connecting national educational institutes to the global network. After 1948 the globalizing tendency was replaced by Czechoslovakia's entry into the bloc of people's democratic countries, especially the Slavonic group. The university presented itself in these forums as a member of a large family of nations on the path to socialism, part of the victorious political camp which would soon embrace the whole world. A trend developed here which might be described today using the slogan "think globally, act locally"[481]: the university joined the international division of research inside the socialist camp and was active in supporting the development of countries through teaching foreign students, etc.

However, it would also be a mistake to imagine that the feeling of national victory over Germany and the globalizing tendencies of the communist era extinguished the local patriotic character of the university's identity. Ladislav Štoll, a powerful man within Czech science, attended a conference of the Czechoslovak Communist Party in Brno on the theme of universities, only to be appalled by what he saw: "*There are strong anti-Prague and anti-centralizing tendencies apparent in the discussions. They talked ironically about the 'Prague comrades'. Typical of Brno students is a strongly anti-Prague local 'patriotism', which Šling indulged in (...)*"[482] A regional Communist leader, Otto Šling's (1912–1952) influence in the university and elsewhere was based on his regional patriotism combined with student left-wing avant-gardism – in the autumn of 1950 he was removed from his post and later hanged.[483] However, this did not mean that the university's identity was separated from Moravian and Brno regional patriotism forever – Šling's era was just one of many short episodes in the long-term development of this identity.

It is obvious from this short detour into the complex web of identities of the Brno university community that it was not easy to lead a discussion on the historical aspects of today's academic community for the 100th anniversary of the university in 2019. In many ways there seems very little convergence between past identities, the victorious struggles of the university and the present political situation. It is difficult to celebrate a historical anniversary in an era when the leading representatives of universities officially demand the development of a spirit of cooperation and the communication of "European values", with all the ambiguity of this term. Perhaps it would be simpler to commemorate an older anniversary, preferably medieval, which would give the organisers more room to manoeuvre and would allow more of a focus on aspects connected with current political re-

---

481 Kellermann, Paul: *Einleitung*, In: Universität und Umland. Beziehungen zwischen Hochschule und Region. Klagenfurt 1982, p. 9.

482 Pernes, *Škola*, p. 65.

483 Šling, Karel: *Otto Šling – příběh jednoho komunisty*. Paměť a dějiny 2012, no. 4, pp. 116–121.

quirements. But this is not at all simple for a university which was founded during a turbulent and tense period at the start of a century which has justifiably been called the century of extremes. However, there is no need to imagine that any potential conflicts related to the commemoration of the university's foundation in 1919 would lead to tension within the academic community – most academics are not interested in the historical aspects of the university's foundation, and if they are, then it is only in connection with the narrow interests of their subject. Only a few voices were raised from the humanities, pointing out that the university emerged firstly as the victory of Czechs over Germans, then as a symbol of the importance of Moravia for the Czech nation and the new state, and thirdly as an expression of the triumph of secular progress over the influence of the Roman Catholic Church.

Globalists and localists

After the fall of communism and the Czech Republic's entry into the European Union, the dividing line between the narrators of the myth of territorial ties was transformed. This quiet transformation occurred in the 1990s when, on the basis of applied research, some disciplines used increased state investment and cooperation with private firms to become so attached to the international network that they became either indifferent to their territorial links or viewed them more as an encumbrance. The university community began to split between the globalists and the localists. Each group interprets the university's past and present in its own way, resembling a mythical narrative, though both stories – fortunately for now – stand more apart from each other than opposed to one other. Rudolf Stichweh believes that in comparison with the top American universities, supporters of locally and regionally focused European universities have more of an influence, which has grown over the past decades, whereas Princeton, Yale and Harvard have become unambiguously global institutions.[484]

The first group would like to see the university develop as an institution which is firmly set within the international community and is ready to profit from the results of globalization. It then sets its priorities for the university's development accordingly: to direct resources towards supporting student and academic mobility, to introduce English as one of the university's official languages and the main language in research, and to focus energy on climbing the ratings ladders. Their goal is to ensure the university has high enough status to access national and international research funding – in the Czech Republic this means a position among

---

484 Stichweh, Rudolf: Universitäten im Zeitalter der Globalisierung, In: Rudersdorf, Manfred – Höpken, Wolfgang – Schlegel, Martin (Hg.): *Wissen und Geist. Universitätskulturen*. Leipzig 2009, pp. 119–138, here 120–121.

the six research institutions aspiring to participate in global affairs.[485] In the USA there are 150 such research institutions from a total of 3,000, in Great Britain approximately 20, in Brazil 6, etc.[486] The objective of the globalist is, therefore, to move step by step away from the university's bond to the territory of the Czech lands or Moravia, as this bond to a small post-communist country in Central Europe does not provide them with a brand equal to their ambitious, and in some cases, excellent research. For the globalists the term national or even "Moravian" university is a millstone, weighed down by history, and for some it is just an unpleasant memory of times which were backward and uniformly grey.

For the localists, on the other hand, globalization represents a series of risks, and they cannot imagine separating the university from its territory. Cutting themselves off from historical traditions is seen as damaging on principle; they see many positives in the national and "Moravian" aspects of the university's history, mainly from the solidarity arising from an awareness of the academic community's heroism when faced by enemies, political oppression and crises. Their arguments are also strong: the large majority of students are from Moravia, in particular South Moravia, while only a handful of courses are taught in English at this large university. The university education also focuses on the needs of the region; the majority of teachers, doctors and lawyers work in Moravian institutions. They point out that for many years the university drew on its strength to overcome crises from its symbolically expressed link to Moravia – the foundation stones of the first university building in 1928 were brought from Moravian towns which symbolized the tradition of education (Nivnice – the birthplace of Comenius; Hodslavice as the birthplace of František Palacký; Hodonín as a reference to T.G. Masaryk, etc.). There were few references to Prague while any international links only appeared in connection with important "Moravian" figures.[487] In a university with a proven structure of traditions and decision-making processes, globalism represents activistic ideas borrowed from who-knows-where and applied haphazardly solely because they are mechanisms which operate in the "developed" environment of Western European or American universities. They are angered by the dominance of English and highlight the importance of other languages that are needed to maintain Europe's great cultural diversity, which is threatened by globalization and digitalization.[488]

485 Charles University in Prague, Masaryk University in Brno, Palacký University in Olomouc, The Czech Technical University in Prague, The Technical University in Brno and the Czech Republic Academy of Sciences.

486 Altbach, Philip: *Tradition und Transition. The International Imperative in Higher Education.* Boston 2007, p. 90.

487 Jordán, *Dějiny university*, pp. 118–119.

488 http://ceskapozice.lidovky.cz/shoda–globalismu–a–lokalismu–je–civilizacni–nezbytnosti–pez–/tema.aspx?c=A180425_151517_pozice–tema_lube (29.4.2018); http://www.ceskatelevize.cz/ct24/

Both positions have their symbolic expressions, and a symbol has the potential to become a bone of contention. As was seen in the story of early-modern Gießen, problems can multiply in the relationship between the university and the inhabitants of a town or region if the university demands privileged treatment, resulting in pressure on the regional and city budget. A poor signal is sent if the buildings disturb the urban appearance, with brutalist buildings disrupting the style of the city and genius loci.[489] Enormous multi-discipline concrete campuses on the outskirts of cities in Germany and Poland (Regensburg, Saarbrücken, Poznań) express doubts about the university community's ability to be part of urban society.[490] If, as in Brno or Vilnius, the university chooses a middle way by leaving the arts and social science departments in the city, then this is beneficial not only for these disciplines and the university, but it also sends a signal that it is willing to "suffer with the city". In the case of science, technical, sports and medical disciplines, a certain distance away in campus areas is required, but even here it is necessary to prevent them from becoming isolated by reaching out into the life of the city through joint projects, celebrations and cultural and sports events. A tendency to become closed off will be met in turn by the town and region also rejecting any notions of solidarity.[491] A special chapter is the role of mass higher education in the development of the relationship between the university and the town: on the one hand – as in the case of the Early Modern Age – the mass of students means increased consumption and an injection of money into certain sectors of the economy, on the other hand, it can put pressure on the city transport network and the entire infrastructure, and also bring noise and night-time disturbance.

By creating such a huge capacity for research, something of a rarity in Central Europe, the university in Brno has become more global than many of its colleagues and competitors from the ranks of regional universities. Even if there is an overly strict dividing line between research universities with global aspirations and regional universities dominated by Bachelor's courses and research in a national

---

veda/2404318-islandstina-vymira-mezi-jazyky-ohrozene-digitalizaci-sveta-patri-i-cestina (29.5. 2018).

489 Geißler, Clemens – Engelbrecht, Gerhard – Kutz, Joachim: Wirtschaftliche und soziale Effekte der Regionalisierung des Hochschulsystems, In: Kellermann, Paul (Hg.): *Universität und Umland. Beziehungen zwischen Hochschule und Region*. Klagenfurt 1982, pp. 40–69, here p. 66.

490 Mayer, Franz: Universität und Gesellschaft: Einige Überlegungen zur Gründung, Planung und Aufbau einer Universität in Regensburg. Zeitschrift für Politik, Neue Folge, Vol. 13, No. 3 (Oktober 1966), pp. 269–284.

491 Cf. Zerlang, Martin: *The university and the city*. GeoJournal, Vol. 43, No. 3 (November 1997), pp. 241–246; Duarte Horta, Regina: *The City Within the City: the University City, History and Urbanism in a Latin American Case Study*. Iberoamericana 2001, Año 13, No. 51 (Septiembre de 2013), pp. 7–25; Berdahl, Robert M. – Cohon, Jared L. – Simmons, Ruth J. – Sexton, John – Berlowitz, Leslie Cohen: *University and the city*, Bulletin of the American Academy of Arts and Sciences, Vol. 64, No. 3 (Spring 2011), pp. 4–18.

context, at least in the Central European and Czech context there is still a significant dividing line in the extent of the territorial bond. The weakening of this bond has the character of symbols signalling to the outside that: we are integrated into the global network of universities! Alongside this we are also integrated into the region and our objectives are the same as the priorities and strategies of the city and region. However, in the competition for a position among the universities this is not mentioned as we are more proud of our globalism. The university in Brno sent a similar signal in 2017 when it became the first university in the Czech Republic to introduce the defence of the thesis in a world language for all subjects, though this was somewhat diluted later by the recognition that some disciplines had specific links to Czech. The idea behind this step, weakening Czech as a language of science and pressurising researchers to distance themselves in their research and publications from the nation and region, provides much food for thought when considering the university's territorial links and identity, the consequences of which are still impossible to foretell.

Conclusion

The two myths standing beside each other, and sometimes opposite each other, are supported by people whose daily lives personify the idea of thinking globally and acting locally. It is rare to find research which purports to be merely provincial in its ambitions, just as one seldom encounters globalist extremism which ignores the needs of the region.[492] Amongst scientists it would be difficult to find either globalists or localists who did not share at least some of the values of the other side. The distinction is not as clear as it might seem and neither myth is aggressive in character. The issue of the territorial bond thus shows the university – as was seen above – as a *multiple hybrid organisation,*[493] i.e. an institution made up of various parts with different missions and internal cultures, in this case in relation to the territorial bond: "*The university is too difficult and complex an organization to be described, let alone governed and administered.*"[494] By choosing their own methods, pace and direction, globalists and localists and university disciplines are striving towards an optimal balance whereby the university is rooted firmly in the region while simultaneously being part of the international debate, where

---

492 Kellermann, *Einleitung*, p. 9.

493 Kleinmann, Bernd: Universitätspräsidenten als „institutional entrepreneurs"? Unternehmensmythen und Führungsaufgaben im Hochschulbereich, In: Scherm, Ewald (Hg.): *Management unternehmerischer Universitäten: Realität, Vision oder Utopie?* München – Mering 2014, pp. 43–62, here p. 48.

494 Delbecq, André – Bryson, Paul – van der Ven, Andrew: *University Governance: Lessons from a Innovative Design for Collaboration,* Journal of Management Inquiry 22, 4, 2013, pp. 382–392, here p. 390.

regional scientific findings will be relevant to the rest of the world due to their general applicability. Such a "fusion" of the university with the city and region is an expression of democracy, but also that the university is not shutting itself away in its ivory tower, but is a valuable actor in improving the lives of the region's inhabitants and taxpayers, who have the right to make demands of the university and expect certain results. In so doing, it can fulfil its fundamental role as the "window" of every region – an innovative intersection between the world of science, the region and the city.

THE HISTORY OF UNIVERSITY CULTURE AND SOME CURRENT ISSUES

Through what are termed "myths", we have attempted to uncover some of the issues for universities which are significant for the (Central) European and especially Czech setting from a historical perspective. In this final, briefer chapter, we will attempt to formulate a number of propositions that stem from our historical knowledge but can actually be viewed as contemporary problems. In doing so, we have made use of publications about the "idea of universities" that have been brought out in Czech and the discussions that have been held for almost three decades in Czech academic circles as well as a survey which we organized among selected colleagues – academics from this country and abroad.

There can be no doubt that the aim of historical research in the field of university culture is to point out continuity and discontinuity in the development of universities, from their medieval beginnings to the present. However, a statement of this kind is not enough to satisfy the historian, who must go on to ask: What exactly does this "continuity" and "discontinuity" consist of? Do we have an adequate understanding of the terms used for university education and research, for example, in the Middle Ages, or even in the nineteenth century? Didn't the modern period and the 20th century witness changes that completely altered the purpose and role of universities and individual faculties as well as public expectations? Didn't mass culture at the turn of the 19th and 20th century, followed by the "massification" of higher education in the second half of the 20th century, change the objectives a university should fulfil in society? But we needn't confine ourselves to the ideological plane. Didn't the "players" in all this – university professors, senior lecturers, other staff and finally students – fundamentally change too? Didn't influences from economics and politics penetrate universities to such an extent that they transformed their internal structure? And aren't present-day reflections about universities, their ideals and needs, their struggle for autonomy and independence, their efforts to be competitive, their search for criteria to evaluate performance and their internal instability actually an expression of the deep crisis the entire university world finds itself in? Are we not then left with mere "myths" which help us to depict the university world of yesteryear but whose present-day form we do not yet have precise words for?

This was accurately described in relation to a specific area by the biologist and philosopher Stanislav Komárek: *"Since the Renaissance...anyone who is unfamiliar with Plato's Dialogues, Virgil's poetry and Livy's chronicles and cannot imitate their style with aplomb is not an educated person... After the Cartesian Revolution and especially with the advent of science and technology in practice, it was repeatedly pointed out that classical texts and culture basically represented an encumbrance... Since the 1920s there has been an increasingly vague notion in Europe about what an educated person should actually know. Which languages should he speak? Or is English enough? Should an educated person be able to name all the lanthanoids? Should he know what photosynthetic phosphorylation is? Should he be familiar with the history of France? And Madagascar? Should he know what a Lombard loan is? Who wrote Crime and Punishment? The constant talk about how the system of teaching should be improved and how it is necessary to "promote education" hopelessly confuses two quite disparate things: namely, the training of specialists in various areas of science and technology (...) and the relics of ideas about education in the original sense of the word, understood as care of the soul or knowledge "just" for the sake of knowledge."*[495]

We could sidestep these and similar questions by saying that it is not for historians to engage in this kind of "philosophizing" – and to some extent we would probably be right. On the other hand, we have written this publication as "interested observers", as active members of the university community who are expressing their views on current issues and have certain ideas about what universities were like in the past, but also what they should and could be like in the near future. We would therefore like to cautiously express our views on the present as well.

Argument One: The "idea of the university" shows up best when it is missing or distorted

It would be possible to compile a hefty anthology containing writings by many thinkers about what a university really "is" and what the ideal or "idea" of the university is.[496] It would undoubtedly make for engaging reading to while away many

---

495 Komárek, Stanislav: *Sloupoví aneb Postila*. Prague 2008, pp. 250–251.
496 In Czech, for example, the subset: Jirsa, Jakub (ed.): *Idea university*. Prague 2015.

evenings. We believe that the most stimulating texts in this imaginary anthology would be those by authors who reflected on colleges and universities at times of their deepest decline or when they ceased to exist. We could cite numerous examples from the early modern period, but let us remain with the twentieth century. This period was – unfortunately – rich in times when the "idea of the university" was heavily distorted or seemed to have completely vanished in some countries. The Second World War was a cruel experience for Central Europe, since in some countries universities were subjected to Nazi ideology and in some countries (e.g. Czechoslovakia) most higher-education institutions were closed as part of Nazi policy. During the communist era, the universities were again subjected to a regime which, declaring class war, limited or abolished some basic university principles – for example, the international exchange of people and ideas. It seems to us that these experiences best illustrate how lively and necessary "ideas" of the university are in cultural settings. During the Second World War, there were students who looked forward to being back at university and teachers who were continually preparing to resume lecturing. In the Stalinist period, it was not exceptional for covert "university" teaching – whose standard was often surprisingly high although it lacked some of the parameters of university communication – to take place in jails and concentration camps.[497] There are Czech as well as Hungarian and Romanian examples of various covert or semi-secret forms of university education from the 1980s intended to make up for the deficiencies of official universities at that time.

This is not to say that the "ideas" of the university cannot be considered – and considered very profoundly – under normal, democratic conditions. An "extreme" example might be the postwar activity of the German philosopher Karl Jaspers, described in the book *The Modern University: Ideal and Reality*.[498] Jaspers' writings are clearly shaped by the crisis German higher education had undergone since 1933 and the failings of some university staff, often outstanding scientists. In the renewed Germany, universities were once again to form the basis of science without ideological influence, the "Humboldtian ideal" of research and teaching was dusted off again, and the relationship between science and "humanitas" was reconsidered in the light of the terrible experience of the loss of humanity. However melodramatic it might sound today, at that time Jaspers again dared to speak of "openness to the truth", human dignity, "mustering all forces" and the "ethos of knowledge". Nowadays these words might have a note of melodrama to them, but it is necessary to ask dispassionately whether certain experiences from

---

497 Cf. Vacková, Růžena: *Vězeňské přednášky*. Prague 1999.

498 Univerzita jako republika učenců: Karl Jaspers. In: Chotaš, Jiří – Prázný, Aleš – Hejduk, Tomáš et al.: *Moderní univerzita. Ideál a realita*. Prague 2015, pp. 197–244.

the past might not help us to consider which elements (of university education and culture) are truly essential and which are not.

So in terms of our first argument, based on our (Central European and especially Czech) experience, we could say that the ideal of the university still consists of a) free access to ideas and the possibility of discussing them on the basis of certain rules, b) respect for the reality we are faced with, c) acceptance of a certain type of "scientific" and human authority and a certain type of mutual communication and sharing, d) the possibility of disseminating ideas and information and continuously exchanging them regardless of national borders, e) equal study opportunities and the building of an (inevitably imperfect) institutional foundation.

Argument Two: It is necessary to listen to criticism

Books by Konrad Paul Liessmann, the Austrian philosopher already mentioned in the main body of this book, tend to be eagerly awaited in the Central European intellectual milieu, especially since his "academic bestseller" *The Theory of Miseducation: The Mistakes of the Knowledge Society*, a Czech translation of which was published in 2008, two years after the German original.[499] As a loose sequel to this book was also released on the Czech market under the title *The Hour of the Ghosts: The Practice of Miseducation – A Polemic*,[500] it is worth outlining the author's basic arguments from the first volume. First and foremost, it is a critique of the contemporary higher-education and academic system, which bears the name "knowledge society" but exhibits a whole range of structural problems which result in education gradually being replaced by half-education or even non-education. There are several reasons for this. The most important are not so much the methods of measuring and weighting scientific results or advancing bureaucratization, but rather the general transfer of humanities disciplines onto an economic ideological basis, which manifests itself in the measuring of education (half-education) by means of questions such as "Where are we in the rankings?" and the revolutionary introduction of the so-called Bologna system, which upset the status quo and introduced a system of never-ending reforms. Liessmann's arguments were compelling, his claims of a Counter-Enlightenment approach within elite education original and accurate. The author did not conceal his conservative conception of education in the humanities as opposed to the natural sciences and was not afraid to expand his topic to take in the whole of society. He did so in a confident tone revealing a detached intellectual view. The persuasive and humorous examples –

---

499 Liessmann, Konrad Paul: *Teorie nevzdělanosti. Omyly společnosti vědění.* Prague 2008.

500 Liessmann, Konrad Paul: *Hodina duchů. Praxe nevzdělanosti. Polemický spis.* Prague 2015. Cf. review by Hanuš, Jiří: *Kdyby se raději rakouský filozof mýlil.* Kontexty 8 (1/2016), pp. 93–96.

for example, about Immanuel Kant, who would scarcely have made it through the current system – are worthy of inclusion in anthologies. Of course, the fact that there was so much discussion about the publication in Central Europe was not only due to its style: it could be said that it was more the author's courage, since he came forward with a critique of newly introduced reforms which European political and academic elites were convinced would bring about the desired progress.

It cannot be said that *The Practice of Miseducation* alias *The Hour of the Ghosts* came up with any radically new arguments – instead, Liessmann expands on what he wrote in the *Theory*. Apart from the old criticism of the Bologna reform and various ways of measuring knowledge (PISA), we also find new phenomena which the author treats with scepticism and irony. Firstly, the so-called education expert – apparently, in Austria this is usually the retired president of the provincial school board, who is now using journalism to catch up on what he missed. The education expert is primarily a disseminator of a rehashed Rousseauistic faith, i.e. the belief that young children are wonderful, broadly competent and multi-talented beings who are only corrupted, broken and destroyed by an antiquated education system and a flawed society; a missionary for the belief in brilliant inclusive teaching which aims to level out all differences within one school; and a promotor of a verdant "tree of life" instead of grey classroom practice. According to the expert, the teacher is a coach, partner and friend, and the pupil or student essentially learns by himself. Liessmann's view of such an expert and his mission is unequivocally negative: the overemphasis on "life", "experience", "autonomy" and "competence" eliminates the very principle of all culture according to which subsequent generations build on the achievements and knowledge of the previous generations: "Giving young people enough time to reinvent the wheel may sound good, but in reality we will only be robbing them of valuable time." What Liessmann considers the second educational folly of the present is the undue emphasis on so-called competences, which in his view have replaced traditional knowledge, learning and curiosity. The third outcome of the new conception of education is the "new undisciplinarity", which the author understands to mean the disintegration and effective elimination of subjects, fields and disciplines, from primary school right up to university. Here there is a paradox: on the one hand, there is a tendency for traditional fields of study to disappear; on the other hand, there are calls for interdisciplinarity and transdisciplinarity, which are impossible without a thorough knowledge of one basic field.

The Czech academic debate about Liessmann harked back to the tradition of this "genre", especially the neo-Marxist criticism of half-education penned by Theodor W. Adorno in the late 1950s. Although it is possible to agree with Michael Hauser that Adorno has some similar themes to Liessmann[501], the contemporary

---

501 Cf. Hauser, Michael: *Věk instrumentální racionality. Moderní univerzita*, c. d., pp. 245–263.

Austrian author is less burdened by a Marxist/sociological class conception and relatively complex terminology, and his analyses are decidedly more "practical", despite also being written by a philosopher. But it is worth recalling that some Czech authors such as Václav Havel also addressed "half-education" in the mid-1960s in an attempt to catch up with (popular) Western European social themes. Havel's Notes on Half-Education, published in the Prague magazine *Tvář* in 1964[502], became a very widely discussed text which the author returned to post-1989.

Although Liessmann's books on non-/half-/education could be assigned to the genre of conservative defences, which have been a part of Central European culture since Baroque times, this is not just about a radical attitude or a sentimental preoccupation with the past. This is clearly demonstrated by the author: because of all the possible criticisms of his opinions, each chapter of *The Practice of Miseducation* includes a very judicious and responsible suggestion for a way out of the crisis. The publication concludes with a pleasing vision of a university or any kind of school that will restore its original mission, become an "island" for encountering and getting to grips with science, create a counterbalance to the volatile virtual world and the "dictatorship of diligence" and once again become a "place of theory" where students will experience the inner and outer discipline of science. This kind of university would supposedly reawaken curiosity and a desire for education and become a hotbed for the intellectual exchange of views – it would cease to slavishly serve bureaucratic and economic interests. One weak point in his otherwise considered analysis might be an underestimation of the market and the alternatives that it presents and creates. In addition to its unquestionably negative effects, the market – especially the laws of supply and demand – may ultimately create a need for alternative models in education which will stand in opposition to both Rousseauistic ideals taken to the extreme and rampant bureaucratization and other strongly negative effects.

Although we can speak of weaknesses in Liessmann's approach (and that of other conservative critics of the current state of affairs) and its limited applicability to the humanities, our next argument is this: let us listen to critics! Some of them are too intelligent for us to dismiss their words with reference to the "automatic progress" which the conservative naysayers object to.

---

502 Havel, Václav: *Poznámky o polovzdělanosti*. Tvář no. 9–10/1964, December 1964, pp. 23–29.

Argument Three: The "Humboldtian ideal" versus the "national interest"

In this work we have frequently used the expression "Humboldtian myth", which we have understood to mean one of the main trends in modern university education which began during the general restoration of the Prussian state at the time of the Napoleonic Wars and was manifested, among other things, in the founding of Berlin University. Although this was originally a Prussian model, it became widespread across the whole of Europe and some elements of it even spread outside Europe. In Central Europe it was still alive in the first half of the 20th century, although some serious shortcomings had already become apparent. It was a system of linking science and teaching which is, of course, still applied and applicable today, although a "harmonious" and optimal version of it is sought. Another rather more problematic aspect was that it was extremely liberal, as is shown by the biographies of many prominent 19th-century Europeans. This is clearly illustrated, for example, by the university courses the young Karel Marx undertook.[503] This system of courses was essentially about a graduate, after several years of selected lectures (and perhaps also private tutoring and parental support), being able to show the results of his work in the form of a book. In short, anyone who wrote a book had it made. The Humboldtian model was also liberal in the sense that it did not really address the graduate's job or profession, partly because in comparison with today there were fewer students at universities.[504]

Apart from this model, however, the "ambivalence of modernity" also manifested itself in another way: in connection with the development of the state and its growing needs. This trend seems to have begun as early as the mid-18th century as part of "state absolutism" (consider Joseph II and his reforming interventions in all areas of state administration) and by the mid-19th century it appeared as a strong trend within the expansion of state bureaucracy and the growing power of the state in almost all European countries. In short, the state developed a need for educated people (in simplified terms, "civil servants") in various positions. The system therefore proved to be different from the "liberal" and "elitist" Humboldtian system, although originally it was also mainly associated with developments in the German lands and Austria. It was based on a particular choice of "profession" or "job" which the "courses" and the form of studies also began to be tailored to. This system increasingly gained ground as the demand for higher education rose, and it was accentuated and refined by twentieth-century political regimes that placed importance on monitoring their citizens and

---

503 Cf. Wheen, Francis: *Marx*. Prague 2002.

504 Cf. Schlerath, Bernfried: (Hg.): *Wilhelm von Humboldt. Vortragszyklus zum 150. Todestag.* Berlin – New York 1986.

incorporating them into the civil service in an organized way. Some Europeans may still remember the communist "placements" used by the state to determine which region a graduate would work in and which post they would take up.

It could be said with some simplification that current developments in higher education are also playing out on this "board", albeit in a more sophisticated form. The liberal tradition is by no means dead – on the contrary, it has taken in new influences from abroad, especially from the USA. The rescue of the Humboldtian model is now being carried out on many levels, with experiments into a looser system of Bachelor's degrees that offers a broader and "freer" foundation for truly scientific Master's degrees. Another aspect intended to increase the liberality of universities is the emphasis on international exchange and interdisciplinarity. Take, for example, the basic Czech higher-education document entitled *A Framework for the Development of Higher Education up to 2020*[505] – although it begins by talking about the labour market and the relationship between higher education and practice (as well as social and gender aspects that are considered important by the current EU elites), it immediately goes on to mention measures to promote the quality of teaching and scientific research, as well as internationalization and other "innovations" and "creative" processes. Despite the focus on the future of graduates, therefore, the document also provides scope for the liberal Humboldtian tradition, albeit supplemented by other elements perceived as up-to-date.

It is our belief that this tradition, however much it is referred to and occasionally applied with varying degrees of success, has relatively powerful "counter-blocs" – not only in strong pressure from the state, as was the case in the past (although even today this cannot be overlooked), but in a whole range of problems associated with the rise in student numbers, the rise in the number of universities, the search for criteria to assess the results of teaching and scientific output, and establishing criteria for the appropriate financial evaluation of the work of universities and especially their staff.

Argument Four: Specific problems of Czech higher education

Within this argument we would like to deal with some challenging trends that have appeared within Czech higher education since 1989, though in the belief that they also affect many Central European countries, especially those which underwent the transformation from a communist to democratic regime in the early 1990s.

Firstly, there is the trend of a rise in the number of university students since 1990. The awareness of new-found freedom opened the "floodgates" with regard to the possibility for personal development, the idea of student life with its social

---

505 http://www.vzdelavani2020.cz/images_obsah/dokumenty/ramec_vs.pdf, downloaded 30. 7. 2018.

opportunities and opportunities for studying abroad, but above all the creation and expansion of state-run and private higher-education institutes. In the 1990s "new foundations" came about in some larger towns and cities with a rather naïve notion of the need for competition and the necessity of supporting some regions through the local school structure. This liberal vision was not entirely misguided, but over time it became apparent that the new universities generally lowered the required higher-education level, despite the fact that some of them aspired to "universal status" without achieving it – it was more a case of specific higher-education institutes reacting to specific regional demand. The creation and development of these institutions burdened the entire system with a "hunt" for accreditation and higher-education specialists, who were in short supply following the communist period. Above all, however, there was a rise in the number of students, and since the early 1990s this number has continued to increase steadily. The sociologist Libor Prudký speaks of the transition from an elite to mass form of education, observing that the process that occurred in the Czech Republic and some other Central European countries took a hundred years in the USA.[506]

The same author describes the growth in student numbers and the creation of schools as parallel processes. In the Czech Republic, public education dominates as a result of historical determinants, but private higher-education institutions have also been created, although they have somewhat different goals and "parameters" – in the Czech Republic, for example, private schools have the opposite ratio of students in full-time and distance learning and a rather different relationship to practical training.

The second most significant aspect of the changes – a long-term one – is the transformation of forms of study, subject preferences and especially the creation of structured courses of the Bologna type. This structural change has been taking place in the Czech Republic since 2001 and from the outset it has had to contend with some difficulties – the Bachelor's degree did not automatically become the basic and most widespread level of study as a large number of students attribute more importance to a Master's degree (partly because by law it is not possible to practise some relatively common types of profession, such as teaching, after only completing a Bachelor's degree.) There have also proved to be significant differences between universities and faculties: some placed importance on experimenting with a "liberal type of study" in the manner of Fareed Zakaria (see The Myth of Indisputable Foundations) while others did not. This is also linked to the issue of graduates. According to data from 2013, public universities accounted for more than eighty per cent of the total number of graduates, and it is interesting to note that in the Czech Republic it is economics subjects which have the largest

506 Prudký, Libor: *Rozvoj osobnosti vysokoškoláků jako součást kvality výuky. Témata a otázky k pojetí vysokoškolského studia jako učení se svobodě.* Brno 2014, p. 53.

share of graduates, followed by technical subjects, with the humanities in third place. One aspect perceived as a deficiency in professional circles is the fact that graduates in teaching subjects come right at the "tail end" of this scale.

For historians specializing in culture and social history, it is also very interesting to observe how social attitudes to the university have transformed with the process of massification, how the social composition of students has changed, and also the changes in the status of teachers, degrees and social rituals. For example, it is worth mentioning the very widespread belief that in a number of fields Bachelor's courses have transformed into a higher form of secondary education, with graduates often achieving the level previously reached by school-leavers. This trend corresponds to personality development, as pointed out by contemporary psychologists – students and young people do not appear to "rush" into adulthood, and some authors speak of adulthood being as late as around 24 years of age. With a few exceptions, this developmental process is not taken very seriously in Czech academic circles.

This is also related to everything that could be termed "student issues". This includes the transformation of the clear vocational focus that was still being employed in Central Europe thirty years ago into a much looser type of study which in practice is often a search for an appropriate form of study even several semesters after it has begun; the change in the chances of securing permanent employment after graduating in particular subject areas (in the scientific sphere, employment is increasingly on a part-time, temporary basis for the duration of a grant, with the insecurity that entails); the pressure to acquire experience abroad, which is associated with the need for language skills; the demands on Bachelor's and Master's theses, which is related to the Bologna system, and so on.

We also believe that, owing to the history of Central European universities, there is still a major shortfall in responsible collaboration between individual fields of study (and hence also faculties and institutes). On the one hand, declarations of interdisciplinarity appear in almost every scientific project; on the other hand, this interdisciplinarity is often superficial – that is, if it does not just remain on paper. Of all people, scientists should know how difficult true disciplinarity is and how exceptional it really is.[507]

---

507 Here it is possible to cite an example from the history of historiography. The most famous French historical school of the 20th century, Annales, arose as a programmatically interdisciplinary school, which was partly a result of the strong personal links between the individual protagonists, the consistent programmatic opposition to the existing historiographical school of thought and the general social demand. Cf. Burke, Peter: *Francouzská revoluce v dějepisectví. Škola Annales 1929–1989.* Prague 2004.

Argument Five: Money "only" comes first

A major and recurring theme in Czech higher education is funding – or rather the lack of it. There is talk of the "underfunding" of education, but this has to be seen in a wider context. Underfunding is a structural problem related to the trend resisting tuition fees within public higher education, to the system of subsidies and grants from Czech and European sources which are intended predominantly for specialist purposes, the minimal involvement of private firms and wealthy entrepreneurs in education, and poor financial management in some schools. However, "underfunding" is a word that keeps cropping up in surveys into problems in education, in regular complaints by academics from various fields and especially among younger teachers who have not yet reached the higher career grades which also entail higher financial remuneration.

One specific and significant aspect of the whole matter is the method of assessing the results of university lecturers'/researchers' work, or rather the lengthy search for an optimal form. Comparative analysis – for example, the most prestigious and best-known world rankings, U21 Ranking of National Higher Education Systems, which compares the quality of higher-education systems in fifty countries around the world – has shown that in 2017, following three years of slight improvement (in 2016 it went up by one place and in 2015 by three places), the Czech Republic dropped two places in the overall assessment from one year to the next and was ranked 24th. The Czech Republic achieved the historically lowest score in the area of connectivity (concerning international cooperation and open access to information) and environment (government policy and regulation, proportion of women, standard of the education system as a whole). The Czech Republic comes off worst in the area of output (which assesses the position of a country's universities in the international rankings, the numbers of scientific articles and citations of them, graduates and their employability on the labour market).[508] This ranking points to weaknesses in some universities when it comes to striking a balance between teaching and scientific research. However, these results do not mean that all universities and colleges are badly off financially, only that there is one basic structural deficiency.

In the chapter on "academic capitalism" we outline numerous problems of history and, in part, of the present too. At this juncture we would also like to mention the inconsistent reception of European projects aimed at increasing the competitiveness of individual fields, improving teaching through innovation and assisting schools financially in the search for new (alternative, more creative) methods of teaching and education. It is no secret that these projects

---

508 https://www.universitas.cz/ze-sveta/85-ceske-vysoke-skolstvi-si-v-porovnani-s-padesatkou-zemi-pohorsilo, retrieved 1.8.2018.

are often viewed with ambivalence – on the one hand, they certainly improve some parameters of teaching, but on the other hand they burden schools with cumbersome bureaucracy, pull apart workplaces set up in the customary way, change their orientation and are sometimes ideologically tinged. The problem of subsidizing through various grants, including European ones, is also related to the widespread vice of "obtaining money at any cost", i.e. circumventing the donor's intentions. In this context there is talk of "wasting" money as well as "underfunding". At first this seems to be a paradox, but in reality it is probably one of the serious problems no-one has really addressed in the Czech Republic.

The funding of schools is directly related to university lecturers' self-esteem, a value that has recently started to be discussed in the Czech Republic – mostly in a wider context that also incorporates the self-esteem of teachers at secondary and primary schools. Generally speaking, it has been shown that an improvement in the relationship in this area cannot come about without establishing clear rules (a high-quality career structure, methodology for assessing teaching and research) and simplifying the entire system ("de-bureaucratizing" projects, etc.). The question of properly funding schools is also largely a political one, and in a system where most of the funding is provided to universities and private schools from the state budget it is dependent on the overall strategic government concept – how the government and the current political elites prioritize the value of education for the country's future. One very obvious problem specific to the Czech Republic remains the all-too-frequent changes in government and ministerial officials, which is largely counterproductive in education. Another factor is political decisions which – unfortunately – often fail to correspond to the condition and possibilities of the Czech economy, especially in the area of so-called basic research and the possibilities of applying science and research in practice.

Argument Six: The need for debate about university culture

As part of the various reforms related to the transition from an elite to mass (universal) type of education, one problem which continually crops up is the re-lationship between the competences of the state and the universities themselves, with existing problems often being swept under the carpet. This is not only about what the state (through its institutions) and elected university bodies should "do" – determining competences is of the utmost importance, as can now be seen in the changes to the accreditation system – but also about the fact that there is no institutionalized discipline (or course) within universities to deal with university culture in its historical and present-day dimension. Although there is specific ex-pertise at individual universities investigating some aspects of the history and present of university culture, systematic research has not been carried out. The historical aspect is usually covered by a "positivistic" description of particular institutions combined with a current need to raise the profile of universities as part of anniversary celebrations, while the present situation is usually examined within traditional disciplines (philosophy, sociology, psychology) or individual theses based on individual study preferences. That is why a number of vital questions remain unasked. A typical example of such a question is the relationship between key groups of subjects (humanities, natural sciences, medical science, technical subjects, new subjects and courses), various facets of which are "tackled" only at an ideological level (European projects) or an entirely practical one (for example, specific relationships between faculties of the same university when the budget for the following year is being set; research carried out by non-university facilities). And yet the relationship between groups of subjects is one of the most traditional and at the same time most current: there is a link between the view of subjects, their identity and self-esteem, society-wide and political support, the perception of access to tertiary education, and student "careers".[509] As part of the transition from elite to mass and universal education, the fundamental problems of "subjects" and their role have been reinstated.

It is true of the Czech setting that in contemporary history these fundamental questions have remained the domain of individuals who (for political or other reasons) have often remained outside universities. For example, thinkers like Jan Patočka (1907–1977), Josef Šafařík (1907–1992), Božena Komárková (1903–1997) and Zdeněk Neubauer (1942–2016) have considered technical developments and the relationship between the humanities and natural sciences (ecology).

In this regard, countries which have undergone the transformation from communism to democracy have one more problematic legacy which they are sometimes at a loss to deal with. In some fields of research, universities have competition from the Academy of Sciences, which carries out basic research as some university departments do. Over the past thirty years this relationship has gone through many twists and turns as the "fields of competence" have been defined, with science and university teaching converging in many subjects (most commonly, some experts from the Czech Academy of Sciences work part-time at universities while some teachers are involved in academy projects). This systemic shift is also directly related to subject identity and scientific and non-scientific interests. Even this specific area requires a continual search for the optimal situation, as is the case in many other areas.

In short, within university culture there are important themes which by their nature lie "outside" the standard and newer disciplines but still require a systemic approach.

---

509 Czech debate on the changes in Czech higher education from elite forms to universal ones, cf. Prudký, Libor – Pabian, Petr – Šíma, Karel: *České vysoké školství. Na cestě od elitního k univerzálnímu vzdělávání 1989–2009*. Prague 2010. Here the authors mainly work with the conception of the American author Martin Trow from the 1970s.

Argument Seven: The wider context of the debate

The wider context of the debate we are instigating consists of several different aspects.

The first aspect is the transformation of higher education and academic education which occurred post-1989 in the countries of the so-called "Eastern Bloc". This makes it possible to compare reforms in various Central European countries which had to fundamentally change their educational priorities and overhaul the entire system in all its constituent parts. It could be provisionally stated that most young people in the Czech Republic managed to adapt quickly to these fundamental changes and adopt most of the basic measures of transformation (eliminating centralism, increasing the range of courses and subjects available, opening up possibilities for studying abroad, increasing the network of schools in regions, etc.) whose basic aim was to liberalize education.[510]

The second factor is the openness of the entire system, which creates sector-specific possibilities. What we have in mind here is primarily the possibility of international cooperation, which is conceivable at the level of individual institutes (departments), faculties and universities, but also at the level of individuals who in principle are not bound by any constraints – on the contrary, in an ideal situation their creativity and international links benefit the institutions they work in. Despite a number of problems, it can be stated that in the Czech Republic anyone (student or researcher) who accepts the basic rules of the game and is willing to put in the work has opportunities for development. Although there are many shortcomings and contradictions, in the last thirty years there have not been any at the systemic level that would prevent research and other work by truly talented and responsible people. In other words, the concept of the "myth" should not and does not aim to disguise the fact that educational processes and specific higher-education and university activities are "real" and are based on the opportunities provided by a free, democratic state.

Cultural history certainly offers a wider range of possibilities than we have put forward in this publication. Its contribution is perhaps to be found in the attempt to link current issues with historical context, the present with the past. This is a reflection of the fact that this text was written on the eve of a certain anniversary – the centenary of the establishment of Masaryk University in Brno, which we have the honour to be part of.

---

510 General context cf. Šafaříková, Vlasta et al.: *Transformace české společnosti 1989–1995*. Brno 1996.

ZUSAMMENFASSUNG

Mythen und Traditionen der mitteleuropäischen universitären Kultur

Die Publikation setzt sich eine Kulturanalyse des universitären Milieus zum Ziel, wobei der Begriff „Mythus" ihr analytisches Hauptinstrument darstellt. Die Autoren fassen den Mythus als eine Kulturerscheinung auf, die die Gegenwart der akademischen Sphäre mit der Vergangenheit verbindet, und als einen Archetyp im Sinne der Psychologie von Carl Gustav Jung, die das Bewusstsein des Einzelnen und die Identität der Kommunität, in diesem Falle der akademischen Gemeinde, als ein Ganzes erscheinen lässt. Sie finden ihre Inspiration bei der modernen Erforschung der Rolle der Mythen beim Konstituieren von nationalen und überhaupt kollektiven Identitäten. Der Mythus weist laut Autoren der Studie feste Bindungen an Symbole auf, die gerade im Bereich des Schulwesens oft in Erscheinung treten, an Rituale, hierarchische Zeichen und Traditionen verschiedenster Art, die die „Gedächtnisstrategien" einer konkreten Institution ermöglichen. Die Mythen sind in der mittelalterlichen Tradition der Universität als eine Gemeinschaft von Wahrheitssuchern verankert, einschließlich aller Widersprüche und Konflikte, die mit der Theorie und Praxis dieser Grundthese an den Wurzeln jeder europäischen Universität vereint sind. Die historische Einsicht in die Problematik der universitären Traditionen und Mythen bildet ein geeignetes Instrument zum Verständnis der mitteleuropäischen universitären Kultur als einer Art Märchen (*Once Upon a Time...*), das in seinem Idealismus und seiner Vertiefung in das Erzählen von den „alten guten Zeiten" gegen die Reformbemühungen beachtlich widerstandsfähig war. Das Buch präsentiert dem amerikanischen und westeuropäischen Leser die universitäre Kultur, die dem sog. humboldtschen Kreis der akademischen Tradition eigen ist, wobei im Zentrum der Aufmerksamkeit vor allem die Situation im tschechischen Hochschulwesen im Vergleich mit der entsprechenden Lage in Deutschland, Polen, Österreich und anderen Ländern steht. Einen bedeutenden Aspekt stellt daher die Charakteristik der mitteleuropäischen Universitäten dar, die im 20. Jahrhundert eine diskontinuierliche Entwicklung erfahren haben. Ein Spezifikum des Buches ist die Präferenz der Betrachtungsweise der akademischen Kultur vorwiegend aus der Perspektive der kleineren Hochschulen, die im 19. und 20. Jahrhundert nicht in einer Metropole entstanden sind. Dies ist als eine Art Ausbalancierung gegenüber der bisher häufig bearbeiteten Geschichte der mitteleuropäischen Hochschulen mit mittelalterlicher Tradition zu betrachten. Die Autoren haben das Buch zwar historisch konzipiert, aber sie wehren sich nicht gegen bedeutende Aktualisierungen. Von besonderem Interesse sind für sie vornehmlich der Widerspruch zwischen dem humboldtschen Ideal und dem „akademischen Kapitalismus", die Suche nach universitärer Einheit im Rahmen des Diversifikationsdrucks, dem sich die Universitäten ausgesetzt sehen, die Tendenz zur Schwächung der universitären Freiheiten und verschiedene Formen und Rollen der universitären Selbstverwaltung. Die Autoren versuchen, mit ihrer Publikation einer Debatte nicht nur in historischen Kreisen, sondern auch unter den Interessenten quer durch die universitäre Kommunität neue Impulse zu geben.

BIBLIOGRAPHY AND SOURCES

Monographs:

Adámek, Vladimír: *Financování veřejných vysokých škol.* Brno 2012.

Altbach, Philip: *Tradition und Transition. The International Imperative in Higher Education.* Boston 2007. https://doi.org/10.1163/9789087903596

Anderson, Robert D.: *European Universities from the Enlightenment to 1914.* Oxford – New York 2004. https://doi.org/10.1093/acprof:oso/9780198206606.001.0001

Arnold, Rolf: *Bildung nach Bologna! Die Anregungen der europäischen Hochschulreform.* Wiesbaden 2015. https://doi.org/10.1007/978-3-658-08978-8

August, Jochen: *Sonderaktion Krakau. Die Verhaftung der Krakauer Wissenschaftler am 6. November 1939.* Hamburg 1997.

Azouvi, Francois – Launnay, Marc de: *Ricoeur, Paul. Myslet a věřit (rozhovor).* Praha 2000.

Badelt, Christian: *Die unternehmerische Universität: Herausforderung oder Widerspruch in sich?* Wien 2004. https://doi.org/10.1007/978-3-322-81900-0_6

Bammer, Gabriele: The Relationship of Integrative Applied Research and I2S to Multidisciplinarity and Transdisciplinarity. In: *Integration and Implementation Sciences for Researching Complex Real-World Problems.* Canberra 2013. https://doi.org/10.22459/DI.01.2013

Banasiewicz, Maria: *Polityka naukowa i oświatowa hitlerowskich Niemiec na ziemiach polskich „wcielonych" do Trzeciej Rzeszy w okresie okupacji (1939–1945).* Poznań 1980.

Barbagli, Marzio: *Educating for unemployment: politics, labor markets, and the school systém – Italy 1859–1973.* New York 1982.

Baumgartner, Marita: *Professoren und Universitäten im 19. Jahrhundert.* Göttingen 1997. https://doi.org/10.13109/9783666357848

Bečvář, Jindřich et al.: *Dějiny Univerzity Karlovy IV (1918–1990).* Praha 1998.

Bendyk, Edwin – Maron, Olaf: *Ranking naukowy uczelni akademickich. Diagnoza stanu szkolnictwa wyższego w Polsce.* Warszawa 2009.

Beránek, Karel (ed.): *Dějiny Univerzity Karlovy II. (1622–1802),* Praha 1995.

Berger, Peter: *Posvátný baldachýn. Základy sociologické teorie náboženství.* Brno 2018.

Bok, Derek: *Universities in the Marketplace. The Commercialization of Higher Education.* Princeton 2003.

Bollenbeck Georg – Wende Waltraud (ed.): *Der Bologna-Prozeß und die Veränderung der Hochschullandschaft.* Heidelberg 2007.

Borovský, Tomáš (ed.): *Historici na brněnské univerzitě. Devět portrétů.* Brno 2008.

Bostan, Grigore: *Der Beitrag der Universität Czernowitz zur Entwicklung der rumänischen Kultur und der ukrainisch-rumänischen Beziehungen.* Bern – Wien 1998.

Bourdieu, Pierre: *Homo academicus.* Frankfurt am Main 1988.

Burke, Peter: *Francouzská revoluce v dějepisectví. Škola Annales 1929–1989.* Praha 2004.

Burke, Peter: *Společnost a vědění II. Od encyklopedie k Wikipedii.* Praha 2013.

Burrow, John W.: *Krize rozumu. Evropské myšlení 1848–1914.* Brno 2003.

Buszko, Józef – Paczyńska, Irena (edd.): *Podstępne uwięzienie profesorów Uniwersytetu Jagiellońskiego i Akademii Górniczej (6.XI.1939 r.): dokumenty.* Kraków 1995.

Campbell, Joseph: *Mýty. Legendy dávných věků v našem denním životě.* Praha 1998.

Cayton, Mary Kupies (ed.): *Encyclopedia of American cultural and intellectual history.* New York 2001.

Cipro, Miroslav: *Idea vysoké školy. Studie o vysokém školství ve světě socialismu a kapitalismu.* Praha 1981.

Connelly, John. *Zotročená univerzita: sovětizace vysokého školství ve východním Německu, v českých zemích a v Polsku v letech 1945–1956.* Praha 2008.

Černý, Václav: *Paměti I–III.* Brno 1992–1994.

d'Elvert, Christian: *Geschichte der Studien-, Schul- und Erziehungsanstalten in Mähren und Oesterr. Schlesien insbesonder der Olmützer Universität. Schriften der historisch-statistischen Section der k.k. mährosch-schlesischen Gesellschaft zur Beförderung des Ackerbaues, der Natur- und Landeskunde.* Bd. X., Brünn 1857.

Davie, Grace: *Výjimečný příklad Evropa. Podoby víry v dnešním světě.* Brno 2009.

Dawson, Christopher: *Pokrok a náboženství.* Praha 1947.

Derwissis, Stergios Nikolaos: *Die Geschichte der griechischen Bildungswesens in neuerer Zeit mit besonderer Berücksichtigung der Einflüsse der deutschen Pädadogik.* Frankfurt am Main 1976.

Domin, Karel: *Můj rektorský rok. Z bojů o Karolinum a za práva Karlovy univerzity.* Praha 1934.

Domin, Karel – Vojtíšek, Václav – Hutter, Josef: *Karolinum statek národní.* Praha 1934.

Dörre, Klaus – Neis, Matthias: *Das Dilemma der unternehmerischen Universität. Hochschulen zwischen Wissenproduktion und Machtzwang.* Berlin 2010. https://doi.org/10.5771/9783845269399

Drtina, František: *Nástin dějin vyššího školství a theorií paedagogických ve Francii o doby revoluce. Díl 1, (1789–1814).* Praha 1898.

Drtina, František: *Organisace školská předních kulturních států.* Praha 1901.

Drtina, František: *Universita a učitelstvo. Soubor statí.* Praha 1932.

Dybiec, Julian: *Finansowanie nauki o oświaty w Galicji 1860–1918.* Kraków 1979.

Elkana, Yehuda – Klöpper, Hannes: *Die Universität im 21. Jahrhundert. Für eine neue Einheit von Lehre, Forschung und Gesellschaft.* Hamburg 2012.

Engelbrecht, Helmut: *Geschichte des österreichischen Bildungswesens, Bd. 4, Von 1848 bi zum Ende der Monarchie.* Wien 1986.

Fallon, Daniel: *The German University. A heroic ideal in conflict with the modern world.* Bouder – Colorado 1980.

Fasora, Lukáš – Hanuš, Jiří: *Masarykova univerzita. Příběh vzdělání a vědy ve střední Evropě.* Brno 2009.

Ferguson, Niall: *The Square and the Tower: Networks, Hierarchies and the Struggle for Global Power.* London 2017.

Fiala, Jiří a kol: *Univerzita v Olomouci 1573–2009.* Olomouc 2010.

Floss, Pavel: *Architekti křesťanského středověkého myšlení 1.* Praha 2004.

Frederick, Rudolph: *The American College and University. A History.* University of Georgia 1990.

Garlicki, Andrzej et all: *Dzieje Unywersytetu Warszawskiego.* Warszawa 1982.

Gawęda, Stanisław (ed.): *Straty wojenne Uniwersytetu Jagiellońskiego i stan powstały na wiosnę 1945 roku.* Kraków 1974.

Goff Le, Jacques: *Intelektuálové ve středověku.* Praha 2009.

Grot, Zdisław (ed.): *Dzieje Uniwersytetu im. Adama Mickeiwicza 1919–1969.* Poznaň 1972.

Halas, František X. – Jordán, František: *Dokumenty k dějinám Masarykovy univerzity v Brně II.* Brno 1995.

Hanuš, Jiří (ed.): *Lidská práva. Národ na obecnou platnost a kulturní diferenciace.* Brno 2001.

Havránek, Jan (ed.): *Dějiny Univerzity Karlovy III. (1802–1918),* Praha 1997.

Heller, Jan – Mrázek, Jiří: *Nástin religionistiky. Uvedení vědy o náboženstvích.* Praha 2004.

Hendrichová, Jana – Čerych, Ladislav et al.: *Terciární vzdělávání ve vyspělých zemích: vývoj a současnost.* Praha 1997.

Herrmann, Hans Peter: *Krisen.* Arbeiten zur Universitätsgeschichte 1933–2010 am Beispiel Freiburgs i. Br. Freiburg i. Br. – Berlin – Wien 2015.

Hobsbawm, Eric: *Věk extrémů. Krátké dvacáté století 1914–1991.* Praha 1998.

Hryniewicz, Janusz – Jałowiecki, Bohdan – Mync, Agnieszka: *Ucieczka mozgów ze szkolnictwa wyższego i nauki. The Brain Drain in Poland. Regional and Local Studies.* Warszawa 1992.

Hüther, Otto – Krücken, Georg: *Hochschulen. Fragestellungen, Ergebnisse, und Perspektiven des sozialwissenschaftlichen Hochschulforschung.* Wiesbaden 2016. https://doi.org/10.1007/978-3-658-11563-0

Charle, Christophe: *Le République des universitaires.* Paris 1994.

Chudoba, Bohdan: *O dějinách a pokroku.* Brno 1939.

Janák, Jan: *Hospodářský rozmach Moravy 1740–1918.* Brno 1999.

Jareš, Jakub – Spurný, Matěj – Volná, Katka: *S minulostí zúčtujeme. Sebereflexe Filozofické fakulty UK v dokumentech sedmdesátých a devadesátých let 20. století.* Praha 2014.

Jaspers, Karl: *Erneuerung der Universität. Reden und Schriften 1945/1946.* Heidelberg 1986. https://doi.org/10.1007/978-3-662-43161-0

Jessen, Ralph: *Akademische Elite und kommunistische Diktatur. Die ostdeutsche Hochschullehrerschaft in der Ulbricht-Ära.* Göttingen 1999. https://doi.org/10.13109/9783666357978

Jirsa, Jakub (ed.): *Idea university.* Praha 2015.

Johnson, Phillip: *Spor o Darwina.* Praha 1996.

Kalemba, Sławomir (ed.): *Miejsce Uniwersytetu Mikołaja Kopernika w nauce polskiej i jego rola w regionie.* Toruń 1989.

Kant, Immanuel: *Der Streit der Facultäten in drei Abschnitten.* Leipzig 1880.

Kerr, Clark: *The Uses of the University.* Harvard 2001.

Kervégan, Jean-Francois: *Co s Karlem Schmittem?* Praha 2015.

Klein, Julia T.: *Interdisciplinarity. History, Theory and Practice.* Detroit 1990.

Kocevová, Marie: *Přehled o aplikovaném výzkumu na univerzitách v USA.* Praha 1978.

Kolář, Zdeněk (ed.): *Hodnocení výchovy na vysokých školách.* Praha 1977.

Komárek, Stanislav: *Evropa na rozcestí.* Praha 2015.

Komárek, Stanislav: *Příroda a kultura. Svět jevů a svět interpretací.* Praha 2000.

Komárek, Stanislav: *Sloupoví aneb Postila.* Praha 2008.

Konrád, Ota: *Dějepisectví, germanistika a slavistika na Německé univerzitě v Praze 1918–1945.* Praha 2011.

Kostner, Maria: *Die Geschichte der italienischen Universitätsfrage in der Österreichisch-ungarischen Monarchie von 1864 bis 1914.* Innsbruck 1970.

Kreiß, Christian: *Gekaufte Forschung. Wissenschaft im Dienst der Konzerne.* Berlin – München – Wien 2015.

Krejčí, Jaroslav: *Mezi demokracií a diktaturou. Domov a exil.* Olomouc 1998.

Křen, Jan: *Dvě století střední Evropy.* Praha 2005.

Křen, Jan: Konfliktní společenství. *Češi a Němci 1780–1918.* Praha 2013.

Laske, Stefan: *Auf der Suche nach der regionalen Identität der Universität.* St. Pölten 1988.

Lears, Jacson T. J.: *No place of grace: antimodernism and the transformation of American culture, 1880–1920.* New York 1981.

Legutko, Ryszard: *Ošklivost demokracie a jiné eseje.* Brno 2009.

Leiß, Jürgen: *Justin-Liebig Universität, Fachhoschule und Stadt.* Giessen 1975.

Lemayer, Karl von: *Die Verwaltung der österreichischen Hochschulen von 1867–1877.* Wien 1878.

Lentze, Hans: *Die Universitätsreform des Ministers Graf Leo Thun-Hohenstein.* Wien 1962.

Liessmann, Konrad Paul: *Hodina duchů. Praxe nevzdělanosti. Polemický spis.* Praha 2015.

Liessmann, Konrad Paul: *Teorie nevzdělanosti. Omyly společnosti vědění.* Praha 2010.

Linnemann, Kai Arne: *Das Erbe der Ostforschung. Zur Rolle Göttingens in der Geschichtswissenschaft in der Nachrkriegszeit.* Marburg 2002.

Lobkowicz: Mikuláš: *Duše Evropy.* Praha 2001.

Loewenstein, Bedřich: *Víra v pokrok. Dějiny jedné evropské ideje.* Praha 2009.

Magris, Claudio: *Habsburský mýtus v moderní rakouské literatuře.* Brno 2001.

Macháček, Jaroslav: *Výzkum na vysokých školách v USA a jiných kapitalistických státech.* Praha 1966.

Majewski, Piotr (ed.): *Dzieje Uniwersytetu Warszawskiego 1915–1945.* Warszawa 2016. https://doi.org/10.31338/uw.9788323522973

Málek, Ivan: *Boj nového se starým v dnešní naší vědě.* Praha 1955.

Málek, Ivan: *Otevřené otázky naší vědy.* Praha 1966.

Málek, Ivan: *Učíme se od sovětské vědy.* Praha 1953.

Marek, Jaroslav: *Česká moderní kultura.* Praha 1998.

McLeod, Hugh: *Sekularizace v západní Evropě (1848–1914).* Brno 2008.

Menand, Louis: *Marketplace of Ideas: Reform and Resistence in the American Universities.* Norton 2009.

Menand, Louis: *The future of academic freedom.* Chicago – London 1996.

Mittelstrass, Jürgen: *Die unzeitgemässe Universität.* Frankfurt am Main 1994.

Moraw, Peter: *Gesammelte Beiträge zur deutschen und europäischen Universitätsgeschichte. Strukturen – Personen – Entwicklung.* Leiden – Boston 2008. https://doi.org/10.1163/ej.9789004162808.i-620

Morée, Peter – Piškula, Jiří: *„Nejpokrokovější církevní pracovník". Protestantské církve a Josef Lukl Hromádka v letech 1945–1969.* Benešov 2015.

Münch, Richard: *Akademischer Kapitalismus. Über die politische Ökonomie der Hochschulreform.* Berlin 2011.

Neave, Guy – Blückert, Kjell – Nybom, Thorsten (ed.).: *The European research university. An historical parenthesis?* New York 2006. https://doi.org/10.1007/978-1-137-10079-5

Nešpor, Václav: *Dějiny university olomoucké.* Olomouc 1947.

Některé zkušenosti z práce SSM na vysokých školách. Praha 1974.

Novák, Mirko: *Úsměvné vzpomínání.* Praha 1998.

Nowak, Manfred: *Universitäten zwischen Freiheit und Verantwortung. Entwicklung und Perspektiven einer Rechtsbeziehung.* Wien 2016.

Oberkrome, Willi: *Methodische Innovation und völkische Ideologisierung in der deutschen Geschichtswissenschaft 1918–1945.* Göttingen 1993.

Ortega y Gasset, José: *Mission of the University.* London 1946.

Otáhal, Milan: *Studenti a komunistická moc v českých zemích 1968–1989.* Praha 2003.

Otruba, Gustav: *Die Universitäten in der Hochschulorganisation der Donau-Monarchie: Nationale Erziehungsstätten im Vielvölkerreich 1850 bis 1914. Student und Hochschule im 19. Jahrhundert: Studie und Materialen.* Göttingen 1975.

Paletschek, Sylvia: *Die permanente Erfindung der Tradition. Die Universität Tübingen im Kaiserreich und in der Weimarer Republik.* Stuttgart 2001.

Paulus, Stefan: *Vorbild USA? Amerikanisierung von Universitäten und Wissenschaft in Westdeutschland 1946–1976.* München 2010. https://doi.org/10.1524/9783486706567

Payne, Thomas: *The Age of Reason.* Peterborough 2011.

Pernes, Jiří: *Nejen rudé prapory aneb Pravda o revolučním roce 1905 v českých zemích.* Brno 2005.

Pernes, Jiří: *Škola pro Moravu. 100 let Vysokého učení technického v Brně.* Brno 1999.

Petráň, Josef: *Filozofové dělají revoluci. Filozofická fakulta Univerzity Karlovy během komunistického experimentu (1948–1968–1989).* Praha 2015.

Petráň, Josef: *Nástin dějin Filozofické fakulty Univerzity Karlovy v Praze do roku 1948.* Praha 1983.

Pipes, Richard: *Dějiny ruské revoluce.* Praha 1998.

Pokludová, Andrea: *Formování inteligence na Moravě a ve Slezsku 1857–1910.* Opava 2008.

Pomian, Krzysztof: *Evropa a její národy. Ve znamení jednoty a různosti.* Praha 2001.

Preisner, Rio: *Americana I. a II.* Brno 1992–1993.

Prudký, Libor – Pabian, Petr – Šima, Karel: *České vysoké školství. Na cestě od elitního k univerzálnímu vzdělávání 1989–2009.* Praha 2010.

Prudký, Libor: *Rozvoj osobnosti vysokoškoláků jako součást kvality výuky. Témata a otázky k pojetí vysokoškolského studia jako učení se svobodě.* Brno 2014.

Rapport, Michael: *Evropa devatenáctého století.* Praha 2011.

Reading, Bill: *The University in Ruins.* Cambridge 1997.

Reuben, Julie A.: *The Making of the Modern University: Intellectual Transformation and the Marginalization of Morality.* Chicago 1997.

Reżimy totalitarne wobec ludzi nauki 1939–1945: Uniwersytet Jagielloński: Sonderaktion Krakau, Zbrodnia Katyńska. Warszawa 2007.

Ringer, Fritz K.: *Die Gelehrten. Der Niedergang der deutschen Mandarine 1890–1933.* Stuttgart 1983.

Rodriguez-Moura, Enrique: *Freiheit und Macht an der Universität.* Berlin 2016.

Röhrs, Hermann: *Einfluss der klasisschen deutschen Universitätsidee auf die Higher Education in Amerika.* Weinheim 1995.

Rolfe, Gary: *The University in Dissent. Scholarship in the corporate university.* London – New York 2013. https://doi.org/10.4324/9780203084281

Rorabaugh, Wiliam Joseph: *Berkeley at War: The 1960s.* New York 1989.

Roth, Oto: *Integrace vysokého školství v EU a česká vysokoškolská politika.* Praha 1997.

Rüegg, Walter (ed.): *A History of the University in Europe. Volume III. Universities in the nineteenth and early twentieth Centuries (1800–1945).* Cambridge 2004.

Rüegg, Walter (ed.): *Geschichte der Universität in Europa, Band II.* München 1996.

Rüegg, Walter (ed.): *Geschichte der Universität in Europa, Band III.* München 2004.

Rüegg, Walter (ed.): *Geschichte der Universität in Europa, Band IV.* München 2008.

Rys, Jan: *Hilsneriáda a TGM.* Praha 2016.

Schatz, Klaus: *Všeobecné koncily. Ohniska církevních dějin.* Brno 2014.

Schlerath, Bernfried: (ed.): *Wilhelm von Humboldt. Vortragszyklus zum 150. Todestag.* Berlin – New York 1986.

Slaughter, Sheila – Leslie, Larry: *Academic Capitalism. Politics, Policies, and the Entrepreneurial University.* Baltimore 1997.

Soukup, Daniel: *Jednota filozofie a různost věd. Úvod ke knize J. H. Newmana Idea univerzity.* Olomouc 2014.

Spunar, Pavel et al.: *Kultura středověku.* Praha 1995.

Spurný, Matěj – Jareš, Jakub – Volná, Katka: *Náměstí Krasnoarmějců 2. 2: Učitelé a studenti na Filozofické fakultě UK v období normalizace.* Praha 2012.

Stanzel, Josef: *Die Schulaufsicht im Reformwerk des Johann Ignaz von Felbiger (1724–1788). Schule, Kirche und Staat in Recht und Praxis des aufgeklärten Absolutismus.* Paderborn 1976.

Stinia, Maria: *Uniwersytet Jagielloński w latach 1871–1914. Modernizacja procesu nauczania.* Kraków 2014.

Svatoš, Michal – Svatoš, Martin: *Živá tvář Erasma Rotterdamského.* Praha 1985.

Svatoš, Michal (ed.): *Dějiny Univerzity Karlovy I. (1347/1348–1622),* Praha 1995.

Szołdrska, Halszka: *Walka z kulturą polską. Uniwersytet Poznański podczas okupacji.* Poznań 1948.

Šafaříková, Vlasta et al.: *Transformace české společnosti 1989–1995.* Brno 1996.

Šima, Karel – Pabian, Petr: *Ztracený Humboldtův ráj. Ideologie jednoty výzkumu a výuky ve vysokém školství.* Praha 2013.

Taylor, Charles.: *Multikulturalismus: Zkoumání politiky uznání.* Praha 2001.

Taylor, Marc C.: *Crisis on Campus. A Bold Plan for Reforming Our Colleges and Universities.* New York 2010.

Teichler, Ulrich: *Hochschulsysteme und quantitativstrukturelle Hochschulpolitik. Differenzierung, Bologna-Prozess, Exzellenzinitiative und die Folgen.* Münster – New York 2014.

Trauner, Karl-Reinhart: *Die Wahrmund-Affäre.* Wien 1992.

Uhde, Milan: *Rozpomínky. Co na sebe vím.* Praha a Brno 2013.

Urban, Otto: *Česká společnost 1848–1918.* Praha 1982.

Urbášek, Pavel – Pulec, Jiří: *Kapitoly z dějin univerzitního školství na Moravě v letech 1945–1990.* Olomouc 2003.

Urbášek, Pavel: *Vysokoškolský vzdělávací systém v letech tzv. normalizace.* Olomouc 2008.

Vacková, Růžena: *Vězeňské přednášky.* Praha 1999.

Veber, Václav et al.: *Dějiny Rakouska.* Praha 2009.

Vlčková, Irena: *Reforma vysokoškolského studia v kontextu evropské vzdělávací politiky.* Liberec 2010.

Walterová, Eliška: *Kurikulum – proměny a trendy v mezinárodní perspektivě.* Brno 1994.

Watrin, Christian: *Studenten, Professoren und Steuerzahler. Die Gruppenuniversität in ökonomischer Sicht.* München 1979.

Wheen, Francis: *Marx*. Praha 2002.

Wolff, Hans J.: *Die Rechtsgestalt der Universität*. Köln 1956. https://doi.org/10.1007/978-3-663-02218-3

Wolff, Robert Paul: *The Ideal of the University*. Boston 1969.

Woods, Thomas Ernest: *Jak katolická církev budovala západní civilizaci*. Praha 2008.

Wróblewska, Teresa: *Die Reichsuniversitäten Posen, Prag und Strassburg als Modelle nationalsozialistischer Hochschulen in den von Deutschland besetzten Gebieten*. Toruń 2000.

Zakaria, Fareed: *Obrana liberálního vzdělání*. Praha 2017.

Anthologies:

Arnswald, Ulrich: Die Geisteswissenschaften – unterschätzte Transmissionsriemen des gesellschaftlichen Wandels und der Innovation, In: Arnswald, Ulrich – Nida-Rümelin, Julian (ed.): *Die Zukunft der Geisteswissenschaften*. Heidelberg 2005, s. 111–162.

Ash, Mitchell G.: Konstruierte Kontinuitäten und divergierende Neuanfänge nach 1945, In: Grüttner, Michael – Hachtmann, Rüdiger – Jarausch, Konrad – John, Jürgen – Middel, Matthias (ed.): *Gebrochene Wissenschaftskulturen. Universität und Politik im 20. Jahrhundert*. Göttingen 2010, s. 215–245.

Barban, Andris: The Magna Charta and the Role of Universities in the Development of Danube Region, In: Rozman, Ivan – Lorber, Lučka (eds.): *The Role of Universities and the Competitiveness of the Danube Region/Vloga univerz in konkurenčnost podonavske regije*. Maribor 2006, s. 55–68.

Barr, Nicholas: Financování vysokého školství z hlediska ekonomické teorie, In: Simonová, Natalie (ed.): *České vysoké školství na křižovatce. Investiční přístup k financování studia na vysoké škole. v sociologické reflexi*. Praha 2005, s. 19–39.

Beran, Karel: Proč je univerzita veřejnoprávní korporací? In: Staša, Josef (ed.): *Historie, současný stav a perspektivy univerzit. Úsvit nebo soumrak akademické samosprávy*. Praha 2008, s. 110–120.

Borek, Zoltán – Lhotka, Jaroslav: Studentské bouře, In: Goldstücker, Eduard (eds.): *Za lepší zítřek. Sborník a vzpomínek na studentské pokrokové hnutí třicátých let*. Praha 1963, s. 96–104.

Briese, Volker: Universität und Umland am Beispiel einzelner Hochschulen: Universität Paderborn, In: Kellermann, Paul (ed.): *Universität und Umland. Beziehungen zwischen Hochschule und Region*. Klagenfurt 1982, s. 107–122.

Brocke, Bernhard von: Die Entstehung der deutschen Forschungsuniversität. Ihr Blüte und Krise um 1900, In: Schwinges, Rainer Christoph von (ed.): *Humboldt International. Der Export der deutschen Universitätsmodells im 19. und 20. Jahrhundert*. Basel 2001, s. 367–401.

Brocke, Bernhard von: Universitäts– und Wissenschaftsfinanzierung im 19./20. Jahrhundert, In: Schwinges, Rainer Christoph (ed.): *Finanzierung von Universität und Wissenschaft in Vergangenheit und Gegenwart*. Basel 2005, s. 343–462

Brocke, Bernhard von: Wege aus der Krise, In: König, Christoph – Lämmert, Eberhard (edd.): *Konkurrenten in der Fakultät. Kultur, Wissen und Universität um 1900*. Frankfurt am Main 1999, s. 191–215.

Bruch, Rüdiger vom: Kommentar und Epilog, In: Weisbrodt, Bernd: *Akademische Vergangenheitspolitik. Beiträge zur Wissenschaftskultur der Nachkriegszeit*. Göttingen 2002, s. 281–288.

Bruch, Rüdiger vom: Langsamer Abschied von Humboldt? Etappen deutscher Universitätsgeschichte 1810–1945, In: Mitchell G. Ash (ed.): *Mythos Humboldt. Vergangenheit und Zukunft deutscher Universitäten.* Wien – Köln – Weimar 1999, s. 29–57.

Bruch, Rüdiger vom: Universitätsreform als Antwort auf die Krise. Wilhelm von Humboldt und die Folgen, In: Sieg, Ulrich – Korsch, Dietrich (edd.): *Die Idee der Universität heute.* München 2005, s. 43–55.

Brzeziński, Jerzy Marian: Od uniwersytetu Humboldta do e-uniwersytetu, In: Drozdowicz, Zbigniew (ed.): *Uniwersytety. Tradycje – dzień dziesiejszy – przyszłość.* Poznań 2009, s. 109–122.

Českým germanistou v Seattlu. Antonín hrubý a Šárka Hrubá, In: *Rozchod 1948. Rozhovory s českými poúnorovými exulanty.* Praha 2006, s. 93–120.

Čikešová, Mária: Aplikácia Bolonského procesu na Filozofickej fakulte Univerzity Komenského, In: Slobodník, Martin – Glossová, Marta (edd.): *95 rokov Filozofickej fakulty UK. Pohľad do dejín inštitúcie a jej akademickej obce.* Bratislava 2017, s. 503–524.

David-Fox, Michael – Péteri, György: On the Origin and Demise of the Communist Academic Regime. In: *Academia in Upheaval. Origin, Transfers, and Transfromations of the Commuist Academia Regime in Russia and East Central Europe.* London 2000, s. 3–38.

Doležalová, Antonie: Fiskální politika, In: Kubů, Eduard – Pátek, Jaroslav (edd.): *Mýtus a realita hospodářské vyspělosti Československa mezi světovými válkami.* Praha 2000, s. 24–40.

Doležalová, Antonie: Ve vleku nemožného čechoslovakismu? Financování Univerzity Komenského v meziválečném období (skrze československý státní rozpočet), In: Slobodník, Martin –Glossová, Marta (edd.): *95 rokov Filozofickej fakulty UK. Pohľad do dejín inštitúcie a jej akademickej obce.* Bratislava 2017, s. 89–103.

Dvořák, Tomáš: Brno a německé obyvatelstvo v květnu roku 1945. Pokus o anatomii historické (ne)paměti, In: Arburg, Adrian von – Dvořák, Tomáš – Kovařík, David: *Německy mluvící obyvatelstvo v Československu po roce 1945.* Brno 2010. s. 89–113.

Erdmann, Eisabeth von: Imagination und Reflexion. Zur Gefangenschaft der Geisteswissenschaften im Nutzen– und Leistungsdenken, In: Gauger, Jörg – Rüther, Günther (edd.): *Warum die Geisteswissenschaften Zukunft haben!* Freiburg – Basel – Wien 2007, s. 180–191.

Friedländer, Saul: The Demise of the German Mandarins. The German University and the Jews, In: Jansen, Christian – Niethammer, Lutz – Weisbrod, Bernd: *Von der Aufgabe der Freiheit. Politische Veranwortung und bürgerliche Gesellschaft im 19. und 20. Jahrhundert. Festschrift Hans Mommsen.* Berlin 1995, s. 69–82. https://doi.org/10.1515/9783050071732-005

Gabriel, Ingeborg: Im Spannungsfeld zwischen Universitärer Freiheit und kirchlicher Bindung. In: Grochlewski, Zenon – Bechina, Friedrich – Müller, Ludger – Krutzler, Martin (edd.): *Katholisch-theologische Fakultäten zwischen „Autonomie" der Universität ud kirchlicher Bindung.* Heligenkreuz 2013, s. 101–105.

Gauger, Jörg – Rüther, Günther: Die Geisteswissenschaften als selbstverständliches Element moderner Kultur. Zur Einführung in die aktuelle Debatte, In: (edd.): *Warum die Geisteswissenschaften Zukunft haben!* Freiburg – Basel – Wien 2007, s. 13–65.

Gawrecki, Dan: Versuche um die Gründung einer Universität in Troppau im 19. und 20. Jahrhundert, In: Schübel, Elmar – Heppner, Harald (edd.): *Universitäten in Zeiten des Umbruchs. Fallstudien über das mittlere und östliche Europa im 20. Jahrhundert.* Wien – Berlin 2011, s. 59–68.

Geißler, Clemens – Engelbrecht, Gerhard – Kutz, Joachim: Wirtschaftliche und soziale Effekte der Regionalisierung des Hochschulsystems, In: Kellermann, Paul (ed.): *Universität und Umland. Beziehungen zwischen Hochschule und Region.* Klagenfurt 1982, s. 40–69.

Gibbons, Michael: A Commonwealth perspective on the globalisation of higher education, In: Scott, Peter (ed.): *The Globalisation of Higher Education.* Buckingham 1998, s. 70–87.

Gjuričová, Adéla: 20. stoletím s čistým štítem i utkvělými představami: Růžena Vacková, In: Marek, Pavel – Hanuš, Jiří (edd.): *Osobnost v církvi a politice.* Brno 2006, s. 546–556.

Goldstücker, Eduard (eds.): *Za lepší zítřek. Sborník a vzpomínek na studentské pokrokové hnutí třicátých let.* Praha 1963.

Grófová, Maria: „... a jako tretia vznikla filozofická fakulta". K počiatkom a prvým rokom FiF UK, In: Slobodník, Martin – Glossová, Marta (edd.): *95 rokov Filozofickej fakulty UK. Pohľad do dejín inštitúcie a jej akademickej obce.* Bratislava 2017, s. 40–72.

Grüttner, Michael: Machtergreifung als Generationskonflikt. Die Krise der Hochschulen und der Aufstieg der Nationalsozialismus, In: Bruch, Rüdiger vom – Kaderas, Brigitte: *Wissenschaften und Wissenschaftspolitik: Bestandsaufnahmen zu Formationen, Brüchen und Kontinuitäten im Deutschland des 20. Jahrhunderts.* Stuttgart 2002, s. 339–353.

Grüttner, Michael: Nationalsozialistische Wissenschaftler: ein Kollektivporträt, In: Hachtmann, Rüdiger – Jarausch, Konrad – John, Jürgen – Middell, Michael (ed.): *Gebrochene Wissenschaftskulturen: Universität und Politik im 20. Jahrhundert.* Göttingen 2010, s. 149–166.

Hauser, Michael: Věk instrumentální racionality, In: Chotaš, Jiří – Prázný, Aleš – Hejduk, Tomáš et al.: *Moderní univerzita. Ideál a realita.* Praha 2015, s. 245–263.

Havránek, Jan: Die tschechischen Universitäten unter der kommunistischen Diktatur, In: Connelly, John – Grüttner, Michael: *Zwischen Autonomie und Anpassung: Universitäten in den Diktaturen des 20. Jahrhunderts.* Paderborn 2003, s. 157–172.

Havránek, Jan: Moravané na pražské univerzitě v 19. a 20. století, In: Malíř, Jiří – Vlček, Radomír (edd.): *Morava a české národní vědomí od středověku po dnešek.* Brno 2001, s. 111–121.

Humboldt, Friedrich von: O vnitřní a vnější organizaci vyšších vědeckých ústavů v Berlíně, In: Jirsa, Jakub (ed.): *Idea university.* Praha 2015, s. 31–39.

Jarausch, Konrad: Das Humboldt-Syndrom. Die westdeutschen Universitäten 1945–1989 – ein akademischer Sonderweg?, In: Ash, Mitchell G. (ed.): *Mythos Humboldt. Vergangenheit und Zukunft der deutschen Universitäten.* Wien – Köln – Weimar 1999, s. 58–79.

Jeskow, Jan: Die Entnazifizierung des Lehrkörpers an der Universität Jena von 1945 bis 1948, In: Hoßfeld, Uwe von – Kaiser, Tobias – Mestrup, Heinz (edd.): *Hochschule im Sozialismus. Studien zur Geschichte der Friedrich-Schiller-Universität Jena (1945–1990).* Wien – Köln – Weimar 2007, s. 71–95.

Jessen, Ralph: Von den Vorzügen des Sozialismus und der deutschen Teilung. Kollaborationsverhältnisse im ostdeutschen Wissenschaftssystem der fünfzigen Jahre. In: Weisbord, Bernd: *Akademische Vergangenheitspolitik. Beiträge zur Wissenschaftskultur der Nachkriegszeit.* Göttingen 2002, s. 39–52.

John, Jürgen: Der Mythos von „rein gebliebenen Geist": Denkmuster und Strategien des intelektuellen Neubeginns 1945, In: Hoßfeld, Uwe von – Kaiser, Tobias – Mestrup, Heinz (edd.): *Hochschule im Sozialismus. Studien zur Geschichte der Friedrich-Schiller-Universität Jena (1945–1990).* Wien – Köln – Weimar 2007, s. 19–70.

Kellermann, Paul: Einleitung, In: (ed.): *Universität und Umland. Beziehungen zwischen Hochsule und Region.* Klagenfurt 1982, s. 9.

Kernbauer, Alois: An elitist group at elitist universities. Professors, Academics an Universities in Habsburg Monarchy from the Middle od 19th Centrury to World War I, In: Bieber, Florian – Heppner, Harald (edd.): *Universities and the Elite Formation in Central, Eastern and South Eastern Europe.* Zürich – Wien 2015, s. 93–110.

Kleinmann, Bernd: Universitätspresidenten als „institutional entrepreneurs"? Unterne-hmensmythen und Führungsaufgaben im Hochschulbereich, In: Scherm, Ewald (Hg.): *Management unternehmerischer Universitäten: Realität, Vision oder Utopie?* München – Me-ring 2014.

Knorre, Dietrich von – Penzlin, Heinz – Hertel, Wieland: Der Lyssenkoismus und die Zoo-logie in Jena, In: Hoßfeld, Uwe von – Kaiser, Tobias – Mestrup, Heinz (edd.): *Hochschu-le in Sozialismus. Studien zur Geschichte der Friedrich-Schiller-Universität Jena (1945–1990).* Köln – Weimar – Wien 2007, s. 1166–1180.

Krull, Wilhelm: Hat das Humboldtsche Bildungsideal noch eine Zukunft?, In: Rudersdorf, Manfred – Höpken, Wolfgang – Schlegel, Martin (ed.): *Wissen und Geist. Universitätskul-turen.* Leipzig 2009, s. 207–219.

Kšicová, Danuše: K některým problémům kulturní politiky SSSR a ČSR v meziválečném ob-dobí, In: Čerešňák, Bedřich (ed.): *Padesát vítězných let: sborník prací z vědecké konference filosofické fakulty Univ. J. E. Purkyně k 50. výročí vzniku KSČ.* Brno 1974, s. 139–144.

Kuhnle, Till: Die ungeliebten Kernfächer – eine Streitschaft zum Ethos der Geisteswissen-schaften, In: Malinowski, Bernadette (ed.): *Im Gespräch: Probleme und Perspektiven.* Mün-chen 2006, s. 127–146.

Langholm, Sivert: The new nationalism and the new universities. The case of Norway in the early 19th century, In: Norrback, Märtha – Ranki, Kristina (edd.): *University and nation: the university and the making of the nation in northern Europe in the 19th and 20th centuries.* Helsinki 1996, s. 139–152.

Lämmert, Eberhard: Geisteswissenschaften in einer industriellen Kultur. Referat anläßlich der Jahresversammlung der Westdeutschen Rektorenkonferenz 1985 in Bamberg, In: Kallischer, Wolfgang (ed.): *Anspruch und Herausforderung der Geisteswissenschaften.* Bonn 1985, s. 127–135.

Liessmann, Konrad Paul: Das Kloster. Über die Zukunft der Universität, In: Kovce, Philip – Priddat, Birger (ed.): *Die Aufgabe der Bildung. Aussichten der Universität.* Marburg 2015, s. 103–114.

Livescu, Jean: Die Entstehung der rumänischen Universitäten im Zussamenhang der europäischen Kulturbeziehungen (1850–1870). In: Plaschka, Richard Georg – Mack, Karlheinz (ed.): *Wegenetz europäischen Geistes. Wissenschaftzentren und geistige Wechsel-beziehungen zwischen Mittel– und Südosteuropa vom Ende des 19. Jahrhunderts bis zum Ersten Weltkrieg.* Wien 1983, s. 21–35. https://doi.org/10.7767/boehlau.9783205158165.21

Loewenstein, Bedřich: Totalitarismus a moderna. In: *My a ti druzí. Dějiny, psychologie, antro-pologie.* Brno 1998, s. 306–313.

Lundgren, Peter: Mytos Humboldt in der Gegenwart. Lehre – Forschung – Selbstverwal-tung, In: Ash, Mitchell G. (ed.): *Mythos Humboldt. Vergangenheit und Zukunft der deutschen Universitäten.* Wien – Köln – Weimar 1999, s. 145–169.

Machula, Tomáš – Machulová, Helena: Hodnoty na univerzitě, In: Hanuš, Jiří et al.: *Jak mohou přežít hodnoty?* Brno 2017, s. 59–69.

Málek, Ivan: Přeměna lékařské výchovy, In: Málek, Ivan – Gutwirth, Alois (ed.): *O nového lékaře. Úvod do studia lékařství.* Praha 1949, s. 97–116.

Malíř, Jiří: Systém politických stran v českých zemích do roku 1918, In: Marek, Pavel: *Po-litické strany. Vývoj politických stran a hnutí v českých zemích a v Československu 1861–2004.* Brno 2005, s. 17–57.

Markschies, Christoph: Was von Humboldt noch zu lernen ist? 11 Thesen, In: Kovce, Philip – Priddat, Birgit (ed.): *Die Aufgabe der Bildung. Aussichten der Universität.* Marburg 2015, s. 239–246.

Marquard, Odo: Einheit und Vielheit, In: *Zukunft braucht Herkunft.* Stuttgart 2003, s. 205–219.

Matuschek, Stefan: Zerreißprobe. Zur gegenwartigen Hochschulreform, In: Jamme, Christoph – Schröder, Asta von (ed.): *Einsamkeit und Freiheit. Zum Bildungsauftrag der Universität im 21. Jahrhundert.* München 2011, s. 125–138.

Melosik, Zbyszko: Uniwersytet i komercjalizacja. Rekonstrukcja zachodniej debaty, In: Drozdowicz, Zbigniew (ed.): *Uniwersytety. Tradicje – dzień dzisiejszy – przyszłość.* Poznań 2009, s. 97–109.

Moklak, Jarosław: Lwów i Triest. Uniwersyteckie dążenia Ukrainców, Włochów, Chorwatów i Słoweńców (1908–1914), In: Pezda, Janusz –Pijaj, Stanisław (ed.): *Europa środkowa, Bałkany i Polacy.* Kraków 2017, s. 241–248.

Müller-Böling, Detlef: Entfesselung der Wettbewerb. Von der Universität zum differenzierten Hochschulsystem, In: Grüttner, Michael – Hachtmann, Rüdiger – Jarausch, Konrad H.: *Gebrochene Wissenschaftskulturen. Universität und Politik im 20. Jh.* Göttingen 2010, s. 353–365.

Nagel, Anne Ch.: Anspruch und Wirklichkeit in der nationalsozialistischen Hochschul- und Wissenschaftspolitik, In: Reulecke, Jürgen – Roelcke, Volker (ed.): *Wissenschaften im 20. Jahrhundert: Universitäten in der modernen Wissenschaftsgesellschaft.* Stuttgart 2008, s. 245–262.

Nantl, Jiří: Mechanismus tvorby vůle orgánů univerzity. (Podmínky jejich legitimity a efektivity), In: Staša, Josef (ed.): *Historie, současný stav a perspektivy univerzit: úsvit nebo soumrak akademické samosprávy?* Praha 2008, s. 54–60.

Newman, Henry John: Idea university. In: Jirsa, Jakub (ed.): *Idea university.* Praha 2015, s. 40–51.

Pešek, Jiří: Prag und Wien 1884 – ein Vergleich zwischen den Universitäten und deren Rolle für die Studenten aus den Böhmischen Ländern, In: Corbea-Hoisie, Andrei – Le Rider, Jacques (edd.): *Metropole und Provinzen in Altösterreich (1880–1918).* Wien – Köln – Weimar 1996, s. 94–109.

Prázný, Aleš: Univerzita jako republika učenců: Karl Jaspers, In: Chotaš, Jiří – Prázný, Aleš – Hejduk, Tomáš et al.: *Moderní univerzita. Ideál a realita.* Praha 2015, s. 197–244.

Shell, Kurt L.: Die amerikanische Universität und die Herausforderung durch den Multikulturalismus, In: Steger, Hans-Albert – Hopfinger, Hans (ed.): *Die Universität in der Welt, die Welt in der Universität.* Neustadt an der Aisch 1994, s. 27–44.

Schütt, Hans-Peter: Der „Geist" der Geisteswissenschaften, In: Arnswald, Ulrich – Nida-Rümelin, Julian (ed.): *Die Zukunft der Geisteswissenschaften.* Heidelberg 2005, s. 63–76.

Schwarz, Karl: Die Bologna-Reform erzwingt die Frage nach einer neuen Universitätskonzeption, In: Kellermann, Paul – Guggenberger, Helmut – Weber, Karl (ed.): *Universität nach Bologna? Hochschulkonzeptionen zwischen Kritik und Utopie.* Wien 2016, s. 74–95.

Snow, Charles Percy: Die zwei Kulturen, In: Kreuzer, Helmut (ed.): *Die zwei Kulturen. Literarische und naturwissenschaftliche Intelligenz.* München 1987, s. 19–58.

Sójka, Jacek: Zarządzenie strategiczne a idea Uniwersytetu. In: Drozdowicz, Zbigniew (ed.): *Uniwersytety. Tradycje – dzień dziesiejszy – przyszłość.* Poznań 2009, s. 169–188.

Spoun, Sascha – Seyfarth, Felix C.: Die Vetreibung aus dem Elfenbeinturm: Sebstverständnis, Attraktivität und Wettbewerb deutscher Universität nach Bologna, In: Jamme, Christoph – Schröder, Asta von (ed.): *Einsamkeit und Freiheit. Zum Bildungsauftrag der Universität im 21. Jahrhundert.* München 2011, s. 193–220.

Starke, Kurt: K vývoji osobnosti socialistických studentů v NDR, In: *Matějovský, Antonín: O komunistické výchově na vysokých školách v BLR a NDR.* Praha 1977, s. 37–79.

Stern, Fritz: Deutschland um 1900 – und eine zweite Chance, In: Hardtwig, Wolfgang – Brandt, Harm-Hinrich (ed.): *Deutschlands Weg in die Moderne.* München 1992, s. 32–44.

Stichweh, Rudolf: Universitäten im Zeitalter der Globalisierung, In: Rudersdorf, Manfred – Höpken, Wolfgang – Schlegel, Martin (ed.): *Wissen und Geist. Universitätskulturen.* Leipzig 2009, s. 119–138.

Stucke, Andreas: Mythos USA – Die Bedetung des Arguments „Amerika" im Hoschulpolitischen Diskurs der Bundesrepublik, In: Stölting, Erhard – Schimank, Uwe (ed.): *Die Krise der Universität.* Wiesbaden 2001, s. 118–138. https://doi.org/10.1007/978-3-663-12044-5_6

Szögi, László: Die Universitäten in Ungarn. Gründungswelle vom späten Mittelalter bis ins 20. Jahrhundert, In: Wörster, Peter (ed.): *Universitäten im östrlichen Europa. Zwischen Kirche, Staat und Nation– Sozialgeschichtliche und politische Entwicklungen.* München 2008, s. 235–268.

Teichler, Ulrich: Bologna – Kontinuität und Wandel der Hochschulentwicklung, In: Kellermann, Paul – Guggenberger, Helmut – Weber, Karl (ed.): *Universität nach Bologna? Hochschulkonzeptionen zwischen Kritik und Utopie.* Wien 2016, s. 74–95.

Turczynski, Emanuel: Czernowitz als Beispiel einer integrativen Universität, In: Seibt, Ferdinand (ed.): *Die Teilung der Prager Universität 1882 und die intellektuelle Desintegration in den böhmischen Ländern.* München 1984, s. 25–36.

Udrescu, Claudia Maria: University and Politics between East and West. Faciing Challenges in post-communist Romania. The Case of University of Bucharest, In: Bieber, Florian – Heppner, Harald (edd.): *Universities and the Elite Formation in Central, Eastern and South Eastern Europe.* Zürich – Wien 2015, s. 215–225.

Walker, Mark: The Nazification and Denazification of Physics, In: Kertz, Walter (ed.): *Hochschule im Nationalsozialismus.* Braunschweig 1994, s. 79–91.

Weisbrodt, Bernd: Der wandelbare Geist. Akademisches Ideal und wissenschaftliche Transformation in der Nachkriegszeit, In: (ed.): *Akademische Vergangenheitspolitik. Beiträge zur Wissenschaftskultur der Nachkriegszeit.* Göttingen 2002, s. 11–38.

Weissinger, Johannes: Die Universität gestern, heute und morgen. Erinnerungen und (un)systematische) Gedanken, In: Kahle, Heinz Gerhard (ed.): *Die Hochschule in der Herausforderungen der 70en Jahre.* Karlsruhe 1980, s. 11–26.

Žilka, Ladislav – Vašek Otakar: O brněnských vysokých školách, In: Goldstücker, Eduard et el. (edd.): *Za lepší zítřek. Sborník a vzpomínek na studentské pokrokové hnutí třicátých let.* Praha 1963, s. 177–184.

Journals:

Beneš, Edvard: *Školské poměry ve Francii. Volná škola: školská revue pro širší vrstvy.* 1908, r. 4, s. 55–57.

Berdahl, Robert M. – Cohon, Jared L. – Simmons, Ruth J. – Sexton, John – Berlowitz, Leslie Cohen: University and the city. *Bulletin of the American Academy of Arts and Sciences.* 2011, r. 64, č. 3, s. 4–18.

Boháček, Miroslav: Založení a nejstarší organisace pražské university. *Acta Universitatis Pragensis.* 1964, r. 5, č. 1, s. 5–31.

Die Clerikalen und die Naturwissenschaften. *Volksfreund.* 1889, r. 9, č. 11, s. 1.

Cyrillo-Methodějská universita na Moravě. *Hlas.* 1894, r. 46, č. 116, s. 1.

Delbecq, André – Bryson, Paul – Van der Ven, Andrew: University Governance: Lessons from a Innovative Design for Collaboration. *Journal of Management Inquiry.* 2013, s. 382–392. https://doi.org/10.1177/1056492612471996

Duarte Horta, Regina: The City Within the City: the University City, History and Urbanism in a latin American Case Study. *Iberoamericana.* 2013, r. 13, č. 51, s. 7–25.

Gumport, Patricia J.: Academic restructuring: Organizational change and institutional imperatives. *Higher Education.* 2000, r. 39, č. 1, s. 67–91. https://doi.org/10.1023/A:1003859026301

Hanuš, Jiří: Kdyby se raději rakouský filozof mýlil. *Kontexty.* 2016, r. 8, č. 1, s. 93–96.

Havel, Václav: Poznámky o polovzdělanosti. *Tvář.* 1964, r. 1, č. 9–10, s. 23–29.

Chlupová, Alena: K volbě rektora a prvnímu otevřenému vystoupení nacistických studentů na Německé univerzitě v Praze roku 1922. *Acta Universitatis Pragensis.* 1978, r. 18, č. 2, s. 78–92.

Isaac, Joel: The Human Sciences in Cold War America. *The Historical Journal.* 2007, r. 50, č. 3, s. 725–746.

Kauppinen, Ilkka: Towards transnational academic capitalism. *Higher Education.* 2012, r. 64, č. 4, s. 543–556. https://doi.org/10.1007/s10734-012-9511-x

Kindl, Vladimír: Pokus o zařazení tzv. dělnického práva do výuky Právnické fakulty UK v období buržoazní ČSR. *Acta Universitatis Carolinae.* 1984, r. 24, č. 1, s. 45–66.

Klabouch, Jiří: K dějinám hospodářství pražské univerzity v 17. a 18. století. *Acta Universitatis Carolinae.* 1963, r. 4, č. 2, s. 87–114.

Klečacký, Martin: Iluze nezávislosti. Sociální status c. k. soudce v konfliktu loajalit mezi národem a státem na přelomu 19. a 20. století. *Český časopis historický.* 2014, r. 112, č. 3, s. 432–462.

Krise zvěrolékařské fakulty v Brně. *Lidové noviny.* 21. 4. 1921, r. 29, č. 197, s. 1.

Kubáček, Vojtěch: Pokrokové tradice Univerzity Jana Evangelisty Purkyně. *Universitas.* 1979, r. 12, č. 1., s. 3–5.

Kučera, Karel: Raně osvícenský pokus o reformu pražské university. *Acta Universitatis Carolinae.* 1963, r. 4, č. 2, s. 61–86.

Kučera, Karel – Truc, Miroslav: Poznámky k fašizaci Německé univerzity pražské. *Acta Universitatis Pragensis.* 1960, r. 1, č. 1, s. 203–223.

Kučera, Martin: K politické činnosti historika Antonína Rezka. *Východočeské listy historické.* 1997, r. 1, č. 11–12, s. 11–33.

Langewiesche, Dieter: Die „Humboldtsche Universität" als nationaler Mythos. Zum Selbstbildt der deutschen Universität in ihren Rektoratreden im Kaiserreich und in der Weimarer Republik. *Historische Zeitschrift.* 2010, r. 151, č. 1, s. 53–91. https://doi.org/10.1524/hzhz.2010.0002

Langewiesche, Dieter: Ende einer Lebensform. Welche Folgen hat der Umbau der europäischen Hochschullandschaft? *Süddeutsche Zeitung.* 29.–30. 12. 2007, r. 63.

Lobkowicz, Nikolaus: Die Idee der Universität. *Vereinszeitung des A. G. V. München*, LIX (1980).

Masaryk, Tomáš: Jak zvelebovati naši literaturu naukovou. *Athenaeum II*, 1885, s. 272–288.

Mayer, Franz: Universität und Gesellschaft: Einige Überlegungen zur Gründung, Planung und Aufbau einer Universität in Regensburg. *Zeitschrift für Politik*. 1966, r. 13, č. 3, s. 269–284.

Milanovic, Branko: Global Income Inequality by the Numbers. *Global Policy*. 2013, r. 4, č. 2, s. 198–208. https://doi.org/10.1111/1758-5899.12032

Morkes, František: Zákony o vysokých školách z let 1948–1989. *Pedagogika*. 1999, r. 41, č. 2, s. 115–127.

Die Naturwissenschaften als Grundlage der Schule. *Volksfreund*. 1887, r. 7, č. 5, s. 2.

Ohrožení britských univerzit (Rada na obranu britských univerzit a Manifest reformy). *Kontexty*. 2013, r. 5, č. 1, s. 45–49.

Představujeme vám... prof. Dr. Arnošta Lamprechta. *Universitas*. 1983, r.16, č. 1, s. 48–51.

Představujeme vám ... prof. Dr. Silvestra Nováčka, CSc. *Universitas*. 1983, r. 16, č. 3, s. 42–45.

Psotová, Věra: Fašizace německého studentstva a ohlas tohoto procesu mezi německými studenty v Československu. *Acta Universitatis Pragensis*. 1980, r. 20, č. 1, s. 31–60.

Raczyńska, Magdalena: Od elitarności do masowości. Stan szkolnictwa wyższego w Polsce po transfomacji ustrojowej z 1989 r. Poliarchia: *Studenckie Zeszyty Naukowe*. 2013, r. 1, č. 1, s. 217–244. https://doi.org/10.12797/Poliarchia.01.2013.01.14

Rhoades, Gary: Capitalism, Academic Style, and Shared Governance. *Academe*. 2005 r. 91, č. 3, s. 38–42. https://doi.org/10.2307/40252785

Rhoades, Gary – Slaughter, Sheila: Academic Capitalism, Managed Professionals, and Supply-Side Higher Education. *Academic Labor*. 1997, č. 51, s. 9–38. https://doi.org/10.2307/466645

Roubal, Ondřej: Když se řekne identita – regionální identita III. část. *SOCIOweb*. 2003, č. 15–16, s. 1–5.

Rubner, Jeanne: Die Märchen-Universität. *Süddeutsche Zeitung*. 6. 1. 2004.

Seibt, Gustav: Ende einer Lebensform. Von Humboldt zu Bologna: Der atemberaubende Untergang der deutschen Universität. *Süddeutsche Zeitung*. 21. 06. 2007.

Seichter, Sabine: Erziehungswissenschaft zwischen Einfalt und Vielfalt. *Vierteljahrsschrift für wissenschaftliche Pädagogik*. 2015. r. 91, č. 2, s. 171–181. https://doi.org/10.1163/25890581-091-02-90000001

Schatz, Gottfried: Skutečné vzdělání namísto pouhého zprostředkování znalostí. *Kontexty*. 2015, r. 7, č. 3, s. 33.

Schmidt, Peter: Zum 100. Todestag von Ernst Ludwig August von Rebeur-Paschwitz. *Nachrichtenblatt zur Geschichte der Geowissenschaften*. 1995, č. 5, s. 58–59.

Schofer, Evan – Meyer John W.: The Worldwide Expansion of Higher Education in the Twentieth Century. *American sociological Review*. 2005, r. 70, s. 898–920. https://doi.org/10.1177/000312240507000602

Sökefeld, Martin et al.: Debating Self, Identity, and Culture in Anthropology. *Current Anthropology*. 1999, r. 40, č. 4, s. 417–447. https://doi.org/10.2307/2991377

Sporn, Barabara: Managing University Culture: An Analysis of the Relationship between Institutional Culture and Management Approaches. *Higher Education*. 1996, r. 32, č. 1, s. 41–61. https://doi.org/10.1007/BF00139217

Spousta, Vladimír: Hodnocení a etika vědecké práce. *Universitas.* 2002, r. 13, č. 2, s. 40–48.

Šling, Karel: Otto Šling – příběh jednoho komunisty. *Paměť a dějiny.* 2012, č. 4, s. 116–121.

Štaif, Jiří: Psaní biografie a autorská sebereflexe. *Dějiny – teorie – kritika.* 2015, č. 1., s. 118–123.

Die tschechischen Ausschreitungen und Gewalttätigkeiten. *Neues deutsches Blatt.* 7. 10. 1905, r. 1, č. 31, s. 4.

Tuunainen, Juha: Hybrid Practices? Contributions to the Debate on the Mutation of Science and University. *Higher Education.* 2005, r. 50, č. 2, s. 275–298. https://doi.org/10.1007/s10734-004-6355-z

Vanderziel, Jeffrey: Senát hájí zájmy univerzity. *MUNI.* 2017, r. 13, č. 12, s. 12.

Vávra, Jaroslav: Zapomenutá doktorská disertace o Jaroslavu Haškovi. Ke vztahům mezi posluchači a profesory Karlovy univerzity za fašistického ohrožení ČSR. *Acta Universitatis Carolinae.* 1984, r. 24, č. 2, s. 55–68.

Vinš, Václav et al.: Vnitřní hodnocení na vysokých školách. Analýza výročních zpráv a dlouhodobých záměrů vysokých škol. *Aula.* 2006, r. 14, č. 14, s. 61–82.

Visingr, Lukáš: Sedm statečných mýtů o Divokém západě: Jak to (možná) bylo doopravdy. *Bobří stopa.* 2017, r. 26, č. 3, s. 3–5.

Vondrák, Ivo: Proč zavádět systém managementu jakosti na univerzitní pracoviště. *Aula.* 2005, r. 13, č. 3, s. 26–31.

Wagner, J. James: Multiversity or University? Pursuing competing goods simultaneously. *The Intellectual Community.* 2007, r. 9, č. 4.

Wolhuter, Charl C. – Mushaandja, John: Contesting Ideas of a University: The Case of South Africa. *Humanities.* 2015, č. 4, s. 212–223. https://doi.org/10.3390/h4020212

Yokohama, Keiko: Entrepreneurialism in Japanese and UK Universities: Governance, Management, Leadership, and Funding. *Higher Education.* 2006, r. 52, č. 3, s. 523–555. https://doi.org/10.1007/s10734-005-1168-2

Závada, Jiří et al.: „Benchmarking" v hodnocení kvality vysokých škol. *Aula.* 2006, r. 14, č. 14, s. 83–96.

Zerlang, Martin: The university and the city. *GeoJournal.* 1997, r. 43, č. 3, s. 241–246. https://doi.org/10.1023/A:1006825013983

Zur Forderung der czechischen Universität in Mähren. *Deutsches Nordmährerblatt.* 12. 3. 1904, r. 6, č. 11, s. 1–3.

Primary sources:

Archiv Masarykovy univerzity (MU), Fond A., Rektorát MU (RMU) II, k.2, sign. 3357/49.

Archiv MU, Fond A., RMU II, k. 2, sign. XIV.

Archiv MU, Fond A2, Filosofická fakulta, k. 1, CSc., i.č. 1/9.

Archiv MU, Fond A3 Lékařská fakulta, k. 1, sign. DXIII.

Archiv MU, Fond A3, Lékařská fakulta, k. 2, sign. B.VI/2.

Archiv MU, Fond A3, Lékařská fakulta, k. 9. sign. B.VI/2.

Archiv MU, Fond A4 Pedagogická fakulta, k. 1, sign. DXIII.

Archiv MU, Fond A6 Přírodovědecká fakulta, k. 4 (Automatizované systémy řízení).

Archiv MU, Fond B100, Otakar Borůvka, i.č. 818.

Archiv MU, Fond ČSM, k. 4, projev prorektora Martince ke studentům VŠ.

Archiv MU, Fond G1, Spolek posluchačů filosofie, k. 1, Jak jsme začínali – vzpomínky na školní rok 1949–1950, příloha k zápisu ze schůze ze dne 5. 3. 1951.

Archiv MU, Fond H3, Sbírka historické dokumentace, sign. 110/7.

Archiv MU, Fond Rektorát A II/2, k. 53, sign. 53/1.

Archiv Univerzity Karlovy (UK), Akademický senát 1882–1945, k. 17.

Archiv UK, Celozávodní výbor KSČ, k. 1, zápis ze dne 28. 3. 1957.

Archiv UK, Fond Akademický senát 1882–1945, k. 31, i.č. 559.

Archiv UK, Fond Akademický senát UK, k. 38, zápis z jednání dne 12. 3. 1948.

Archiv UK, Fond Čestný soud vysokých škol, i.č. 421–423.

Archiv UK, Fond Kolegium rektora, k. 38, zápis z jednání dne 9. 4. 1990.

Archiv UK, Fond Vědecká rada UK, zápis ze dne 31. 3. 1960.

Archiv UK, Ústav sociálně politických věd, i.č. 471, 474.

Archiv UK, Ústav sociálně-politických věd, k. V/53, i.č. 471, 475.

Archiv Univerzity Palackého (UP), FF UP, k. 59, i.č. 71, sign. C/I/3.

Archiv UP, k. 441, i.č. 1488, sign. D/II/5.

Archiv UP, Rektorát UP I., k. 41, i.č. 83, sign. III/25.

Archiv UP, Rektorát UP II., k. 56, i.č. 141, sign. I/9A.

Národní archiv (NA), Fond Ministerstvo školství a národní osvěty, k. 1115, sign. 5I2A, č. j. 138493/23.

NA, Fond Ministerstvo školství a kultury (MŠK), k. 27, zápisy z jednání kolegia ministra z 28. 4. 1960 a 5. 5. 1960.

NA, Fond MŠK, k. 2085a, i.č. 44 I., Výzkum 1945–1948.

NA, Fond MŠK, k. 2085a, i.č. 44 I., Výzkum 1950–1952.

NA, Fond MŠK, k. 2086, i.č. 44, Výzkum 1953.

NA, Fond MŠK, k. 2086, i.č. 44, Výzkum 1954.

NA, Fond MŠK, k. 2089 (1958), dokument Zhodnocení práce na Filozoficko-historické fakultě UK.

Zemský archiv Opava, pobočka Olomouc, KV KSČ, schůze byra, k. 54, zápis z jednání dne 14. 11. 1955.

Internet addresses:

https://aktualne.centrum.sk/status-univerzit-ohrozil-najma-vysoky-pocet-studentov/sloven-sko/spolocnost/ (5. 5. 2018).

https://amu.edu.pl/__data/assets/pdf_file/0004/239755/STRATEGIA-ROZWOJU--UAM_NOWELIZACJA.pdf (15. 8. 2017).

https://archiv.ihned.cz/c1–64640160-slovenska-vysoka-skola-danubius-uz-nesmi-rozda-vat-doktorske-tituly-doktorat-z-ni-ma-i-hejtman-hasek (21. 12. 2017).

https://brno.idnes.cz/daniel-kretinsky-pravnicka-fakulta-masarykovy-univerzity-poh-/br-no-zpravy.aspx?c=A180207_381505_brno-zpravy_dh (8. 2. 2018).

http://ceskapozice.lidovky.cz/akademicka-samosprava-musi-byt-stavovska-nikoli-demokra-ticka-p6q-/tema.aspx?c=A160623_165535_pozice-tema_lube (6. 1. 2018).

http://ceskapozice.lidovky.cz/shoda-globalismu-a-lokalismu-je-civilizacni-nezbytnosti-pez-/tema.aspx?c=A180425_151517_pozice-tema_lube (29. 4. 2018) http://fajnova.cz/historicke-centrum-mesta-ozivi-ostravska-univerzita-jeji-studenti/ (10. 5. 2018).

https://financialobserver.eu/cse-and-cis/serbia/serbia-experiencing-health-sector-brain-drain/ (2. 1. 2018).

https://restartregionu.cz/univerzita-karlova-zahaji-vyuku-ve-varech-pomoci-muze-program-restart/ (5. 5. 2018).

https://slovacky.denik.cz/zpravy_region/zlinska-univerzita-roste−20071.html (5. 5. 2018).

https://technet.idnes.cz/volebni-pruzkumy−0zx-/veda.aspx?c=A131016_152300_veda_pka (20. 12. 2017).

https://uniba.sk/o-univerzite/poslanie/ (15. 8. 2017).

https://vsmonitor.wordpress.com/2014/05/13/jak-v-nizozemsku-urcuji-pocty-prijatych-na-vysoke-skoly/ (5. 7. 2017).

https://web.natur.cuni.cz/student/studentska-komora-akademickeho-senatu-prf (31. 3. 2018).

https://www.aktuality.sk/clanok/518391/kiska-by-zrusil-tretinu-univerzit-ktore-by-to-mohli-byt/ (5. 5. 2018).

https://www.ceitec.cz/evaluace/t1133 (20. 12. 2017).

http://www.ceskatelevize.cz/ct24/nazory/1368357-byznys-a-pruzkum-verejneho-mineni;

http://www.ceskatelevize.cz/ct24/veda/2404318-islandstina-vymira-mezi-jazyky-ohrozene-digitalizaci-sveta-patri-i-cestina (29. 5. 2018).

http://www.ehea.info/pid34248/history.html (6. 7. 2017).

http://www.fu-berlin.de/universitaet/profil/gesellschaft/index.html (16. 8. 2017).

https://www.giessen.de/index.phtml?La=1&mNavID=640.4&object=tx%7C684.4427.1&sub=0 (25. 5. 2018).

http://www.harvard.edu/media-relations/media-resources/quick-facts (29. 6. 2017). https://www.chronicle.com/blogs/innovations/the-privatization-of-state-universities-it-makes-sense/31744 (20. 12. 2017).

https://www.lidovky.cz/superplat-dekanky-na-dotaz-na-neumerne-vysoke-odmeny-jsem-odpoved-nedostal-rika-byvaly-rektor-iga-/zpravy-domov.aspx?c=A180323_115043_ln_domov_mpr (23. 3. 2018).

http://www.lnu.edu.ua/about/ (14. 6. 2018).

http://www.msmt.cz/ministerstvo/novinar/poslanci-schvalili-novelu-vysokoskolskeho-zakona (6. 7. 2017).

http://www.msmt.cz/vzdelavani/vysoke-skolstvi/prehled-vysokych-skol-v-cr−3

http://www.muni.cz/media/docs/1110/Dlouhodoby_zamer_MU_2016_2020.pdf (15. 8. 2017).

http://www.nefmi.gov.hu/felsooktatas/felsooktatasi-intezmenyek

https://www.online.muni.cz/udalosti/382-v-brne-zacina-teologicke-studium-na-akademicke-pude (11. 5. 2018)

https://www.ox.ac.uk/about/facts-and-figures/student-numbers?wssl=1 (29. 6. 2017).

https://www.parlamentnilisty.cz/politika/politici-volicum/Babis-ANO-Ridit-stat-jako-firmu-A-proc-ne−499512 (20. 12. 2017).

https://www.polityka.pl/tygodnikpolityka/nauka/1621163,1,ranking-naukowy-uczelni-akademickich.read (5. 5. 2018).

http://www.psp.cz/eknih/1918ns/ps/stenprot/022schuz/s022007.htm (10. 5. 2018).

http://www.psp.cz/eknih/1918ns/ps/stenprot/022schuz/s022008.htm (7. 1. 2018).

http://www.shanghairanking.com/ARWU-Methodology–2016.html (15. 6. 2017).

http://www.telegraph.co.uk/education/educationnews/12059161/Politically-correct-universities-are-killing-free-speech.ht (18. 7. 2017).

http://www.ubalt.edu/about-ub/docs/Strategic%20Plan_FINAL.pdf (16. 8. 2017).

https://www.uni-lj.si/o_univerzi_v_ljubljani/poslanstvo__vrednote_in_vizija_ul/ (15. 8. 2017).

https://www.universitas.cz/ze-sveta/85-ceske-vysoke-skolstvi-si-v-porovnani-s-padesatkou--zemi-pohorsilo (1. 8. 2018).

http://www.vysokeskoly.sk/katalog

http://www.vzdelavani2020.cz/images_obsah/dokumenty/ramec_vs.pdf (30. 7. 2018).

https://www.yale.edu/about-yale/yale-facts (29. 6. 2017).

https://zpravy.idnes.cz/kvuli-plzenskym-pravum-se-poprve-sejde-komise-titul-zatim-odebran-nebyl–14s-/domaci.aspx?c=A100626_171702_studium_jan (21. 12. 2017).

NAME INDEX

Myths and Traditions of Central European University Culture

Lukáš Fasora – Jiří Hanuš

Published by the MASARYK UNIVERSITY PRESS,
Žerotínovo nám. 617/9, 601 77 Brno, CZ
in the monographic series **Opera Facultatis philosophicae Universitatis Masarykianae (Spisy Filozofické fakulty Masarykovy univerzity)** / Number 494 and
KAROLINUM PRESS, Ovocný trh 560/5, 116 36 Prague, CZ

Editor in charge / doc. Mgr. Jana Horáková, Ph.D.
Editor in chief / doc. Mgr. Katarina Petrovićová, Ph.D.
Editorial assistant / Mgr. Vendula Hromádková
Translation / Graeme Dibble
Cover illustration / Miroslav Huptych
Series graphic and cover design / Mgr. Pavel Křepela
Typesetting / Dan Šlosar

First published / 2019
Number of copies / 350
Printing and bookbinding / Tiskárna KNOPP s.r.o., U Lípy 926, 549 01 Nové Město nad Metují, CZ

ISBN 978-80-210-9412-3 (Masarykova univerzita. Brno) (paperback)
ISBN 978-80-246-4380-9 (Karolinum. Praha) (paperback)
ISBN 978-80-210-9413-0 (Masarykova univerzita. Brno) (online : pdf)
ISBN 978-80-246-4497-4 (Karolinum. Praha) (online : pdf)

ISSN 1211-3034
https://doi.org/10.5817/CZ.MUNI.M210-9413-2019